Other military reference books by William E. Hamelman:

•• Of Red Eagles and Royal Crowns

•• The History of the Prussian Pour le Mérite Order,
      Volume I, 1740-1812
      Volume II, 1813-1888
      Volume III, 1888-1918

Matthaeus Publishers
Post Office Box 1361
Dallas, TX 75221

Printed in the United States of America

ISBN 0-931065-06-2

✠ ✠ ✠

GERMAN IRON CROSS DOCUMENTS
OF
WORLD WAR I

A comprehensive study of the various documents
of the German Iron Cross awarded during
World War I and a brief history of the
units in which the brave
soldiers served.

by

William E. Hamelman

✠ ✠ ✠

Dedicated to

CHARLES E. & BETTY ANN DUNN

for still being there
after so many years.

✠ ✠ ✠

CONTENTS

✠ ✠ ✠

Edited by

KATHERINE GODBY

✠ ✠ ✠

ACKNOWLEDGEMENTS

The author is very grateful to the many individuals, fellow collectors, and friends who assisted, by word and deed, during the compiling and completion of this book.

A very special thanks goes to *Steve Fore* who provided one of the most important tools in this project, the primary reference source.

My sincere thanks to *Brad Yahn*, for his greatly appreciated assistance and especially for finding many of the documents which are shown in this book; *Jeff Eicher*, for his stimulating encouragement, continuous interest, and use of several documents shown in this book; *Danny Priozzo*, for always having a big smile and making me feel this project was well worth the effort. As well as *Dennis Martin*, for his valuable suggestions and research assistance.

Also special thanks to *Eugene Hamelman* and *Christian Hamelman* and most especially to their wonderful wives, *Jean* and *Cyndi*, for keeping them out of my hair. Also to *John Tank, Ron Scott, Richard Etier, Joy Wyse*, and others too numerous to name.

My deepest appreciation and heartfelt thanks, however, goes to *Helaine Hamelman*, "the best wife in the world" for allowing me to pursue the dream of an author. For her unwavering and unselfish support and loyalty, her smiling personality, her understanding and help during the researching and writing of this book.

William E. Hamelman
Dallas, TX

✠ ✠ ✠

GRADES OF OFFICERS IN THE GERMAN ARMY DURING WORLD WAR I

General Officers

1.	Generalfeldmarschall (Field Marshal)	Commands a Group of Armies
2.	Generaloberst (Colonel General)	Commands an Army
3.	General der Infanterie(Infantry) General der Kavallerie (Cavalry) General der Artillerie (Artillery)	Corps Commander Same Same
4.	Generalleutnant (Lieutenant General)	Division Commander
5.	Generalmajor (Major General)	Brigade Commander

Regimental Officers

6.	Oberst (Colonel)	Regimental Commander
7.	Oberstleutnant (Lieutenant Colonel)	Second-in-command of Regiment
8.	Major (Major)	Battalion Commander
9.	Hauptmann (Captain) Rittmeister (Captain)	Captain of Infantry, Artillery or Engineers Captain of Cavalry or Trains
10.	Oberleutnant (1st Lieutenant)	Company Officer
11.	Leutnant (2nd Lieutenant)	Company Officer
12.	Feldwebelleutnant	In all arms vacancies in the grade of 2nd Lieutenant were in part filled by promoting Feldwebel (Sergeant Major) or Vizefeldwebel (Assistant Sergeant Major) who had retired before the war after 12 years service, to the rank of Feldwebelleutnant (Sergeant Major Lieutenant).
13.	Offizierstellvertrater (Acting Officer)	Utilized where needed.

Generally by 1918 lieutenants commanded companies, captains commanded battalions, and majors commanded regiments, et cetera.

✠ ✠ ✠

GRADES OF NON-COMMISSIONED OFFICERS IN THE GERMAN ARMY DURING WORLD WAR I

1.	Feldwebel *(Infantry)* *(Sergeant Major)* Wachtmeister *(Artillery & Cavalry)*	First sergeant
2.	Vizefeldwebel *(Infantry)* *(Assistant Sergeant Major)* Vizewachtmeister *(Artillery & Cavalry)*	Senior duty sergeant
3.	Fähnrich *(Officer Candidate)*	
4.	Sergeant *(Sergeant)*	Platoon sergeant
5.	Unteroffizier *(Corporal)*	Section leader
6.	Gefreiter *(Private First Class)*	Squad leader

Collectively, *Unteroffizier* stands for "non-commissioned officer," however, in referring to an individual the term invariably means "corporal."

The *Fähnrich* was a man with certain educational qualifications who had been accepted for enlistment as *"Fahnenjunker"* (officer candidate or candidate for a commission), and upon approval of his officers was sent to a military school after having served six months, half that time as a corporal, with a regiment. He was returned to company duty as a Fähnrich after successfully completing a nine month course at the school. After a further short period of active service performing duties of a non-commissioned officer, he was given a commission as a leutnant (lieutenant).

✠ ✠ ✠

ORGANIZATION OF THE GERMAN ARMY UNITS IN 1914

Infantry

Squad	8 men under the command of a Corporal *(Unteroffizier)*.
Section	16 men under the command of a Sergeant *(Sergeant)*.
Platoon	50-75 men under the command of a Lieutenant *(Leutnant)*.
Company	200-250 men (3 platoons) under the command of a Captain *(Hauptmann)*.
Battalion	4 or more companies under the command of a Major *(Major)*.
Regiment	3 or more battalions under the command of a Lt. Colonel or Colonel *(Oberst)*.
Brigade	2-3 regiments under the command of a Brigadier General.
Division	2 or more brigades under the command of a Major General.
Corps	2 or more divisions under the command of a Lt. General.

Artillery

Battery	130-280 men (4-6 cannon) under the command of a Captain *(Hauptmann)*.
Battalion	3-4 batteries under the command of a Major *(Major)*.
Regiment	3-4- battalions under the command of a Colonel *(Oberst)*.

Cavalry

Section	8 men under the command of a Corporal *(Unteroffizier)*.
Platoon	36-50 men under the command of a Lieutenant *(Leutnant)*.
Troop	3-4 platoons, 125-150 men under the command of a Captain *(Rittmeister)*.
Squadron	3 troops under the command of a Major *(Major)*.
Regiment	4-6 squadrons under the command of a Colonel *(Oberst)*.
Brigade	3 regiments under the command of a Brigadier General.
Division	2-3 brigades under the command of a Major General.

✠ ✠ ✠

DISTINCTIONS BETWEEN REGULAR ARMY AND RESERVE COMPONENTS OF THE GERMAN ARMY IN 1914

REGULAR

The standing army is composed of regular and active reserve troops. Each German male citizen must serve in the German military service for a period of two years. The obligation begins upon completion of his 17th year. After completing two years active military service, the soldier is placed in the reserves.

RESERVE

The reservist serves five years. Each year he is required to participate in two field maneuvers of eight weeks each. Upon completion of this phase, the reservist is assigned to the Landwehr.

LANDWEHR

Landwehr I: The reservist serves in the Landwehr I for a minimum of five years. During this time he is required to participate in field maneuvers of two weeks duration once or twice a year. Upon reaching the age of 32 the citizen soldier can be transferred to the Landwehr II. If not transferred to Landwehr II, he remains assigned to Landwehr I until he reaches the age of 39 and is then placed in the militia or Landsturm II.

Landwehr II: Transferred to the Landwehr II, the 32 year-old citizen soldier is usually assigned to a garrison near his home. He serves in this capacity until age 39 and is then placed in the militia or Landsturm II.

LANDSTURM (MILITIA)

Landsturm I: Consists of all men ages 18 to 45 who are physically unable to serve in the regular army formations. They could have served in the regular army but due to injury were assigned to the Landsturm I.

Landsturm II: Following his 39th birthday, the citizen soldier is assigned to the Landsturm II and serves until he reaches his 45th year. The Landsturm II is used in reinforcing the regular army during wartime. It is utilized as occupation troops or in the homeland as guard units.

✠ ✠ ✠

PREFACE

Over the years there have been many books written about the history of the German Iron Cross, but for some vague reason, very little, if anything, has been written regarding the documents awarding the Iron Cross. Most books covering the Iron Cross, if they do mention documents, will perhaps show one or two, possibly three, documents and then dismiss them with no explanation.

It seems a travesty that the World War I memorabilia collectors have not been afforded the opportunity to learn more about the many different types of documents and certificates authorizing the Iron Cross. These documents were given to the soldier along with the actual award in recognition of his bravery and leadership on the field of battle. The documents are just as much a part of the collector's estate as is the actual Iron Cross itself. In fact, the document makes the man live again because now his name is known. The collector can now question, dream if you please, when he holds the Iron Cross document in his hand: who was this person, what was he like, where was he from, was he married, did he have children, whatever happened to him?

This book is not meant to show all the variations of the Iron Cross documents. However, the author has assigned a category to documents in order to allow the collector to better identify each as a specific type. The documents will also bring alive the memory and history of a soldier. The documents shown in this book briefly trace, where possible, the soldiers' unit history. The time period when he was decorated with the Iron Cross is shown, and an attempt has been made to pinpoint the specific action.

Again, it must be pointed out that this is not a definitive history of the many units described herein but only the tip of the iceberg. Perhaps a new door will be opened to the collector to better understand the significance of that long-neglected little piece of paper with a man's name on it. Also, the collector can pursue a quest for knowledge and make history live again.

William E. Hamelman
Dallas, TX

✠ ✠ ✠

The bridegroom wears the Iron Cross 2nd Class from the buttonhole of his civilian coat.

The bridegroom, in uniform, wears a Bavarian helmet and the Iron Cross 2nd Class. Note that the ribbon is formed into a bow and suspended from the second buttonhole of the military tunic.

1914 SECOND CLASS IRON CROSS SINGLE DOCUMENTS

1914 Iron Cross 2nd Class

During World War I, the types of documents used to authorize, award and verify the receipt of the Iron Cross were almost endless.

Many Iron Cross documents were printed in very ornate and beautiful styles - some, as a large diploma for framing and others very plain to be carried by the recipient.

The documents and certificates were printed at both civilian printing companies as well as by military printing units. Many varieties were used by the armies, corps, occupation forces, regiments, battalions and so on down the line; companies mimeographed, stenciled and duplicated simple documents, and many were just plain handwritten authorizations.

Presented here are only some of the many variations. Where possible, a brief history of the unit in which the recipient served is outlined.

✠ ✠ ✠

The Iron Cross certificates illustrated in this book have been catagorized as **eleven** basic types.

Type 1.	Preliminary Authorization Certificate	*Vorläufiges Besitzzeugnis*
Type 2.	Preliminary Identification Certificate	*Vorläufiger Ausweis*
Type 3.	Preliminary Authorization Certificate	*Vorläufige Urkunde*
Type 4.	Authorization Certificate	*Besitz-Zeugnis*
Type 5.	Identification Certificate	*Ausweis*
Type 6.	Authorization Certificate	*Urkunde*
Type 7.	Confirmation of Bestowel Certificate	*Verleihungs Bestätigung*
Type 8.	Letter of Transmittal	*Übersendungsschreiben*
Type 9.	Official Certificate	*Offiziell Urkunde*
Type 10.	Privately Purchased Certificate	*Privat Urkunde*
Type 11.	Generic Multiple Award Certificate	*Ausweis*

The classifications are as follows:

PRELIMINARY AUTHORIZATION CERTIFICATE

Types 1 and **3**, *(Vorläufiges Besitzzeugnis or Besitz-Zeugnis and the Vorläufige Urkunde)*, advised the recipient that he had been recognized to receive the Iron Cross. The recipient was authorized to wear the new decoration beginning on the date of the document.

PRELIMINARY IDENTIFICATION CERTIFICATE

Type 2, *(Vorläufiger Ausweis)*, was, as the name implies, an identification certificate.

AUTHORIZATION CERTIFICATEE

Types 4, 5 and **6**, *(Besitz-Zeugnis, Ausweis, and Urkunde)*, were usually given the recipient at a later time.

CONFIRMATION OF BESTOWAL CERTIFICATE

Type 7, *(Verleihungs Bestätigung)*, was an official confirmation of having received the award.

LETTER OF TRANSMITTAL

Type 8, *(Übersendungsschreiben)*, was a letter advising the recipient that the award was being sent to him or indicating a time and place where he would be receive the decoration.

OFFICIAL CERTIFICATE

Type 9, *(Offiziell Urkunde)*, did not state a heading, such as *"Vorläufiges Besitzzeugnis," "Ausweis," "Verleihungs Bestätigung"* or any other heading, and was usually issued from a military headquarters.

PRIVATELY PURCHASED CERTIFICATE

Type 10, *(Privat Urkunde)*, could be purchased by the recipient to be framed and/or displayed, whereas the issued documents were usually kept in the military file or in a personal file.

GENERIC MULTIPLE AWARDS CERTIFICATE

Type 11, *(Ausweis)*, shows one or more awards were authorized and was used as identification for other than the Iron Cross.

✠ ✠ ✠

The attractive document shown below is an Official Certificate, Type 9, named to Lieutenant Colonel *(Oberstleutnant)* **EBERHARD KINTZEL**, who was the commander of the 4th Reserve Light Infantry *(Jäger)* Battalion, 14th Reserve Infantry Brigade, 7th Reserve Infantry Division.

The large document, awarded very early in the war, is printed on heavy white cardboard stock, measures 30.2 cm. wide x 21.8 cm. high. It was signed on 7 October 1914 at the headquarters on the front at Vanzezis and signed in black ink by the commanding general of the 14th Reserve Infantry Brigade. In the lower center between the signature block and the date, is the purple ink official stamp of the 14th Reserve Infantry Brigade.

Document 1   *Official Certificate, Type 9, to Lt. Col. Eberhard Kintzel*

At the beginning of World War I the 7th Reserve Infantry Division was part of the 4th Reserve Corps. By 19 August 1914, the division reached Brussels and advanced towards Paris through Enghien, Ath, Conde, Amiens. By 30-31 August, it had reached Clermont, Creil, and by 4 September 1914 had reached Senlis. At the battle of the Marne, the division was engaged northwest of Crouy sur Ourcq and suffered heavy losses on 6-7 September 1914. It was during this engagement on the Marne that Lt. Col. Kintzel was decorated with the Iron Cross 2nd Class for distinguished leadership and bravery in action.

Between 8 and 11 September 1914, the division withdrew traveling through Villers Cotterets, Coeuvres, Port Fontenoy in the region of Nouvon. The division fought several engagements over a rather long period of time. After the front was stabilized, the division held the line between the Soissons-Laon Road to the southwest of Nouvron. On 12 November 1914, the division suffered heavy losses in its attack on the plateau of Nouvron. The division remained on the western front until the end of the war.

✠ ✠ ✠

The document shown below is an Official Certificate, Type 9, to Private (Second Line Reserve) *(Landwehrmann)* **HEINRICH METHNER** who was serving in the 8th Company, 20th Landwehr Infantry Regiment, 21st Landwehr Infantry Division when he was awarded the Iron Cross 2nd Class on 5 September 1917.

Div.-St.-Qu., *5. Septbr.* 191*7*.

Im Namen

Seiner Majestät des Kaisers und Königs

habe ich am *5. Septbr.* 191*7*.

dem *Wehrm. Hinrij Methner, L. J. R. 20 8. Komp.*

das Eiserne Kreuz II. Klasse

verliehen, was hiermit bescheinigt wird.

Generalmajor u. Div.-Kdeur.

Felddruckerei Bugarmee.

Document 2   *Official Certificate, Type 9, to Landwehrmann Heinrich Methner*

The document was signed at the Division Staff Headquarters on the same date by either the commanding general of the division or his representative. The official 21st Landwehr Infantry Division stamp in purple ink is adjacent to the signature block. The document measures 21.4 cm. wide x 17.0 cm. high, and was printed by the Bug Army Military Field Printers *(Felddruckerei Bugarmee)* as shown by the small print in the lower left-hand corner of the certificate.

The 21st Landwehr Division was formed during April 1917. The 20th Landwehr Infantry Regiment was transferred to the new 21st division from the 3rd Corps District in Brandenburg. The division was stationed in the area of Arras during early 1917. On May 16th the division was transferred to the eastern front arriving at Brest-Litovsk on 21 May 1917. Here the division remained and rested for ten days, and after completing additional training was sent to the Nieman front where it occupied the Vichnev sector until March 1918. It appears that Landwehrmann Heinrich Methner was awarded the Iron Cross 2nd Class for distinction in action while serving on the Russian front.

✠ ✠ ✠

The decorative document shown below is a Preliminary Authorization Certificate, Type 1, *(Vorläufiges Besitz-Zeugnis)* named to Driver *(Fahrer)* **FRIEDRICH FRENGER** serving at the time he was decorated with the Iron Cross 2nd Class, in the 9th Infantry Light Artillery Battery, *(Infantrie Geschütze Batterie)*, 14th Assault *(Sturm)* Battalion. The division to which the battalion is assigned is not identified.

Document 3   *Preliminary Authorization Certificate, Type 1, to Fahrer Friedrich Frenger*

The large document measures 26.9 cm. wide x 22.4 cm. high, and appears to have been originally hand-drawn and then printed. It is printed in brown ink on tan paper. The document is dated 2 April 1918 and is signed in black ink by Freiherr von Puttkamer, Captain *(Hauptmann)* and battalion commander.

Below the date is the purple ink official stamp, barely discernible, of the 14th Assault Battalion. The document shows that Fahrer Frenger was awarded the Iron Cross 2nd Class on 26 March 1918 in recognition of bravery in action. Unfortunately, no information was found on the 14th Assault Battalion or to which division it was assigned.

✠ ✠ ✠

The document shown below actual size, is a Preliminary Authorization Certificate, Type 1, *(Vorläufiges Besitzzeugnis)* awarding the Iron Cross 2nd Class to Private *(Pionier)* * **HEINRICH DESCHLER**, serving in the Mortar *(Minenwerfer)* Company, 4th Bavarian Reserve Infantry Regiment, 199th Infantry Division.

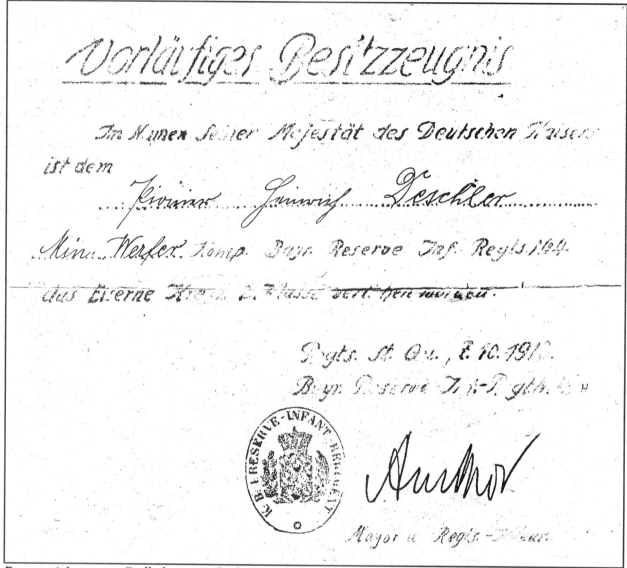

Document 4　　*Preliminary Authorization Certificate, Type 1, to Pionier Heinrich Deschler*

The document measures 19.8 cm. wide x 15.2 cm. high, and was printed on a mimeograph (duplicator) with the usual purple lettering. The paper is of poor quality. The name of the recipient is written in blue ink. The document was signed at the regimental headquarters and has the official regimental stamp of the 4th Bavarian Reserve Infantry Regiment, stamped in purple ink, in the lower center to the left of the signature block. The document is signed with a purple indelible pencil by Major Amthor, the regimental commander, and dated 7 October 1918.

The 4th Bavarian Reserve Infantry Regiment was transferred from the Bavarian Replacement *(Ersatz)* Division to the 199th Infantry Division in August 1916. The 199th Infantry Division was created in August 1917 in the region of Stryi-Halicz in Galicia (a region in Eastern Central Europe) with troops from various units transferred from the western front.

---

* The term "Pionier" indicated a member of an engineering battalion and was usually composed of two engineering *(pionier)* companies, a searchlight *(scheinenwerfer)* company, and a mortar *(minenwerfer)* company.

From the end of August 1916 until the beginning of November, the 199th Infantry Division fought in Galicia and suffered heavy casualties. In early November the division was replaced. After a rest and replacements the division was sent to the western front. The division arrived at Dun and remained in billets for three weeks in the vicinity of Spincourt. In the latter part of November 1916, the 199th Infantry Division was sent to the Champagne area and assigned to the Bohaine region. It went into the front lines in the Rancourt-Sailliz sector on the Somme by the end of December 1916. In early 1917 the 4th Bavarian Reserve Infantry Regiment was relieved and returned to the Bavarian Replacement *(Ersatz)* Division.

Assigned to the Aisne front, east of Craonne, the Bavarian Replacement Division was able to successfully check the French April 1917 Offensive. The fierce fighting of the division earned the commanding general the Pour le Mérite Order.* On 12 April 1917, Colonel Jordan was appointed regimental commander. Relieved at the end of April, the division occupied a sector in the Apremont Wood from the middle of May until the end of August 1917. On 1 September, the division was in Belgium where it fought on both sides of the Ypres-Menin Road until September 25th. The 3rd Battalion of the 4th Bavarian Reserve Infantry Regiment was almost destroyed during a major engagement on 20 September 1917.

In October, the division was transferred to the eastern front and sent into the front line southeast of Tarnopol during December 1917.

Major Amthor *(see document 4)* was appointed regimental commander on 21 January 1918. The division was then returned to the western front where it held a part of the Verdun sector. This area was quiet with no major engagements taking place. Relieved from the front by the 231st Infantry Division, the Bavarian Replacement Division was moved to the Vesle front on 25 July 1918 and remained in this sector until 12 August 1918. The division was then sent to the vicinity of Meubeuge to rest, be refitted, and receive replacements. On 1 September 1918, the division was again sent to the front lines near Perthes.

It was between 23 September and 30 October 1918, during a major engagement in the Champagne sector that the division lost around 2000 men. It was during this engagement that Pionier Deschler was awarded the Iron Cross 2nd Class in recognition of his bravery in action. The division was now so reduced in strength that it was dissolved shortly after it was withdrawn from the front in mid October 1918.

✠ ✠ ✠

---

* Bavarian Lt. General Hermann Ritter von Burkardt, Commanding General of the Bavarian **Ersatz** (Replacement) Division was awarded the Prussian Pour le Mérite Order on 12 May 1917. The citations reads in part:

> "... in recognition of distinction during the battle and withdrawal at
> Craonne on April 16, 1917..."

"The History of the Prussian Pour le Mérite Order, 1888-1918," Volume III, W.E. Hamelman, pp.489-490, entry 239.

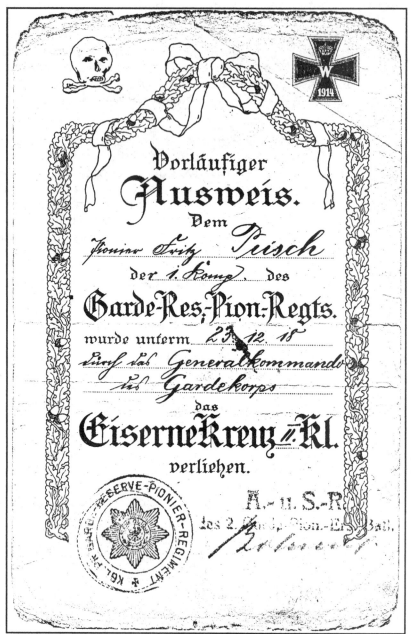

**Document 5   Preliminary Identification Certificate, Type 2
to Pionier Peisch**

The document shown at the left is a Preliminary Identification Certificate, Type 2, *(Vorläufiger Ausweis)* named to Private *(Pionier)* **FRITZ PEISCH**, serving in the 1st Company, 2nd Guard (Garde) Reserve Engineer ((Pionier) Regiment, 1st Guard Reserve Infantry Division.

This small, decorative document shows that Pionier Pusch was awarded the Iron Cross 2nd Class on 23 December 1918, over a month after the armistice. It was awarded through the authority of the Guard Corps General Command. The document measures 10.5 cm. wide x 16.3 cm. high. In the lower left corner is the official regimental stamp. To the right is the signature block with the official stamp of the 2nd Guard Engineer *(Pionier)* Replacement Battalion. Pionier Pusch's unit became a part of the 1st Guard Reserve Division during 1915.

It appears that Pionier Peisch carried this well worn document for quite some time after the war to provide proof of his award of the Iron Cross 2nd Class.

Moving ahead to 1917, the division began its withdrawal from the Hindenburg Line and engaged in a rear guard action in the active Pys-Grevillers region.

On 20 March 1917, the division was removed from the line and sent to a rest area near Tournai. The 1st Guard Reserve Division, on 25 April 1917, took over the Oppy-Gavrelle sector and successfully repulsed several British attacks. Relieved in early May, the division was again sent for rest and refitting at Templeuve and later began construction of defensive positions near Cambrai. The 8th of June found the division assigned to the front, east of Messines. On 12 June 1917, the division was withdrawn and returned to Artois, holding the Moeuvres-Pronville front from 21 June until 16 August 1917. During this time the division took part in no major actions. Sent to the Lens front on 21 August 1917, the division suffered heavy losses resulting from gas attacks during September and October 1917.

The 1st Guard Reserve Division left the Lens sector at the beginning of 1918. The opening day of the Somme Offensive found the division at Lagnicourt northeast of Bapaume. While in heavy action at Lagnicourt the division suffered very heavy losses and required the pioneer regiment to be utilized as infantry in order to stabilize and hold the front. By November 1918, the division was north of Landrecies and participated in the general retreat until the end of the war. It appears that Private Fritz Peisch was decorated for bravery with the Iron Cross 2nd Class during the last days of the war.

✠ ✠ ✠

Document 6   *Preliminary Identification Certificate, Type 2 to Jäger Adolf Emrich*

The above document is the Preliminary Identification Certificate *(Vorläufiger Ausweis)* named to Light Infantryman *(Jäger)* **ADOLF EMRICH**, who was serving in the 2nd Company, 14th Grand Duchy of Mecklenburg Light Infantry *(Jäger)* Battalion, 6th Light Infantry *(Jäger)* Regiment, 195th Infantry Division.

The document shows that Jäger Emrich was authorized to wear the Iron Cross 2nd Class on 3 October 1917. It was signed on the same date by the battalion commander. The document measures 20.8 cm. wide x 16.5 cm. high. Along the lower left border is the printer of this document, Brothers Saupe of Strassburg i.G. and printed in accordance with special military formats. It is interesting that the document does not show a battalion or regimental stamp.

The 195th Infantry Division was formed in July 1916. It was transferred shortly after its formation to Galicia where the division took part in several engagements during August 1916. The division was then sent to the Zloczov sector and went into the front line with Austrian troops. At the end of April 1917, the division was transferred to the western front. In May 1917, the division was successively in the front lines in the Ypres sector, in the Wytschaete sector during June and July, and in the St. Quentin sector during August 1917. By late August, it was relieved from the front and rested in the Walincourt area. It appears that Jäger Emrich received his Iron Cross 2nd Class during one of these actions. From 3 through 12 October 1917, the division was on the front line and enagaged in several actions in the Passchendaele sector. Relieved on October 12th, the division was reorganized at Meulebecke and was transferred to Gand, Belgium.

✠ ✠ ✠

The printed document shown below is an Official Certificate, Type 9, named to Private *(Reservist)* **HEINRICH GEORG FAUL**, serving, at the time he was awarded the Iron Cross 2nd Class on 27 September 1917, in the 12th Company, 120th Württemberg Reserve Infantry Regiment, 204th Infantry Division.

Im Namen Seiner Majestät des Kaisers

habe ich

am 2. September 1917,

dem Reservist Heinrich, Georg F a u l,

12. Kompagnie, Württ.Res. Jnf.Regts. Nr. 120, das

Eiserne Kreuz 2. Klasse

Verliehen.

204. Jnf.-Division,

St. Qu., den 27.9.1917.

Generalmajor
und Divisions-Kommandeur.

Document 7   *Official Certificate, Type 9, to Reservist Heinrich Faul*

The document measures 20.5 cm. wide x 16.5 cm. high. It was dated 27 September 1917 and signed at Staff Headquarters of the 204th Infantry Division by Major General von Stein, the division commander, in black ink and between the signature and date is the purple ink stamp of the 204th Infantry Division.

A brief divisional history shows that the 204th Infantry Division was formed during June and July of 1916 entirely of soldiers from Wurttemberg. The division was sent to Belgium, arriving at Cortemarck on 27 July 1916. Almost immediately, the division was placed in the front line where it occupied the Dixmude-Bixschoote sector until 1 October 1916. At the end of 1916, the 415th and 416th Infantry Regiments were relieved and replaced by the 120th Reserve Infantry Regiment and at this time that the unit of Reservist Heinrich Faul was assigned to the 204th Infantry Division.

After four weeks rest in the area of Ghent, the division returned to the sector southeast of Ypres during February 1917. Three days after the British attack against the German positions at the heights of Wytschaete-Messines, the 204th Infantry Division was relieved on 10 June 1917. The division took part in repulsing several British attacks while in this area. Losses suffered resulted mostly from the British artillery bombardment. Relieved and sent to Gheluvelt until 20 June 1917, the 204th Infantry Division was transferred to the vicinity of Sarreberg. From 20 July until 15 August 1917, the 204th was assigned to a sector north of the Rhone-Rhine Canal in upper Alsace. Again returning to Belgium at the end of August 1917, the division was assigned to the front line sector north of St. Julian where it participated in no major engagements other that patrol activities and small minor actions. It was during one of these minor actions that Reservist Faul was decorated for bravery with the Iron Cross 2nd Class. On September 13, 1917, the 204th Infantry Division was relieved from the Ypres front and assigned to a sector near Cambrai from 24 September 1917 until 13 November 1917.

During this period, the 204th Infantry Division was rated a good fighting division as shown in the records of the Intelligence Section, General Staff, American Expeditionary Forces in France.

✠ ✠ ✠

The document shown below is the Preliminary Authorization Certificate, Type 1, *(Vorläufiges Besitzzeugnis)* named to a Bavarian Private First Class *(Gefreiten)* **ADAM LANG**. He was serving at the time in the 6th Company, 15th Bavarian Landwehr Infantry Regiment, 30th Bavarian Reserve Division when decorated with the Iron Cross 2nd Class. Only two months before the end of World War I, Gefreiten Lang was awarded the decoration on 8 September 1918.

The document was issued on 12 September 1918 and signed in ink by the colonel commanding the 15th Infantry Regiment. It shows the purple stamped official regimental seal of the 15th Bavarian Landwehr Infantry Regiment. The certificate measures 18.0 cm. wide x 14.0 cm. high.

Document 8   *Preliminary Authorization Certificate, Type 1, to Gefreiten Adam Lang*

The 15th Bavarian Landwehr Infantry Regiment, which had been a part of the 39th Bavarian Division, was attached to the 30th Bavarian Reserve Division during December 1916 where the division was serving in the Vosges sector of the front. It was at this time Corporal Lang joined the division. In April 1917, the division was relieved from the front and after a short rest, sent to the front lines at Lorraine in the Seille sector.

At the end of October 1917 the 30th Bavarian Reserve Infantry Division was transferred to Upper Alsace north of the Rhone-Rhine Canal where it relieved the 3rd Reserve Division.

During 1918 the 30th Bavarian Reserve Division remained on the front until the armistice was signed in November 1918. The majority of the men in the 15th Bavarian Landwehr Infantry Regiment were over 30 years old. It was necessary to establish assault detachments using the younger men of the regiment in order to accomplish the required patrol activities. Since Gefreiten Lang was decorated so late in the war, we can assume that it came as a result of his patrol activities.

✠ ✠ ✠

The document shown below is an Authorization Certificate, Type 4, *(Besitzzeugniz)* named to Private First Class *(Gefreiten)* **MAX SÖLL**, who, when decorated with the Iron Cross 2nd Class, was serving in the 1st Assault *(Sturm)* Battalion.

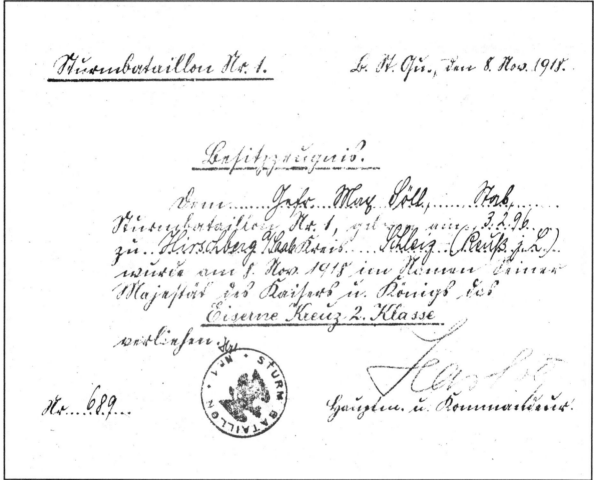

Document 9   *Authorization Certificate, Type 4, to Gefreiten Max Söll*

The document is produced from a mimeograph duplicator and the printing is the usual purple lettering. It measures 20.4 cm. wide x 16.4 cm. high. The document was signed on 8 November 1918, three days before the war ended, at the battalion headquarters by the battalion commander with a purple indelible pencil. The document has been numbered 689. In the center between the number and the signature block is the purple ink official stamp of the 1st Assault Battalion. When Gefreiten Söll was decorated with the Iron Cross 2nd Class for bravery in action, he was 22 years old and received his award three days before the war ended.

No information regarding the 1st Assault Battalion was found.

✠ ✠ ✠

$\mathbf{T}$he document shown below is a Preliminary Identification Certificate, Type 2, *(Vorläufiger Ausweis)* named to Corporal *(Unteroffizier)* **PAUL BIEMANN**, who was serving in the 47th Bavarian Flying Service Section *(Fliegerabteilung)*, Army Group "Linsingen."

```
        V o r l ä u f i g e r   A u s w e i s !
        ===========================================


        Es wird hiermit bescheinigt, dass dem Unteroffizier

        Paul  B i e m a n n, bayr.Fliegerabteilung 47, am 24.12.17

             das Eiserne Kreuz zweiter Klasse
             ====================================

        gemäss Oberkommando Heeresgruppe Linsingen IIa Nr.50487 K

        verliehen worden ist.

                          O.U., den 24. Dezember 1917.


                                    Hauptmann
                                       und
                              Kommandeur der Flieger
                             bei Heeresgruppe Linsingen
```

Document 10   *Preliminary Identification Certificate, Type 2, to Unteroffizier Paul Biemann*

The plain, typed document measures 20.6 cm. wide x 15.1 cm. high. It was signed with a pencil on 24 December 1917 by the commander of the Flying Service Section. To the left of the signature block is the purple ink official stamp of the Flying Section of the Army Group "Linsingen." The document shows that Unteroffizier Biemann was authorized to wear the Iron Cross 2nd Class on 24 December 1917, a rather nice Christmas gift.

The 47th Bavarian Flying Section *(Fliegerabteilung)* was a defensive unit for the protection of the air strips. The unit utilized anti-aircraft defenses and was also responsible for transportation services.

✠ ✠ ✠

$\mathbf{O}$n the following page is the Preliminary Identification Certificate, Type 2, *(Vorläufiger Ausweis)* named to Corporal *(Unteroffizier)* **HEINRICH GANTERT**,who was serving in the 6th Company, 470th Infantry Regiment, 240th Infantry Division.

The document measures 21.5 cm. wide x 18.3 cm. high. It shows that Unteroffizier Gantert was awarded the Iron Cross 2nd Class on 31 October 1917. It was signed at divisional staff headquarters by Major General Müller, commander of the 240th Division. The purple ink official stamp of the 240th Infantry Division is shown in the lower left-hand corner.

The 470th Infantry Regiment was composed of men from the Grand Duchy of Baden. The 240th Prussian Infantry Division was created in early 1917. After a period of intensive training from 4 February until 28 March 1917, the division was sent to Mulhousen during the latter part of March 1917. It was assigned to the front line between the Rhone-Rhine Canal and Hirzbach until 20 August 1917. On 25 August 1917, the division was reassigned to Woevre in the Calonne Trench sector. On October 5th the division left the area of Conflans and was assigned in Flanders on 9 October 1917. The 240th Infantry Division went into action between the Ypres-Staden railroad and Poelcappelle where it suffered heavy losses during the battles fought on 9 October and 12 October 1917. It was during one of these battles that Unteroffizier Gantert was cited for bravery and awarded the Iron Cross 2nd Class.

Document 11   *Preliminary Identification Certificate, Type 2, to Sergeant Heinrich Gantert*

Relieved on 14 October 1917, the division was sent to Artois, and by the 23rd of October, the division was reassigned to the Bullecourt sector southeast of Arras, where on 20 November 1915 the sector was attacked by British units. Here the division again suffered heavy losses and in mid December the 240th Infantry Division was relieved and sent for rest, replacements and refitting.

During 1918 the division was sent to various sectors on the front serving as reinforcements and was engaged in several actions. In November 1918 the division withdrew toward Mouzon on its return to Germany.

✠ ✠ ✠

The document shown below is a handwritten Identification Certificate, Type 5, *(Ausweis)* named to Staff Physician *(Stabarzt)* Dr. **KARL SPILLER**, who was serving on the medical staff of the 247th Squadron Staff *(Staffelstab)*.

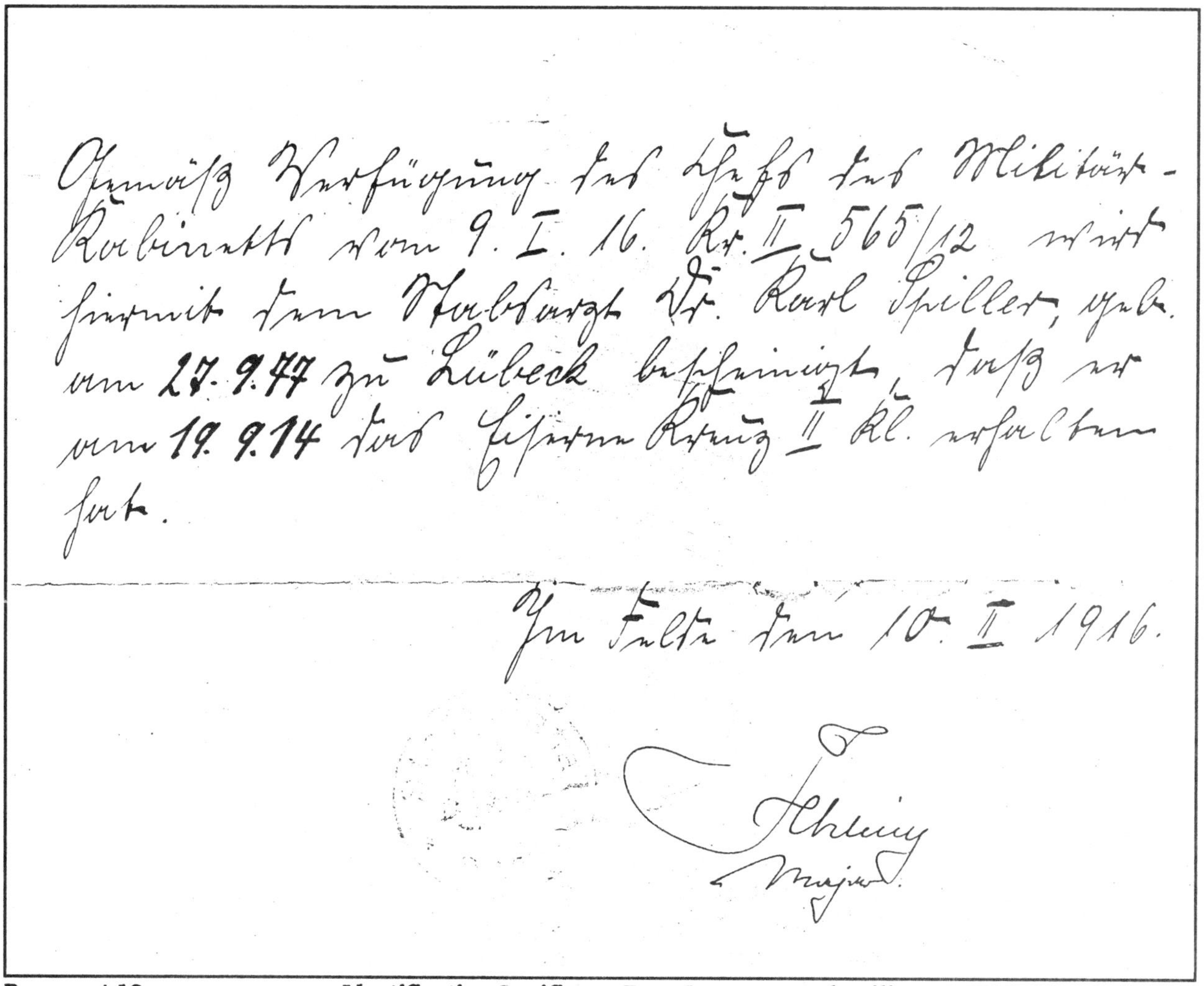

Document 12   *Identification Certificate, Type 5, to Dr. Karl Spiller*

The certificate measured 21.0 cm. wide x 15.5 cm. high. The plain, handwritten certificate was signed in the field *(Im Felde)* on 10 February 1916 and by a major. The document shows adjacant to the signature block, a faded purple ink official stamp of the 247th Squadron Staff. The document shows that Dr. Spiller was born on 9 September 1877, and therefore 37 years old when he was awarded the Iron Cross 2nd Class on 19 September 1914.

It appears that Dr. Spiller carried this certificate as identification in the event he was asked to produce proof of having been awarded the Iron Cross 2nd Class.

✠ ✠ ✠

The document shown below is an Official Certificate, Type 9, of the German Alpine Corps *(Das Deutsche Alpenkorps)* which has been given to Acting Officer (Offizierstellvertrater) **GERMAN SOLCHER**, born in Oberroning on 22 May 1886. As shown on the document, Solcher was almost 29 years

Document 13   *Official Document, Type 9, to Offizierstellvertrater German Solcher*

old when awarded the Iron Cross 2nd Class for bravery on 24 December 1914. He was serving in the Bavarian Life Infantry Regiment, 1st Bavarian Division, 1st Bavarian Corps which was a part of the

6th Army. The document is very decorative and measures 36.0 cm. widw x 28.0 cm. high, and has a yellow border with the center illustration in yellow and brown tones. On either side of the document in yellow highlights are battle credits. The purple ink official regimental stamp of the Bavarian Life Infantry Regiment is in the lower left hand corner. To the left is the original ink signature of the regimental commander, Colonel Ritter von Epp *(pictured at right). In the right hand corner at the bottom is the facsimile of the commanding general of the Alpine Corps. Ritter von Epp officially took command of the regiment on 26 December 1914, therefore, this was probably one of the first award documents for the Iron Cross signed by the new regimental commander.

Colonel Franz Ritter von Epp

The division arrived at Saarbrücken on 8-9 August 1914, crossed the French border, attacked Badonviller on the 12th of August, and withdrew north of Saarbrücken on August 17th. It saw action again on the 20th of August against the French at Saarbrücken. The division again crossed the French frontier and advanced to Nossoncourt and Xaffévillers by way of Ballarat. On 12 August 1914 the division was withdrawn and reassembled at Peltre by the city of Metz. The division moved from Metz to Namur on the 14-15 September 1914 reaching Péronne on the 24th.

The 1st Bavarian Infantry Division was heavily engaged at Combles on 24 October 1914 and at Mericourt on December 17th. It is most likely during one of these battles that Officer Candidate Solcher was noticed for his leadership and bravery in the field and subsequently recommended for the Iron Cross 2nd Class.

✠ ✠ ✠

---

* Bavarian Colonel Franz Ritter von Epp served in China during the 1900-01 Boxer Rebellion and also saw service in the campaigns against the Herero and Hottentots in German Southwest Africa during 1904-06. On 23 June 1916, he was awarded the Bavarian Military Max Joseph Order. Colonel Ritter von Epp was also awarded the Prussian Pour le Mérite Order on 29 May 1918. The citation reads in part:

"...for outstanding leadership ... on the western front and
during the battles of Armentières and Bailleul."

"The History of the Prussian Pour le Mérite Order, 1888-1918, Volume III, W.E. Hamelman, p. 576, entry 563.

Note: The German Alpine Corps was not actually an Alpine Corps as such but rather the Bavarian Life Infantry Regiment. The actual Alpine Corps was not formed until May 1915 when the High Command recognized the need for experienced mountain troops. In October 1915 the Bavarian Life Infantry Regiment was transferred into the Alpine Corps which fought in Italy and other mountainous areas until the end of the war. The Alpine Corps was considered as a first class fighting unit by the US Army Intelligence Section of the American Expeditionary Forces.

The attractive red and black document shown below is an Official Certificate, Type 9, awarding the Iron Cross 2nd Class to Sergeant Major Lieutenant *(Feldwebelleutnant)* **SCHLICKUM**. He was ser-

1914 — 1915

Im Namen   Sr. Majeſtät

des Kaiſers und Königs

iſt durch den

Kommandierenden Herrn General

des 24. Reſerve-Armeekorps das

Eiſerne Kreuz 2. Klaſſe

dem *Feldw. Ltn. Schlickum, R. Jäg. B. 20*

am *26. Dezember* 19 *14*

verliehen worden.

Diviſions-Stabs-Quartier, den *30. Juli* 19 *16.*
48. Reſerve-Diviſion.

Generalleutnant und Diviſionskommandeur.

A. LÜBER

Document 14   *Official Certificate, Type 9, to Feldwebelleutnant Schlickum*

ving, at the time of the award of the Iron Cross 2nd Class, in the 20th Reserve Light Infantry *(Jäger)* Battalion, 48th Reserve Infantry Division, which was assigned to the 24th Reserve Corps.

The document has a wide black border with red leaves and berries enclosing the text and measures 21.6 cm. wide x 30.2 cm. high. At the center of the top frame is an Imperial Crown. It is interesting that Feldwebelleutnant Schlickum received the certificate a year and a half after actually being awarded the Iron Cross 2nd Class since the document shows he was authorized the award on 26 December **1914** but the official certificate was not issued until 30 July **1916**.

The document was signed at division staff headquarters by the division commander. To the left, barely visible, is the black ink official stamp of the 48th Reserve Infantry Division. The authorization came through the 24th Reserve Army Corps Staff Headquarters.

The 48th Reserve Infantry Division was formed between August and October 1914. It trained at the Oberhofen Training Camp. In the middle of October 1914, the division was concentrated in the area near the city of Metz and on the 25th of October was assigned the area between Armentières and La Bassée. On 1 November 1914 the division held the front line at Neuve Chapelle. Some units of the division were assigned further north and west of Wytschaete by mid-November. By the end of November the 48th Reserve Division left the western front for duty in Russia.

On 3 December 1914 the division was in Poland near Kalish. It was made a part of the Xth Army and was engaged in several actions during the latter part of December. It was in one of these actions that Feldwebelleutnant Schlickum distinguished himself in action and was recognized by being awarded the Iron Cross 2nd Class. The 20th Reserve Jäger Regiment remained with the 48th Reserve Division only through 1916 when it was transferred to another division.

✠ ✠ ✠

The document shown below is a Preliminary Identification Certificate, Type 2, *(Vorläufiger Ausweis)* named to Corporal *(Unteroffizier)* of the Landwehr I **HOLZMANN**, who was serving in the 3rd Company, 412th Infantry Regiment, 202nd Infantry Division.

Vorläufiger Ausweis

Dem Unteroffz. d. L. I Holzmann der 3. Kompagnie Inf.-Regt. 412 ist durch Verfügung der 202 Inf.Div. vom 9. März 191[illegible] das Eiserne Kreuz II. Klasse verliehen worden.

Regts.-St.-Qu., den 23. März 191[illegible]

Hering

Oberstleutnant und Regiments-Kommandeur

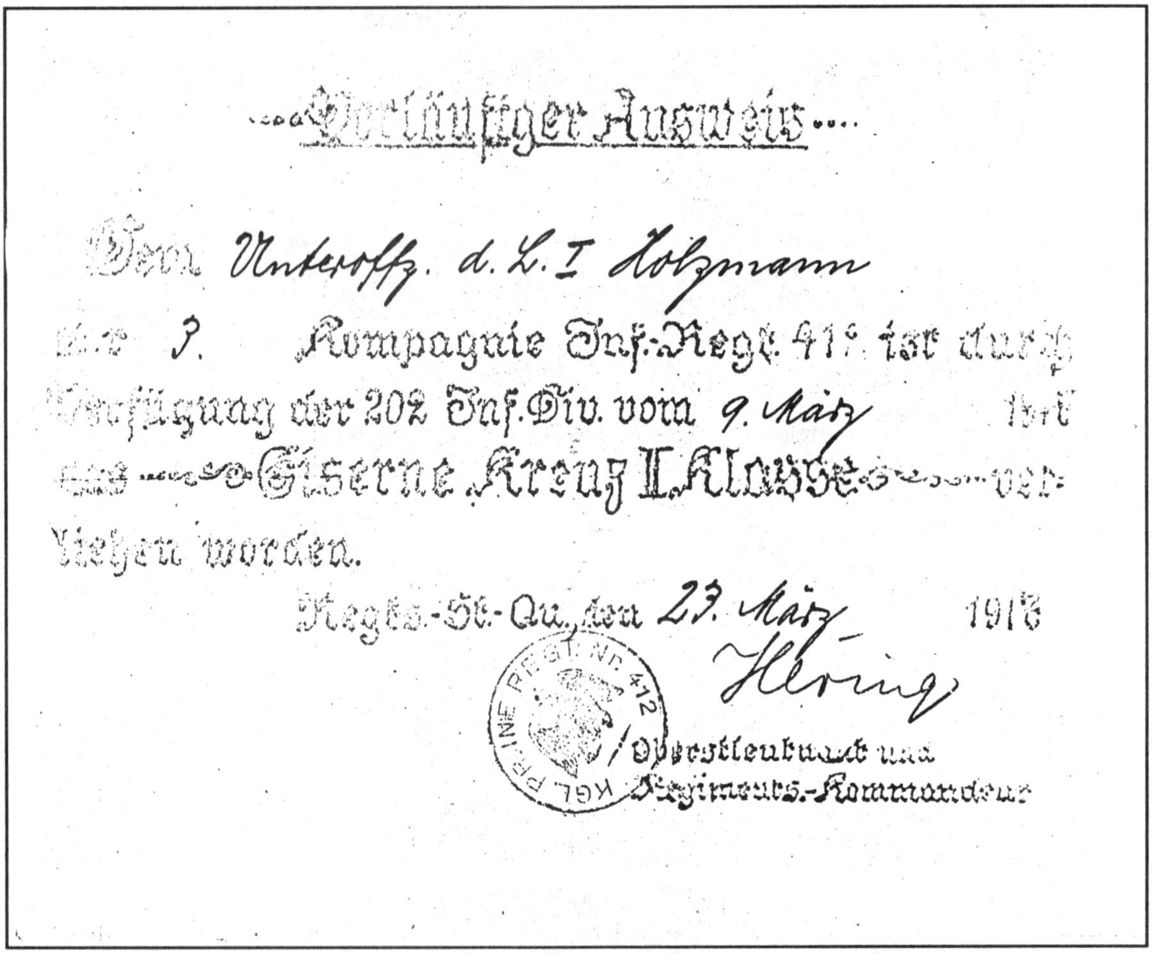

Document 15 Preliminary Identification Certificate, Type 2, to Unteroffizier Holzmann

The document measures 20.7 cm. wide x 16.4 cm. high. It shows that Unteroffizier Holzmann was awarded the Iron Cross 2nd Class on 9 March 1917. It is of the usual purple ink mimeograph duplicator type and on poor quality paper. The document was issued on 23 March 1917 and signed at the regimental staff headquarters by the regimental commander using a purple indelible pencil. In the bottom center, adjacent to the signature block, is the official stamp of the 412th Infantry Regiment stamped in green ink.

The 412th Infantry Regiment did not join the 202nd Infantry Division on the eastern front until early 1917. From March until the end of September 1917, the division occupied a sector near Toukkoum in Courland and took part in several actions. It was during one of these battles that Unteroffizier Holzmann displayed bravery in the field for which he received the Iron Cross 2nd Class. During late September 1918 the division was transferred to the western front and fought in several major actions in eastern Champagne, during which time the division was nearly destroyed. As a result, the 412th Infantry Regiment was dissolved, the surviving troops were distributed between the 408th and 411th Infantry Regiments.

✠ ✠ ✠

On the left is a recent Iron Cross 2nd Class recipient with two previous recipients and in the rear an undecorated comrade. Note the walking sticks.

Seated to the left is a recipient of the Iron Cross 2nd Class. Note he is wearing a shooting lanyard. Seated to the right is a wounded comrade.

✠ ✠ ✠

The document shown below is an Identification Certificate, Type 5, *(Ausweis)* named to Private First Class *(Gefreiter)* **TEGLMEYER** serving in the 10th Company, 74th Infantry Regiment (1st Hanovarian Infantry Regiment), 19th Infantry Division.

Document 16　　　　*Identification Certificate, Type 5, to Gefreiter Teglmeyer*

The document measures 20.5 cm. wide x 16.4 cm. high. It shows that Gefreiter Teglmeyer was awarded the Iron Cross 2nd Class on 4 September 1916. It is signed by the regimental commander with a purple indelible pencil while the unit was in the field *(Im Felde)*. To the left of the signature block is the purple ink official stamp of the 1st Hanovarian Infantry Regiment Number 74. The document shows the usual two holes punched in the left margin indicating that it had been placed in the soldier's military records.

The 19th Infantry Division was formed at the outbreak of World War I and was assigned to the western front as part of the 2nd Army. In April 1915, the 19th Infantry Division was sent to Galicia where it took part in the Mackensen Offensive. On 17 September 1915, the division was reassigned to the western front and sent to Antwerp. Then, by way of Namur and Givet, it went to the Champagne area. The 19th Infantry Division remained behind the front reinforcing the 3rd Army until the division was relieved on 17 October 1915. After a few days rest in the area of Grandlup, it was sent to the front where it held the Hurtebise-Vauclerc sector until the end of October 1915. In mid-December the division was withdrawn from the front lines.

At the beginning of January 1916, the 19th Infantry Division was returned to the Hurtebise-Vauclerc sector where it remained until the middle of May. It was then sent to Sissonne for additional training until 7 June 1916. Entraining on June 8th, the division was sent again to the eastern front arriving at Kovel on 12 June 1916. The division remained on the Russian front from June until November 1916.

At this time the division was assigned to the 4th Austrian Army on the Volhynia front. It was during this time on the Russian front that Gefreiter Teglmeyer was cited for bravery in action and awarded the Iron Cross 2nd Class.

On the 8th of November 1916, the division returned to the western front where it remained in action in various sectors until the end of the war. The 19th Infantry Division was classified as one of the best divisions in the German armies. Morale was high until the end of the war.

✠ ✠ ✠

Letter from home

✠ ✠ ✠

The document shown below is an Official Certificate, Type 9, named to Private *(Musketier)* **WILHELM GRUNENBERG**, serving in the 1st Company, 463rd Infantry Regiment, 238th Infantry Brigade, 238th Infantry Division. The document shows that he was decorated with the Iron Cross 2nd Class for "bravery before the enemy" *(Tapferkeit vor dem Feinde)* on 17 January 1918.

The document measures 21.2 cm. wide x 16.6 cm. high. The lettering and border is printed in blue ink. It was signed in black ink by the regimental commander on 20 February 1918. In the bottom center is the purple ink official stamp of the 463rd Infantry Regiment.

Document 17   *Official Certificate, Type 9, to Musketeer Wilhelm Grunenberg*

The 238th Infantry Division was formed at the beginning of January 1917. Its infantry regiments were taken from the 9th and 10th Corps districts on 13 April 1917. After three months training, the 238th Infantry Division was sent to Cambrai on 20 April 1917. The division went into the front line in the Vendhville-Bellicourt sector. It was relieved on May 20th and rested in the vicinity of Douai until 28 May 1917. On 6 June 1917, the 463rd Infantry Regiment suffered heavy losses during a fierce engagement in the Roeux-Gavrelle sector. Sent to Flanders, the division rested at Roulers and was then placed in reserve in the area of Westroosebeke. On October 13th the division returned to the front lines southwest of Passchendaele. While there it was engaged in a major action which successfully stemmed the British attack on 30 October 1917. After being relieved on November 6th, the division was given a few days rest and on 11-12 November occupied the sector south of St. Quentin-Itancourt. It was during this period that Musketeer Grunenberg was decorated for bravery in action.

The division rested in the vicinity of Origny-St. Benoite from February 1 until March 19, 1918. It was now sent to the front south of St. Quentin. On March 21st, the division attacked at Grugies and in two days advanced by Grand-Serancourt and across the canal near St. Simon. From the 23rd until the 29th of March, the division advanced in reserve by Libermont-Beaulieu les Fontaines-Beuvraignes.

The division was reengaged in battle on the 29th of March at Rollot and Boulogne la Grasse until mid-April. It was active in several other major actions and engagements and was on November 6, 1918, on the front line at Buironfosse until the war ended.

Since the 238th Infantry Division was composed primarily of young recruits, the division was given the nickname "The Division of First Communicants." Note that the recipients, Musketeer Grunenberg was 20 years old and Musketeer Grotefend was only 19 years old when decorated with the Iron Cross 2nd Class.

✠ ✠ ✠

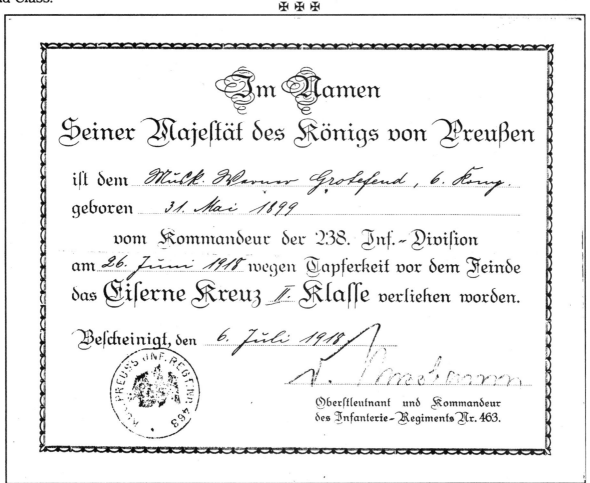

Document 18   *Official Certificate, Type 9, to Musketeer Werner Grotefend*   J. Eicher Collection

The above document is an Official Certificate, Type 9, named to Private *(Musketier)* **WERNER GROTEFEND**, serving in the 6th Company, 463rd Infantry Regiment, 238th Infantry Division. The document shows that he was decorated with the Iron Cross 2nd Class for "bravery before the enemy" *(Tapferkeit vor dem Feinde)* on 26 June 1918.

The document measures 21.2 cm. wide x 16.6 cm. high, and the text and border is printed in blue ink. It is signed by the regimental commander using a purple indelible pencil on 6 July 1918. In the bottom center is the purple ink official stamp of the 463rd Infantry Regiment.

Note that the above document is the same as Document 17. Note, however, that the two stamps of the 463rd Infantry Regiment are different. Here are two identical documents given to different individuals, who could possibly have known each other, being purchased by collectors at different times and at different places, coming together years later in the same place.

✠ ✠ ✠

The poor quality document shown below is an Authorization Certificate, Type 4, *(Besitzzeugnis)* named to Acting Officer *(Offizier-Stellvertrater)* **KARL REHFELD**, who was serving in the 10th Company

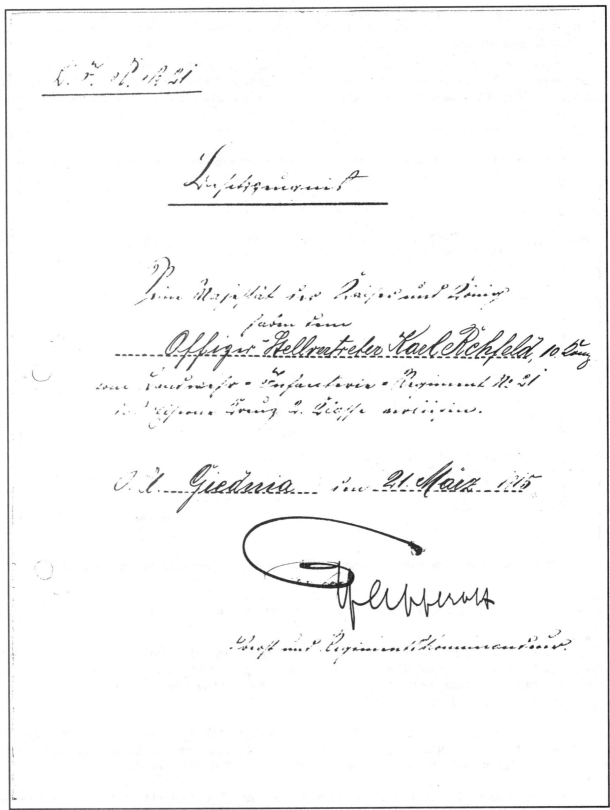

Document 19   *Authorization Certificate, Type 4, to Offizier-Stellvertrater Karl Rehfeld*

of the 21st Landwehr Infantry Regiment, 60th Landwehr Infantry Brigade, 85th Landwehr Infantry Division.

The document measures 21.0 cm. wide x 27.6 cm. high, and is the usual purple ink mimeograph duplicator type certificate that is completely handwritten. It shows that Acting Officer Rehfeld was awarded the Iron Cross 2nd Class on 21 March 1915. The document was signed at field regimental headquarters on the eastern front in Giednia by the colonel commanding the 21st Landwehr Infantry Regiment. There is no regimental stamp, but the left margin shows the usual two holes indicating that the document was attached to the military records of Acting Officer Rehfeld.

The 85th Landwehr Division was stationed in Poland at Presnysz in the Mlawa region during early 1915. The division was engaged in several actions, and it was during one of these actions that Karl Rehfeld was recognized for his distinguished conduct and leadership and decorated with the Iron Cross 2nd Class.

During July 1915, the 85th Landwehr Infantry Division took part in the offensive against the Russians, advancing to the west of Pultusk. By September 1915, with the front being stabilized, the division occupied the Vichnev sector south of Krevo. The division remained on the Vichnev-Deliatitchi front for more than two years, from September 1915 to October 1917.

Toward the end of January 1918, the division was still in the Vidzy region. In early May 1918, the division, except some units, was moved to the Polotsk region where it remained until the end of the war.

✠ ✠ ✠

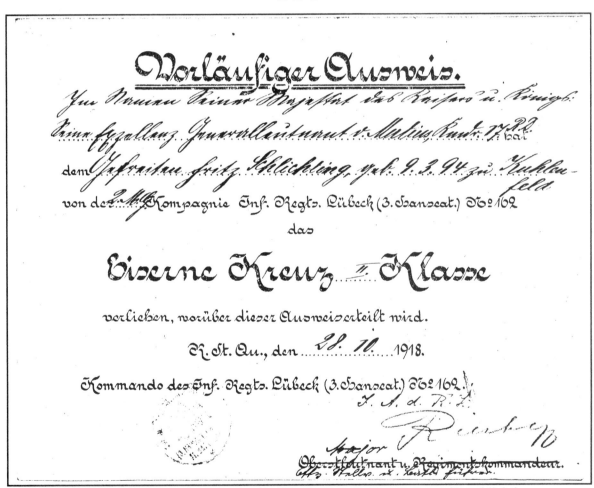

Document 20   Preliminary Identification Certificate, Type 2, to Gefreiten Fritz Schlichting

The document shown above is a Preliminary Identification Certificate, Type 2, *(Vorläufiger Ausweis)* to Private First Class *(Grefreiten)* **FRITZ SCHLICHTING**, while he was serving in the 2nd Machine Gun Company, 2nd Battalion, 162nd Infantry Regiment Lübeck (3rd Hanseatic), 81st Infantry Brigade, 17th Reserve Infantry Division.

The document measures 20.5 cm. wide x 16.1 cm. high. It was issued and signed with a purple indelible pencil at the 162nd Infantry Regiment (Lübeck) on 28 October 1918. Notice the signature block where the regimental commander and his replacement has been lined out. The certificate has been authorized by an Acting Officer and acting battalion commander. This speaks for the heavy losses the division must have suffered during October 1918. In the lower left hand corner is the official regimental stamp in the usual purple ink.

The beginning of 1918 found the 17th Reserve Infantry Division holding a quiet sector of the front during the winter months prior to the German offensive on the Lys, which began 9 April 1918. On 22 April 1918, the division was relieved and on April 24th arrived in the area of Maldeghem. The division suffered heavy casualties.

On 4 June 1918, the division was sent to Tergnier at which time the June German Noyon offensive was being organized. The division, marching by night, arrived at Boulogne la Grasse on the 10th of June and went into the front line during the evening of the 11th. The 17th Reserve Infantry Division, by the 18th of June, was engaged in a major action against the French counter-offensive. In August, the French mounted another major attack against the sector of the 17th Reserve Infantry Division and forced the division to withdraw to Canny sur Matz and later to north of Fresnieres. The division was assigned to second line defenses on 31 August 1918. By the 5th of September, the division was again engaged in action at Esmery-Hallon and was relieved from the front on 9 September 1918.

Subsequently, the 17th Reserve Infantry Division was sent to Lorraine where it rested for a month, was refitted and received replacements. On 10 October 1918 the division returned to the front at Le Cateau. On 11 October, the 17th Reserve Infantry Division was attacked during a major British assault which continued until 3 November 1918. The division was engaged in several actions near Le Cateau on October 18th, Bazuel on October 21st, Forest on October 23rd, Landrecies on October 24th, and Bois L'Eveque on 27 October 1918. It was during one of these actions that Private First Class Schlichting, who was 24 years old at the time, was decorated for bravery in action with the Iron Cross 2nd Class.

The 17th Reserve Infantry Division was removed from the front lines on 3 November 1918 and remained behind the lines until the end of the war.

The document shown below is an Authorization Certificate, Type 4, (Bestizzeugnis) named to Artillery Assistant Sergeant Major (Vizewachtmeister) **HANSEN** serving in the 65th Reserve Field Artillery Regiment, 80th Reserve Artillery Brigade, 80th Reserve Infantry Division, attached to the XXXXth Reserve Corps.

The document measures 17.5 cm. wide x 10.7 cm. high. It was signed on 1 May 1915 in Kemping. It is signed by the regimental commander and the award was authorized through the XXXXth Reserve Corps "Orders of the Day." It showed that Vizewachtmeister Hansen was awarded the Iron Cross 2nd Class on 13 March 1915. What is interesting is that Hansen was authorized to wear the Iron Cross 2nd Class but did not receive the Authorization Certificate until six weeks later. In the lower left hand corner is the blue ink official 65th Reserve Field Artillery Regiment stamp.

| Document 21 | Authorization Certificate, Type 4, to Vizewachtmeister Hansen | J. Eicher Collection |

The 80th Reserve Infantry Division was organized during the 1914-1915 winter. After completion of training at Lockstedt, the division was sent to Eastern Prussia in early February, 1915. It took part in the Masurian Lakes battle from the 7th to the 17th of February 1915. From the end of February to the beginning of March, the 80th Reserve Infantry Division was actively engaged in actions along the Polish frontier until the Russian retreat. In March 1915, the division was reassigned to the Eastern Prussian boundaries and took part in several actions in the area of the Suvalki government until July. It was during one of these engagements that Vizewachtmeister Hansen was cited for bravery in action and rewarded with the Iron Cross 2nd Class.

At the time of the 1915 German summer offensive, the division participated in the capture of Kovno on 18 August 1915. The 80th Reserve Infantry Division fought on the Niemen from the 19th of August until the 8th of September 1915 when it captured the city of Vilna. The division occupied this area until March 1916. In March 1916 the division opposed the Russian offensive in the Narotch Lake front and occupied this new sector until December 1916. On December 23rd, the 80th Reserve Infantry Division was sent to the western front where it was engaged in several major engagements in various sectors. The division stayed on the western front until the end of the war.

✠ ✠ ✠

The document shown below is a Preliminary Identification Certificate, Type 2, *(Vorläufiger Ausweis)* to Replacement Reserve Private *(Ersatz Reserve)* **HANS ROTHMANN**. He was serving, when awarded the Iron Cross 2nd Class, in the 8th Company, 75th Reserve Infantry Regiment, 211th Infantry Brigade, 211th Infantry Division.

Document 22   *Preliminary Identification Certificate, Type 2, to Reservist Hans Rothmann*

The decorative black ink printed on creme paper document measures 21.4 cm. wide x 18.5 cm. high. It was authorized by the commander of the 211th Infantry Division and signed and issued in the field on 25 February 1918. The certificate is signed in ink by the regimental chief and to the left of the signature block is the official purple ink stamp of the 75th Reserve Infantry Regiment.

The 211th Infantry Division was organized on 15 September 1916 at Tournai. The 75th Reserve Infantry Regiment had been assigned to the 27th Infantry Division, a part of the 4th Army Corps. The regiment had seen action on the front during the British Somme offensive from July to August 1916. By 20 September 1916, the division's reorganization had been completed; it was immediately sent to the front at the Nublu-Manancourt sector of the Somme where it set up defensive positions.

During January until June 1917 the division was engaged in several major actions and by 25 June the division held the forest of St. Gobain. By the end of July, the division was reassigned to the Cernay-

Malval Farm sector. At the end of December 1917, the 211th Infantry Division was relieved from the front and sent to rest, receive replacements, and be refitted. The division stayed at Gizy, west of Liesse for four weeks. It appears that Reservist Hans Rothmann was decorated with the Iron Cross 2nd Class for his bravery in action during one of the battles fought in the fall of 1917. In August 1918 the 75th Reserve Infantry Regiment was broken up and the men were sent as drafts to the 42nd Infantry Division and the 87th Infantry Division.

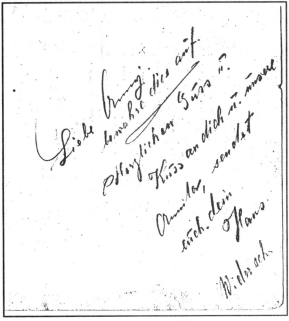

Shown at left is the reverse lower right hand corner of the document shown on the preceding page (Document 21). It is a note, shown actual size, written by Reservist Hans Rothmann to his wife.

"Dear Anny (?)
Keep this!
I send heartfelt greetings and
a kiss to you and our
Anita.
Your Hans
Til we meet again."

It makes one wonder if they did ever meet again. Many documents have interesting snippets such as this which make them mean so much more.

Exhibit 1   **Note to Frau Rothmann**

✠ ✠ ✠

The document shown on the following page appears to be an Authorization Certificate, Type 4, *(Besitz-zeugnis)* named to Ordnance Expert *(Waffenmeister)* **HOLDER** serving on the staff of the 51st Replacement *(Ersatz)* Infantry Regiment, 8th Replacement *(Ersatz)* Infantry Division (243rd Infantry Division).

The large format document measures 19.7 cm. wide x 27.3 cm. high, which when compared with Document 23 appears to have been made smaller. It was signed in pencil on 30 September 1915 at the divisional headquarters by an unidentified officer. To the left of the signature is the purple ink official stamp of the 8th Ersatz Infantry Division. Directly below the stamp is the registration number (2939) of the award indicating its official registration in the Orders (Awards) List of the 8th Ersatz Division. **(See important note below.)**

Note: Upon closer examination, the Holder document discloses that it is **not** an original document but a **photocopy** of an original. It has been doctored to appear as an original by being dampened, crumpled, and then smoothed with a hot iron. There is on the photocopy what appears to be lemon juice added to stain the paper and make it appear older. The signature has been traced, compare it with Document 23, with a pencil. The size is also suspicious since it is smaller than the original as shown on page 32. The decorative rose border has had pencil lines added in several places where the photocopy did not show all the border. The ink stamp of the division has been traced with purple ink with the result that the ink has run. Even three letters of "Preussische"in the stamp have been added to replace those possibly washed out. There is no question as to whether or not this is an actual document, but what is important is that this photocopy was sold as an original document.This shows how, if the collector is not astute and aware, he will be cheated by dealers and even other collectors, and sold a very clever photocopy for an original. *Therefore be careful!*

The 8th Ersatz Division was formed in August 1914. On 17 August 1914, the division was sent to Saarbrücken, as part of the rear of the 6th Army. Elements of the division went into action on 20 August 1914. It was engaged at Hoeville and Serres, north of Luneville on the 25th of August. In September the division took part in the attacks upon the town of Nancy. The division was subsequently relieved and sent to the rear in the vicinity of Morhange, then it was transferred to Haye at the end of September to relieve the 14th Corps. The division was assigned the sector between Limey, on the west,

Besitzeugnis

Im Namen

Seiner Majestät des Kaisers

habe ich

dem Waffenmeister Holder

Ersatz Infanterie Regiment 51, Stab

das eiserne Kreuz II. Klasse von 1914 verliehen.

8. Ersatz=Division.

Div. St. Qu. .... , den 30. September 1915

nr. 2930 der Ordensliste der 8. Erf. Div.

Spezialfabrik für Militärformulare Gebr. Saupe, Men.

Document 23   *Authorization Certificate, Type 4, to Waffenmeister Holder*

and La Pretre Woods, on the east, for two years. It was during this time period that Waffenmeister Holder was awarded the Iron Cross 2nd Class.

The document shown below is a Authorization Certificate, Type 4, *(Besitzzeugnis)* named to Reserve Corporal *(Unteroffizier d. Reserve)* **LANZ** who was serving in the 165th Artillery Ammunition Column *(Artillerie Munitions Kolonne 165)*, attached to the 238th Artillery Command, 8th Replacement *(Ersatz)* Division (243rd Infantry Division).

The large format document measures 21.5 cm. wide x 27.8 cm. high. The faded document appears to have been framed and exposed to sunlight. The ink in the recipient's name, unit, date and Orders

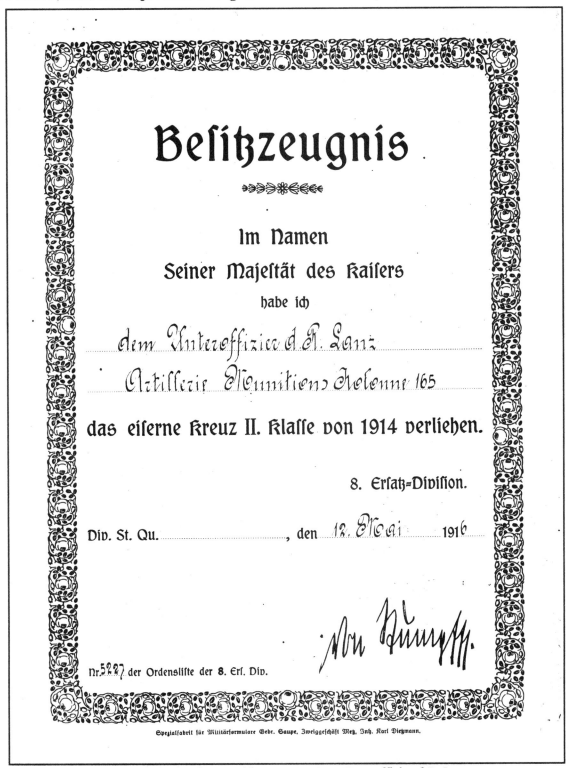

Document 24   *Authorization Certificate, Type 4, to Unteroffizier d.R. Lanz*

List number have faded to a brownish color. The document was signed in ink by an unidentified officer on 12 May 1916. It is interesting that the document does not have an authenticating stamp. In the lower left-hand corner is the official registration number (5227) for the Orders List of the 8th Replacement (Ersatz) Division.

By comparing this document with Document 22 it appears that the same clerk filled in the recipient's names and the same officer signed them.

During 1916 the 8th Replacement (Ersatz) Division occupied the sector of the Pretre wood, north of Fey en Haye until the beginning of October 1916. It appears that Reserve Corporal Lanz was cited for bravery or distinguished service during the period that the division was in the La Pretre wood. No specific information was found regarding the 165th Artillery Ammunition Column.

✠ ✠ ✠

Note: It should be pointed out that **not all** documents relating to the awarding of the Iron Cross were stamped with an authenticating stamp. However, the great majority of award documents do have either a regimental, battalion, or division authenticating stamp.

The document shown below is an Authorization Certificate, Type 4, *(Besitz-Zeugnis)* named to Private *(Fusilier)* **GOLDMANN**. He was serving, at the time of the award of the Iron Cross 2nd Class, in the 10th Company, 408th Infantry Regiment, 406th Infantry Brigade, 202nd Infantry Division.

Besitz-Zeugnis.

Im Namen Sr. Majestät des Kaisers und Königs wurde am 16. September 1917, dem

Fusilier Goldmann

10. Komp. Infanterie-Regiment 408

für hervorragende Tapferkeit vor dem Feinde das unterm 6. August 1914 gestiftete

Eiserne Kreuz II. Klasse

verliehen, über dessen rechtmäßigen Besitz ihm dieses Zeugnis ausgefertigt worden ist.

Für die Richtigkeit:

Major u. Regts.-Kommandeur.

Formular-Lager Julius Wangnid, Königsberg i. Pr., Französische Straße 8.

Document 25   *Authorization Certificate, Type 4, to Fusilier Goldmann*

The document shows that Fusilier Goldmann was decorated with the Iron Cross 2nd Class "for outstanding bravery before the enemy" *(für hervorragende Tapferkeit vor dem Feinde)* on 16 September 1917. The decorative and large document measures 21.5 cm. wide x 33.8 cm. high. It is interesting that where the date, name, unit, class, and signature block are seen, the areas are lined to prevent erasures or changes. It is dated 16 September 1917 and was signed in black ink by the regimental commander. To the left of the signature block is the purple ink stamp of the 408th Infantry Regiment. The document was printed in Königsberg, Prussia.

The 202nd Infantry Division was formed during October 1916 at the Lockstedt cantonment in the 9th Corps District in Altona. The 408th Infantry Regiment was assigned to the division from the Guards depot. By late October 1917, the division was sent to the Russian front. In December 1916 the 202nd Infantry Division was in the area of Riga. From March until the end of August 1916, the division occupied a sector near Toukkoum in Courland where it saw only minor actions and mostly patrol activities. In September 1916, the division was east of Riga where it again engaged in several minor actions. It was during one of these actions that Fusilier Goldmann distinguished himself and was recommended for the Iron Cross 2nd Class.

In November 1917 the 202nd Infantry Division was transferred to the western front. It arrived in the vicinity of Dieuze on 20 November 1917. The division stayed to the rear of the front until the middle of January 1918. The division was assigned to the Lorraine sector where it held the line until being relieved on 19 May 1918. On May 23, 1918, the division was sent to a sector west of Noyon and was in the front line when the German June offensive was made. It advanced by way of Orval as far as Bethencourt. Here it remained until July 10th when it exchanged sectors with the 105th Infantry Division at Autreches. In this sector the division was attacked in mid-August and forced back to Audigncourt. The division suffered very heavily and by late September 1918 was effectively destroyed. The troops remaining were assigned to other units as replacements.

✠ ✠ ✠

The document shown on the following page is an Official Certificate, Type 9, named to Private First Class *(Gefreiten)* **JOHANNES GLINDEMANN**, who was serving in the 2nd Machine Gun Company, 84th Infantry Regiment, 108th Infantry Brigade, 54th Infantry Division.

The document measures 20.8 cm. wide x 16.5 cm. high. It shows that Gefreiten Glindemann was awarded the Iron Cross 2nd Class on 2 August 1917. The document was signed in ink at Division Staff Headquarters by Major General Theodor von Watter*, the commanding general of the 54th Infantry Division. To the left of the signature is the purple ink official stamp of the 54th Infantry Division.

The 54th Infantry Division was formed in March 1915. The 84th Infantry Regiment was transferred from the 18th Infantry Division in the 9th Army Corps District. After organization, the 54th Infantry Division was assigned, by the middle of April 1915, to the Champagne area in the vicinity of Perthes where it remained until July 1915. In July 1915, the division was sent to Russia where it saw action on the Neraw during July and August, and on the Nieman, southeast of Grodno, in September 1915. Returned to France at the beginning of October, the division went into the front line on 12 October 1915 on the left bank of the Oise.

By May of 1916, the 54th Infantry Division saw action while it occupied the sector of Hill 304 at Verdun. On September 11th, it crossed the right bank of the Meuse and advanced north of Fleury. On October 24, 1916, the division was dislodged by French attacks and driven back with heavy losses to north of Fort Douaumont. It was relieved in early November and, hardly having received enough replacements, was again sent into the line on 5 November 1916 north of Flirey em Haye.

---

* Württemberg General Freiherr Theodor von Watter was awarded the Prussian Pour le Mérite Order on 1 September 1916.

"The History of the Prussian Pour le Merite Order, 1888-1918," Volume III, p. 463, entry 158.

Moving ahead to the year 1917, we find the 54th Infantry Division assigned to a relatively quiet sector of Fleury during the winter of 1916-1917. Relieved during the middle of April 1917, the division was sent behind the Champagne front near Asfeld. On 21 April 1917, the division reenforced the front

Im Namen Sr. Maj. des Kaisers und Kœnigs ist verliehen das

Eiserne Kreuz 2. Klasse

dem _Gefreiten Johannes Glindemann der 2.M.G.K._

Jnfanterie-Regiments von Manstein (Schlesw.) Nr. 84.

Div.St.Qu. , den   2.8.   1917

Kœnigl. württ. Generalmajor und Divisions - Kommandeur

Document 26   *Official Certificate, Type 9, to Gefreiten Johannes Glindemann*

lines at Berry au Bac. The French attacked the sector on May 4th but were repulsed. It was during this engagement the division suffered moderate losses. On 10 May 1917, the division was withdrawn from the Aisne front for a short rest and refitting. From May 15th until July 24th, the 54th Infantry Division occupied the sector south of Somme Py. While holding this sector the division received around 2,000 replacements.

On 25 July 1917 the division was sent to Belgium for rest. It was in action again east of Ypres from the 5th to the 19th of August and suffered heavy casualties especially during the British attack on 16 August 1917. It was during this major engagement that Gefreiten Glindemann was recommended for the Iron Cross 2nd Class. The division was relieved and after a short rest was sent back into the frontline in the Cambrai sector at the end of August 1917. It suffered heavy losses during the British tank attack in November 1917.

During 1918 the division fought in many major engagements on the western front. In February 1918, the division was relieved from the frontline sector north of Nancy. It rested and was returned to the front in the area of Moreuil on 3-4 April 1918, taking part in the German attack against the British lines. It was involved in several other engagements in various sectors of the front. The division fought in the Le Cateau area until 12 October 1918, when it was placed in reserve in the vicinity of Landrecies. On 2 November 1918 it was reengaged in several actions in the Ors area until the end of the war.

✠ ✠ ✠

The document shown below is a Preliminary Identification Certificate, Type 2, *(Vorläufiger Ausweis)* named to Artillery Assistant Sergeant Major *(Vizewachtmeister)* **FABER**, who was serving

Document 27   *Preliminary Identification Certificate, Type 2, to Vizewachtmeister Faber*

in the 4th Battery, 21st Reserve Field Artillery Regiment, 21st Reserve Infantry Division when awarded the Iron Cross 2nd Class on 22 August 1917.

The very ornate document measures 16.4 cm. wide x 20.8 cm. high. It was signed with a purple indelible pencil by the section commander on 22 August 1917. To the left of the signature is a blue ink official stamp of the 21st Reserve Field Artillery Regiment.

The 21st Reserve Infantry Division was formed at the beginning of World War I and became a part of Prince Albrecht of Württemberg's 4th Army. On 10-12 August the division entered Belgium. After an action at Neufchateau on 22 August 1914, the 21st Reserve Infantry Division reached Carignan on the 25th of August and saw action again on the 28th of August at Mouzon. It crossed the Meuse at that point, and from there, via Grandpré, swinging around the Argonne to the west, arrived at the Marne-Rhine Canal on 6 September 1914. After several actions, the division held the heights to the south of Cernay en Dormois by 14 September 1914. The 21st Reserve Infantry Division consolidated its positions in the sector of Ville sur Tourbe and at the end of September 1915 took part in the Champagne offensive.

During August 1916 the division was in the vicinity of Senon-Foamix and occupied the Hardaumont sector on the Verdun front until 7 December 1916. During January 1917, the 21st Reserve Infantry Division left the Verdun front very exhausted and on 24 February 1917, occupied the rear sector of Letriecourt-Moncel in Lorraine. From 19 July until 22 October 1917, the division occupied a sector in Champagne southwest of Navroy where it engaged in several major actions. During one of these actions Vizewachtmeister Faber was cited for bravery and subsequently decorated with the Iron Cross 2nd Class.

In the March 1918 offensive the division advanced from la Vacquerie to Beaumont Hamel, which it reached on 27 March 1918. Here the line was stabilized and the division held this sector throughout April, May, and June of 1918. The division remained on the western front until it withdrew toward Germany on 8 November 1918.

✠ ✠ ✠

The document below is a Preliminary Identification Certificate, Type 2, *(Vorläfiger Ausweis)* named to Private *(Musketier)* **HANS STÜBEN** of the 12th Company, 76th Reserve Infantry Regiment, 33rd Reserve Infantry Brigade, 17th Reserve Infantry Division. It shows that he was cited for bravery in action and awarded the Iron Cross 2nd Class on 8 March 1918.

Vorläufiger·Ausweis.

Im Namen Seiner Majestät des Kaisers und Königs ist dem

Walther Hans Stüben

der *12.* Kompagnie Reserve-Infanterie-Regiments Nr. 76 das

EISERNE KREUZ II. KLASSE

verliehen worden, worüber ihm dieser vorläufige Ausweis ausgefertigt wird.

Regts.-Stabsquartier, den *8 März* 1918.

Major und Regimentskommandeur.

Korpsdruckerei XVIII. R. K.

Document 28　　*Preliminary Identification Certificate, Type 2, to Musketier Hans Stüben*

The document measures 20.3 cm. wide x 15.1 cm. high, and, as shown in the lower left corner, was printed by the Corps Print Section. It was authorized on 8 March 1918 at the regimental staff headquarters and signed with an indelible purple pencil by the regimental commander. To the left is the official stamp, in blue ink, of the 76th Reserve Infantry Regiment.

During early August 1914, the 17th Reserve Infantry Division was used to guard the Schleswig-Holstein coast. On 23 August 1914, the division was sent to Belgium and by September 4th reached Termonde outside of Antwerp. About the middle of November the division occupied the front between the Avre and Roye. On December 20, 1914, the division was in the front line between Ribécourt and Thiescourt. On 6 February 1915, the division left the banks of the Oise river to return to the area south of the Avre, between Lassigny and Roye. It remained in this sector until the month of October 1915. During October, the 17th Reserve Infantry Division was withdrawn from the front south of Roye and sent to Artois, near Lens (Liévin-Givenchy).

The division remained in Artois until the battle of the Somme. In February 1916, it launched several attacks against the British. In July the division was sent to Valenciennes for rest, replacements, and refitting. At the end of August 1916, it occupied the sector of Loos-Hulluch, north of Lens. Around September 21st, the division returned to the Somme where it suffered 51% casualties. Relieved, it was transferred to Belgium.

Note: The above history of the 17th Reserve Infantry Division also relates to the 162nd Infantry Regiment document (Example 20) as shown on page 27.

The beginning of 1918 found the 17th Reserve Infantry Division holding a quiet sector of the front during the winter months where it saw several actions. It was during one of these actions that Musketeer Stüben was decorated for bravery in action. This was prior to the German offensive on the Lys which began 9 April 1918. On 22 April 1918 the division was relieved and by April 24 the 17th Reserve Infantry Division arrived in the area around Maldeghem. It is of interest that the division suffered many casualties; death notices in German newspapers revealed that two battalion and several company commanders were lost during the Lys offensive.

On 4 June 1918 the division was sent to Tergnier where, at this time, the June 9th Noyon offensive was being organized. The division, marching by night, arrived at Boulogne la Grasse on the 10th of June and went into the front line during the evening of the 11th. The 17th Reserve Infantry Division by the 18th of June was engaged in a major action against the French counter-offensive.

In August, the French mounted another major attack against the sector of the 17th Division and forced the division to withdraw back to Canny sur Matz and later north of Fresnieres. The division was assigned to second line defenses around 31 August 1918. By September 5th, the division was again in action at Esmery-Hallon and was relieved from the front on 9 September 1918.

The 17th Reserve Infantry Division was sent to Lorraine where it rested for a month and was refitted and received replacements. On 10 October 1918, the division returned to the front at Le Cateau. On October 11th it was attacked by a major British assault which lasted until November 3rd. The division was engaged in actions near Le Cateau on October 18th, Bazuel on October 21st, Forest on October 23rd, Landrecies on October 24th, and Bois L'Eveque on 27 October 1918.

The 17th Reserve Infantry Division was removed from the front lines on 3 November 1918 and remained behind the lines until the end of the war.

✠ ✠ ✠

A. REICH

The document shown below is an Official Document, Type 9, named to Corporal (*Unteroffizier*) **GEORG FRIEDRICH GOHDE**. When awarded the Iron Cross 2nd Class, he was serving in a Telephone and Telegraph Section (*Fernsprech - Abteilung*) attached to the VIIIth Army Corps.

The unusual document measures 21.2 cm. wide x 13.5 cm. high. It is unique in that it has been printed on a type of cloth paper. The document has the texture of cloth but appears to be a heavy paper-like substance. It was issued through the authority of the commanding general of the VIIIth Army Corps and was signed on 27 October 1915, in black ink by the communications section commander. To the left of the signature block is the purple ink stamp of the Telephone and Telegraph Section of the VIIIth Army Corps.

Im Namen Seiner Majestät
des Kaisers und Königs

ist durch den Kommandierenden General des VIII. Armeekorps

dem *Unteroffizier Georg. Friedrich G o h d e.*

Fernsprech - Abteilung VIII. Armeekorps

das Eiserne Kreuz II. Klasse

am *27. Oktober 1915* verliehen worden.

Hauptmann d.Res.u.Abtlgs.Komdr.

Document 29   *Official Certificate, Type 9, to Unteroffizier Georg Gohde*

The VIIIth Army Corps was composed of the 15th Infantry Division and the 16th Infantry Division, and was part of the 4th Army of the Duke of Württemberg.

During 1915, the Telephone Section was assigned to the western front and saw action in the sectors of Champagne (April), St. Mihiel (April), Artois (May), and the Aisne (June).

There is no way to determine where Corporal Gohde served or to what unit he was attached with the information available.

✠ ✠ ✠

The document shown below is an Official Certificate, Type 9, named to Cavalry Assistant Sergeant Major *(Vizewachtmeister)* **VOLLRATH** who was decorated with the Iron Cross 2nd Class while serving at the Veterinary Hospital (Pferde Lazarett 2), Munitions and Transportation Columns, XVIIIth Army Corps.

Seine Exzellenz der Herr kommandierende General

hat im Namen

Seiner Majestæt

des Kaisers und Kœnigs

dem _____

_____ das

Eiserne Kreuz 2. Klasse

verliehen. — Tagesbefehl des ____ v. 26. 7. 16.

Document 30   *Official Certificate, Type 9, to Vizewachtmeister Vollrath*   W. Shannon Collection

The very interesting document measures 20.8 cm. wide x 16.4 cm. high. Printed in black ink and signed with a purple indelible pencil by the column commander on 26 July 1916. Below the date is the purple ink stamp of the Headquarters of the Munitions and Transportation Column. The award was authorized through the daily orders of the XVIIIth Army Corps. The document has in the left margin the usual two punched holes indicating that the certificate was a part of the military records of Vizewachtmeister Vollrath.

What makes this document so unique is that the recipient was assigned to a veterinary hospital treating horses. It makes one wonder what duties Vizewachtmeister Vollrath was assigned to in order for him to have been awarded the Iron Cross 2nd Class. There is no indication whether the award was for combatant or noncombatant actions.

✠ ✠ ✠

The document shown below is a Confirmation Bestowal Certificate, Type 7, *(Verleihungs Bestätigung)* named to Captain *(Hauptmann)* **RUDOLF WETZERICH**, Battery Commander, 4th Battery, 22nd Reserve Field Artillery Regiment, 22nd Reserve Infantry Division. He was born on 29 July 1869 in the Pomeranian town of Negrep and was 45 years old when decorated for bravery with the Iron Cross 2nd Class on 16 September 1914.

The beautiful entirely hand-written document is in black ink and measures 20.9 cm. wide x 16.5 cm. high. The document is dated 29 January 1915 and was signed in black ink by the regiment commander on the Aisne front. It shows that Captain Wetzerich received the Iron Cross 2nd Class on 16 September 1914. To the left of the signature block is the black ink stamp of the 22nd Reserve Field Artillery Regiment.

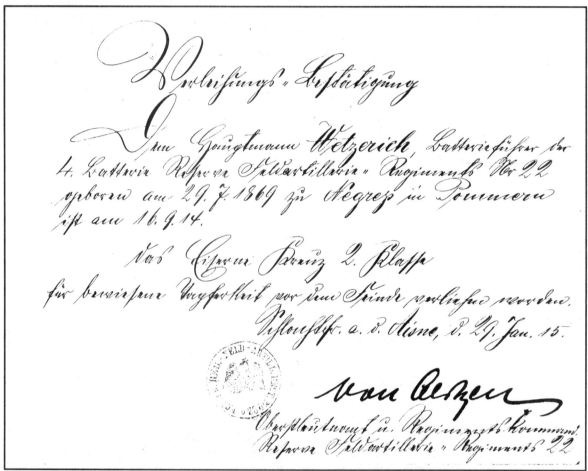

Document 31   *Confirmation Bestowal Certificate, Type 7, to Hauptmann Wetzerich*

At the outbreak of World War I, the 22nd Reserve Infantry Division along with the 7th Reserve Infantry Division formed the 4th Reserve Corps of the 1st Army. The division took part in the battle of the Marne on 6 September 1914. Following the Marne, the division was concentrated on the Nouvron plateau. It was during this time that Captain Wetzerich* was decorated for "demonstrated bravery before the enemy" *(für bewiesene Tapferkeit vor dem Feinde)*. On 12 November 1914, elements of the division took part in the attack on the Nouvron Plateau and suffered heavy losses. The 22nd Reserve Infantry Division occupied the front between the Aisne and the Oise rivers until the autumn of 1915. At the end of October the division left the area northwest of Soissons to go to Champagne (Souain sector).

From March 1 until 5, 1916, at the height of the Verdun offensive, the division was reassembled between Dun and Vilosnes behind the front. On 6 March 1916, it attacked on the left bank of the Meuse. Until the end of the war, the division occupied several sectors of the western front and was active in several major battles and many minor actions. It suffered heavy losses but maintained a high morale.

---

* Promoted to Major on 27 January 1915.

Rudolf Gustav Albert Wetzerich was a career officer. He was married to **Antonie Peters** on 5 October 1890. They had one issue, a daughter, Edda, born on 26 June 1897. He entered the military as an officer candidate on 1 October 1890 in the 19th Thuringen Field Artillery Regiment and sworn in on 17 October 1890. On 17 December 1891, Wetzerich was promoted to the rank of Second Lieutenant.

On 26 September 1912, Wetzerich, now holding the rank of Captain, was decorated with the House and Merit Order of Duke Peter Friedrich Ludwig 2nd Class with the Silver Crown from the Duchy of Oldenburg. In recognition of his abilities as an instructor of artillery at the War College in Hersfeld, he was decorated with the Prussian Red Eagle Order 4th Class on 18 January 1914.

Shortly after World War I began, Captain Wetzerich was recognized for his leadership and the command of his artillery battery, and awarded the Iron Cross 2nd Class on 16 September 1914.

His records show that he participated in several major engagements. Beginning in August 1914, from the 28th through the 30th, his artillery unit fought in the engagement at Solesmes. Then from the 5th through 9th of September 1914, he fought at the battle of the Somme and on the 12th of September at the engagement at Ourcq. His unit was engaged from the 11th through the 12th of November 1914, at Chevillecourt.

On January 1, 1915, Captain Wetzerich commanded his battery at the engagement at Nouvron. It appears from his records that Captain Wetzerich was hospitalized on the 23rd of January 1915 for a nervous condition. While in the hospital, Wetzerich was promoted to the rank of Major. He was released from the hospital on April 8, 1915 and he returned to command his artillery unit.

Later the unit commanded by Major Wetzerich fought in the major battle of the Aisne on 21-27 May 1917. One day later his artillery battery was engaged in the double battle on the Aisne and Champagne which lasted from the 28th of May until the 6th of July 1917.

His artillery unit settled down to the static trench bombardments in the Chemin des Dames sector. It seems that his leadership during the assault on the French position south of Vauxaillon on the 1st of June 1917 was especially noted, and we can assume that it was during this engagement that he was recommended for and received the Iron Cross 1st Class.

On 26 November 1917, Major Wetzerich was awarded the War Merit Cross 2nd Class from the Duchy of Brunswick. The Kingdom of Saxony decorated him with the Royal Albrecht Order Knight 1st Class on 18 September 1918. On 19 October 1918, shortly before the war ended, Major Wetzerich received from Austria the Military Merit Cross 3rd Class with the War Decoration.

From 11 August until 15 October 1917, Major Wetzerich was active in the static position bombardments at Verdun and from 17 October 1917 until 10 January 1918, his unit engaged in defensive bombardments in the Lothringen area. Major Witzerich was given leave from his artillery unit from 26 October until 22 November 1917.

From the 11th of January until the 20th of March 1918, Major Wetzerich and his artillery battery engaged in static trench bombardments in the Lothringen sector and on the 29th of March 1918, Major Wetzerich was relieved from front line duty because of his health problems and did not return to the front or his unit again.

His military record shows that he was also awarded the Iron Cross 1st Class. However, no date is given as to when he received it. Wetzerich was the recipient of the Friedrich August War Cross in both the 1st and 2nd Classes from the Duchy of Oldenburg.

✠ ✠ ✠

The document shown below is an Official Certificate, Type 9, named to Private (*Musketier)* **HEINRICH RIEBE**, serving in the 8th Company (machine gun), 69th Infantry Regiment *(Rheinish),* 80th Infantry Brigade, 15th Infantry Division.

The document measures 20.5 cm. wide x 16.4 cm. high. It is a very decorative document and was signed in black ink by the commanding general of the 15th Infantry Division at division staff headquarters on 14 September 1918. In the lower center adjacent to both the date and signature block is the purple ink official stamp of the 15th Infantry Division. The document has in the left-hand margin the two punched holes indicating that the certificate had been placed in the military records of Musketier Riebe.

| Document 32 | Official Certificate, Type 9, to Musketier Heinrich Riebe |

In the official Order of Battle records of the 15th Infantry Division, the 69th Infantry Regiment was not assigned to the division until 1917. In February 1917, the division was in Transylvania and by April it was being held in reserve at Vladimir-Volynski. The division was then transferred to the western front in France at the end of April 1917 and occupied the sector of Vaux les Palaneix on the Meuse. At the end of May the division was relieved and sent to the Vauclerc Plateau where it took up positions on the front line. On 2-3 June 1917, the division successfully attacked in this sector . The division renewed these attacks again on July 3rd which resulted in heavy losses. By 8 July 1917, the division was relieved and sent to the Lys area from where it was transferred to the Richecourt-Avricourt sector. It was placed back in the front lines on 15 July 1917 near Blamont.

On 4 September 1917, the division was sent to the Verdun area to rest and be refitted. Later it was transferred to Belgium on 7 October 1917, where it saw action and suffered heavily on the Ypres front until November 13th. The division was then sent to the rear for rest, replacements and refitting in the area of Brueges-Knocke. The 15th Infantry Division was sent back into the front line east of Ypres on December 18th. By the middle of January 1918, it was withdrawn from this sector and returned to the Brueges (Bruges) sector.

Moving ahead to September 1918, the division was in the Damvillers sector north of Verdun, and on 26 September 1918 it was reassigned to Flabas east of the Meuse. It was during this period that Musketeer Reibe was decorated with the Iron Cross 2nd Class. The division held a sector in the Bois des Caures area until the end of the war.

✠ ✠ ✠

In defense of the regimental standard

The document shown below is a simple handwritten Preliminary Identification Certificate, Type 2, *(Vorläufiger Ausweis)* showing that Mounted Light Infantryman *(Jäger zu Pferde)* **WALTER STARK** was awarded the Iron Cross 2nd Class on 4 April 1918. He was serving in the 3rd Squadron, 6th Mounted Light Cavalry Regiment *(Jäger Regiment zu Pferde)*, Guard Cavalry Division.

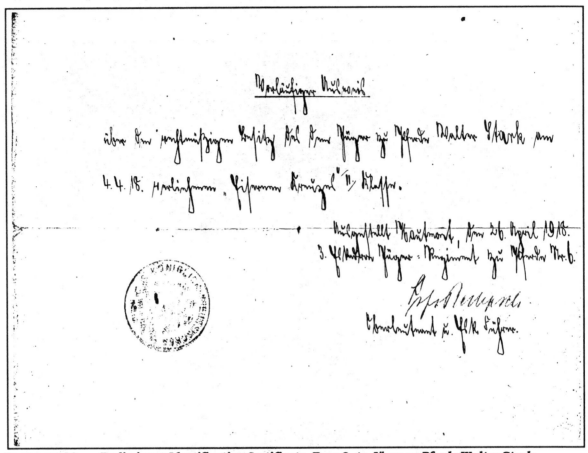

Document 33 *Preliminary Identification Certificate, Type 2, to Jäger zu Pferde Walter Stark*

The document measures 20.2 cm. wide x 16.4 cm. high, and the text is written in black ink. It was signed with an indelible purple pencil on 26 April 1918 by the squadron commander. In the lower left-hand corner is the official stamp of the 6th Light Cavalry Regiment in green ink. The document is worn and appears to have been carried by Jäger Stark as a means of producing proof of his authorization to wear the Iron Cross.

The Guard Cavalry Division had been reformed during early 1918 when the division left the eastern front in mid-March. After being reformed the division was assigned to the western front arriving at the Meubeuge area where it underwent six weeks' training for open warfare. On 28 May 1918 the division relieved the 23rd Infantry Division east of the Suippe. The Guard Cavalry Division was relieved about 2 July 1918 and on 15 July 1918 returned to the front to strengthen the line near Souain. It was then relieved on 20 July 1918. The division was moved to the Soissons area and on 22 August 1918 relieved the Light Infantry *(Jäger)* Division east of Soissons.

The Guard Cavalry Division was withdrawn from the western front on September 5, 1918.

✠ ✠ ✠

The document shown below is a Authorization Certificate, Type 4, *(Besitz-Zeugnis)* named to War Volunteer Private*(Kriegs-freiwilliger)* **HEINRICH GRAU,** who was serving in the 2nd Company, 123rd Grenadier Infantry Regiment, *(King Karl of Württemberg),* 53rd Infantry Brigade, 27th Infantry Division, XIIIth Army Corps.

Document 34   *Authorization Certificate, Type 4, to War Volunteer Heinrich Grau*

The very colorful and ornate document measures 20.5 cm. wide x 21.4 cm. high. The document shows that Volunteer Grau was awarded the Iron Cross 2nd Class on 25 February 1917. The award was not authorized until it was signed on 25 April 1917, two months later, at the regimental headquarters by the authorization of the XIIIth Army Corps. The document is signed in black ink by the Lt. Colonel commanding the regiment. To the left is seen the purple ink oval official stamp of the 123rd Württemberg Grenadier Regiment. At the top is the Imperial Crown colored in yellow, the laurel leaves on the left and the oakleaves on the right are tinted green. The outer border is black, the thinner inner border brown and the body of the document is a patterned browntone. The document was printed in Stuttgart as barely seen in the middle of the bottom thin inner border.

During 1917, the 27th Infantry Division was on the Somme until the beginning of 1917. At this time it was transferred east of Cambrai. During the month of March, the division was in line in the Roisel area. After a short rest in the vicinity of Valenciennes, the division went into action in the Bullecourt sector southeast of Arras where the division suffered heavy losses between 7 April and 11 May 1917. It appears that during this battle, Volunteer Private Heinrich Grau was decorated for bravery with the Iron Cross 2nd Class.

Withdrawn 11 May 1917 from the Arras front and after a rest, the 27th Infantry Division by the beginning of June, occupied a sector in the vicinity of Le Catelet which was located between Gonnelieu and Honnecourt. In early August, the division was relieved and transferred to Flanders, arriving on 12 August 1917. On 26 August 1917, the division went into action northeast of Ypres, southeast of St. Julien. In this sector it did not take part in any important engagements but was subjected to heavy enemy artillery fire and sustained many casualties. The 27th Infantry Division was sent to the rear on 12 September 1917 and rested for a month northeast of Ghent. On October 11th the division went back into the line northeast of Ypres near the Ypres-Thourout railroad and remained there until 11 November 1917. When relieved it was sent almost immediately to Alsace where the division arrived by mid-November 1917. The 27th Infantry division remained on the western front seeing action in various sectors until the end of the war.

✠ ✠ ✠

The document shown below is a Preliminary Identification Certificate, Type 2, *(Vorläufiger Ausweis)* named to Artilleryman *(Kanonier)* **ALBRAND**, who was serving, at the time of his being de-

Document 35   *Preliminary Identification Certificate, Type 2, to Kanonier Albrand*

corated with the Iron Cross 2nd Class, in the 6th Battery, 63rd Field Artillery Regiment *(2nd Nassau)*, 21st Brigade, 21st Infantry Division.

The document is of the mimeograph duplicator type having the usual purple lettering with the name and the battery written in black ink. It measures 21.0 cm. wide x 16.0 cm. high. What is interesting and unusual about this document is that the line "Eiserne Kreuz II. Klasse" is not in the purple lettering but in a very faint green. The document was signed and authorized at regimental staff headquarters on 13 June 1918. The document is signed with a purple indelible pencil by the regiment commander. To the left is the purple ink official stamp of the 63rd Field Artillery Regiment.

The 21st Infantry Division, along with the 25th Infantry Division, was a part of the 18th Army Corps District. Looking at the activities of the division in 1917 we find that on 19 April 1917 the 21st Infantry Division was relieved from the western front, rested a few days in Neufchâtel, and then was sent to the eastern front reaching Vilna on 9 May 1917. In 1917 the division was reorganized and occupied a sector of the front on 14 June 1917 in the Postavy area north of Lake Narotch. The division occupied this sector until the end of September 1917. During this period there were no major engagements other than patrol actions.

On 25 September 1917, the division was again transferred back to the western front. It was assigned to the front line on 28 October 1917 in a sector northeast of Rheims. After being relieved and rested in January 1918, the division returned to this sector in February 1918. The division held the Clonay-La Pompelle until 23 April 1918. The 21st Infantry Division was relieved on 23 April 1918 and sent to the rear where it rested several days at Warnerville before being sent to St. Quentin. From there it marched to Rosieres en Santerre and later moved to the Avre front. The division relieved the 2nd Bavarian Infantry Division in the sector south of Thennes on 3-4 May 1918, and held that sector for approximately five weeks. On June 12th, the division moved into second line positions and reappeared on the front west of Castel-Bois Senecat by mid-June 1918.

Artilleryman Albrand was awarded the Iron Cross 2nd Class for distinction in action during patrol activities in the sector of Thennes. The division was relieved by the end of June 1918 and remained on the western front until the end of the war when it was withdrawn by stages towards Germany.

✠ ✠ ✠

The document shown below is an Identification Certificate, Type 5, *(Ausweis)* named to Sergeant Major Lieutenant *(Feldwebel-Leutnant)* **SCHMELZPFENNIG**, serving in the Landsturm Infantry Battalion "Göttingen" under the command of the German Occupation Forces in Lille, Belgium.

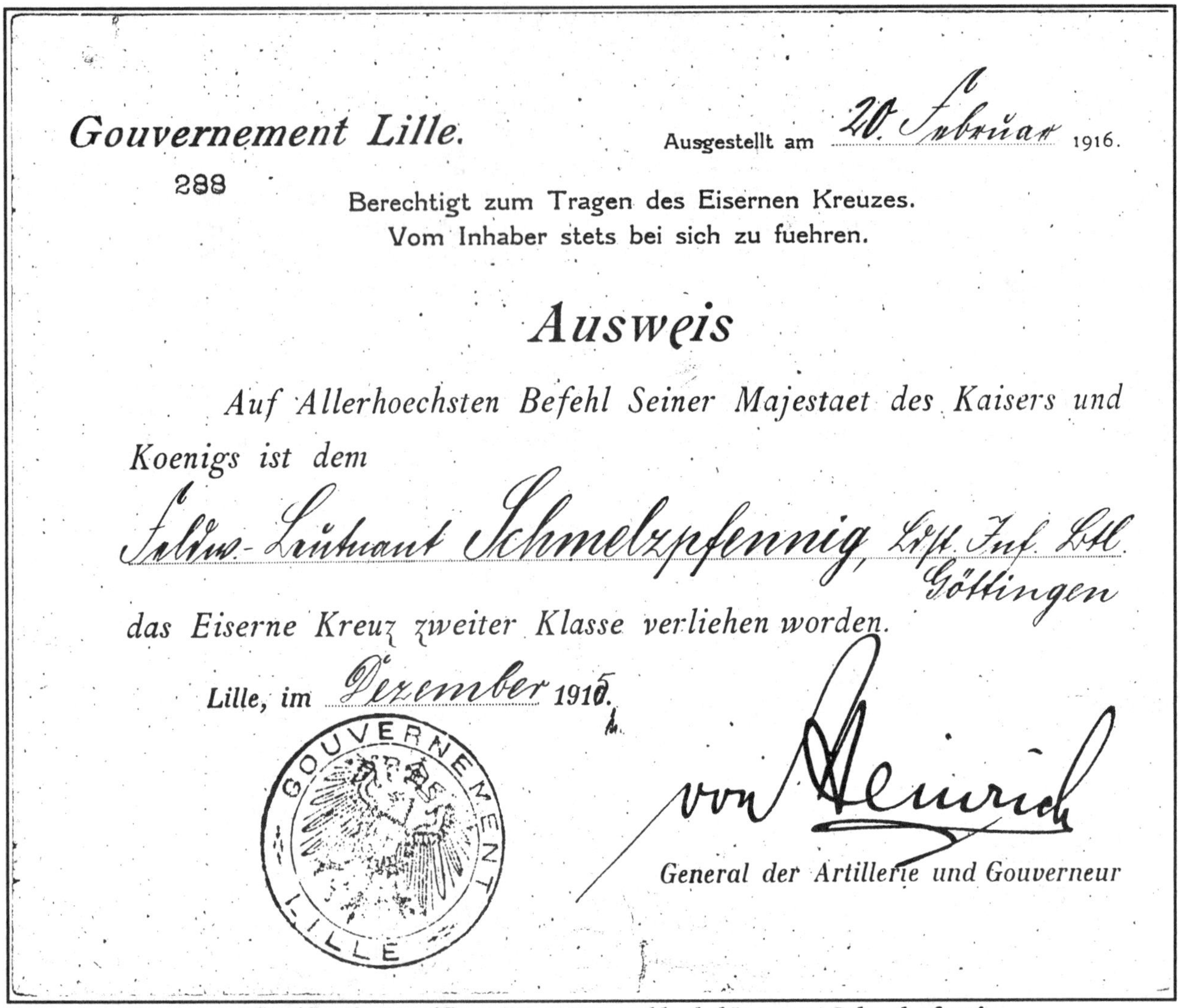
Gouvernement Lille. Ausgestellt am 20. Februar 1916.

288

Berechtigt zum Tragen des Eisernen Kreuzes.
Vom Inhaber stets bei sich zu fuehren.

Ausweis

Auf Allerhoechsten Befehl Seiner Majestaet des Kaisers und Koenigs ist dem

Feldw.-Leutnant Schmelzpfennig Ldst. Inf. Btl. Göttingen

das Eiserne Kreuz zweiter Klasse verliehen worden.

Lille, im Dezember 1915.

GOUVERNEMENT LILLE

von Heinrich

General der Artillerie und Gouverneur

Document 36 ***Identification Certificate, Type 5, to Feldwebel-Leutnant Schmelzpfennig***

The document shows that Feldwebel-Lieutenant Schmelzpfennig was authorized the Iron Cross 2nd Class sometime in December 1915 (no date is shown). Note that the printed year 1916 has been changed to 1915 and initialed. The document measures 16.8 cm. wide x 13.6 cm. high, and was signed in ink by General von Heinrich, General of Artillery and Governor of Lille. The certificate is numbered 288 and was issued on 20 February 1916. To the lower left is the purple ink official stamp of the Occupation Government of Lille.

✠ ✠ ✠

Note: The Landsturm Infantry Battalion "Göttingen" was composed mainly of older men and the unit was utilized primarily for occupation duties. No other specific information was found.

The document shown actual size is a Preliminary Identification Certificate, Type 2, *(Vorläufiger Ausweis)* to Territorial Reserve Private First Class *(Gefreiten der Landwehr 2)* **WILHELM SCHWEERS** serving in the Supply Park and Transport Column 80, 5th Bavarian Reserve Division, 1st Bavarian Reserve Corps. He was awarded the Iron Cross 2nd Class on 9 May 1917.

The document measures 14.5 cm. wide x 23.3 cm. high, and is printed on heavy paper stock. It was authorized and stamped on 9 May 1917. The signature is a stamped facsimile signature of General of Infantry Ritter von Fasbender in purple ink as is the official stamp of the 1st Bavarian Reserve Corps. The document appears to have been carried by Gefreiten Schweers.

Example 37   *Preliminary Identification Certificate, Type 2, to Gefreiten Wilhelm Schweers*

Looking at 1917 when Gefreiten Schweers was decorated with the Iron Cross 2nd Class, we find the 5th Bavarian Reserve Division was withdrawn from the Somme front at the end of January, 1917, and sent to rest in the vicinity of Cambrai until April. At the beginning of April the division was sent east of Laon to the region of St. Erme, and reinforced the front south of Juvincourt between the Miette and Aisne rivers by 12 April 1917 in anticipation of the French offensive.

Withdrawn on 20 April 1917 from the Aisne front after suffering heavy losses, the division was reinforced and refitted in an area north of Laon. On 1 May 1917 the division was assigned the St. Mihiel sector. It appears that Gefreiten Schweers was decorated for bravery in action during the French offensive in April. On 7 October 1917 the division left the St. Mihiel sector and sent to Flanders and into the front line on 12 October 1917 near the Ypres-Roulers railroad. In November the division was in the area near Artois, where it held a sector north of the Scarpe (from Gavrelle to Acheville). It remained in this area until the end of February.

The 5th Bavarian Reserve Division remained on the western front and was engaged in several major actions until the end of the war where on 1-2 November it held a position on the east bank of the Meuse.

✠ ✠ ✠

The document shown below is a Preliminary Identification Certificate, Type 2, *(Vorläufiger Ausweis)* named to Corporal *(Unteroffizier)* **KARL HEINRICH FRIEDRICH FRENZEL** serving on the staff of the 238th Infantry Division.*

Document 38   *Preliminary Identification Certificate, Type 2, to Unteroffizier Karl Frenzel*

The attractive document is printed on heavy paper stock and measures 21.2 cm. wide x 16.6 cm. high. It shows that Unteroffizier Frenzel was awarded the Iron Cross 2nd Class on 24 September 1917, when he was 24 years old. The document was signed in ink by the commanding general of the 238th Infantry Division at divisional headquarters on 4 June 1918, being issued almost nine months later. In the lower center between the date and signature is the purple ink official stamp of the 238th Infantry Division. At the top, the decorative leaves are printed in green.

The 238th Infantry Division was formed at the beginning of January 1917. After almost three months training the division was sent on 13 April 1917 to the western front where it arrived on 16 April 1917. On 20 April 1917, the division went into the front line in the sector of Vendhuille-Bellicourt. It was relieved on 20 May for a rest in the vicinity of Douai where it remained until 28 May 1917. At the end of May the division was assigned to the sector Roeux-Gavrelle, north of the Scarpe. It remained on this part of the front until 27 September 1917. During this time the division was mostly engaged in patrol activities. The 238th Infantry Division was then sent to Flanders where it remained for a short rest at Roules, then was placed in reserve in the vicinity of Westroosebeke. On 13 October 1917 the division went back into the front lines southwest of Passchendaele. Having suffered heavily from the British attack of October 30, the 238th Infantry Division was relieved on the 31 October 1917. On 6 November 1917, the division was sent to the rear where it rested a few days and was then reassigned

---

* See pp. 24-25 for documents also relating of the 238th Infantry Division.

to occupy the sector south of St. Quentin-Itancourt on 11 November 1917. During 1918 the division remained on the western front and was engaged in several major battles during the middle and latter part of 1918; on 6 November 1918, the 238th Infantry Division held the sector of Buironfosse until the end of the war.

✠ ✠ ✠

The document shown below is an Official Certificate, Type 9, named to Second Lieutenant *(Leutnant)* **HAUSMANN**, serving at the time of his being decorated with the Iron Cross 2nd Class on 5 March 1917, in the 2nd Company, 32nd Reserve Engineer *(Pionier)* Battalion, 197th Infantry Division.

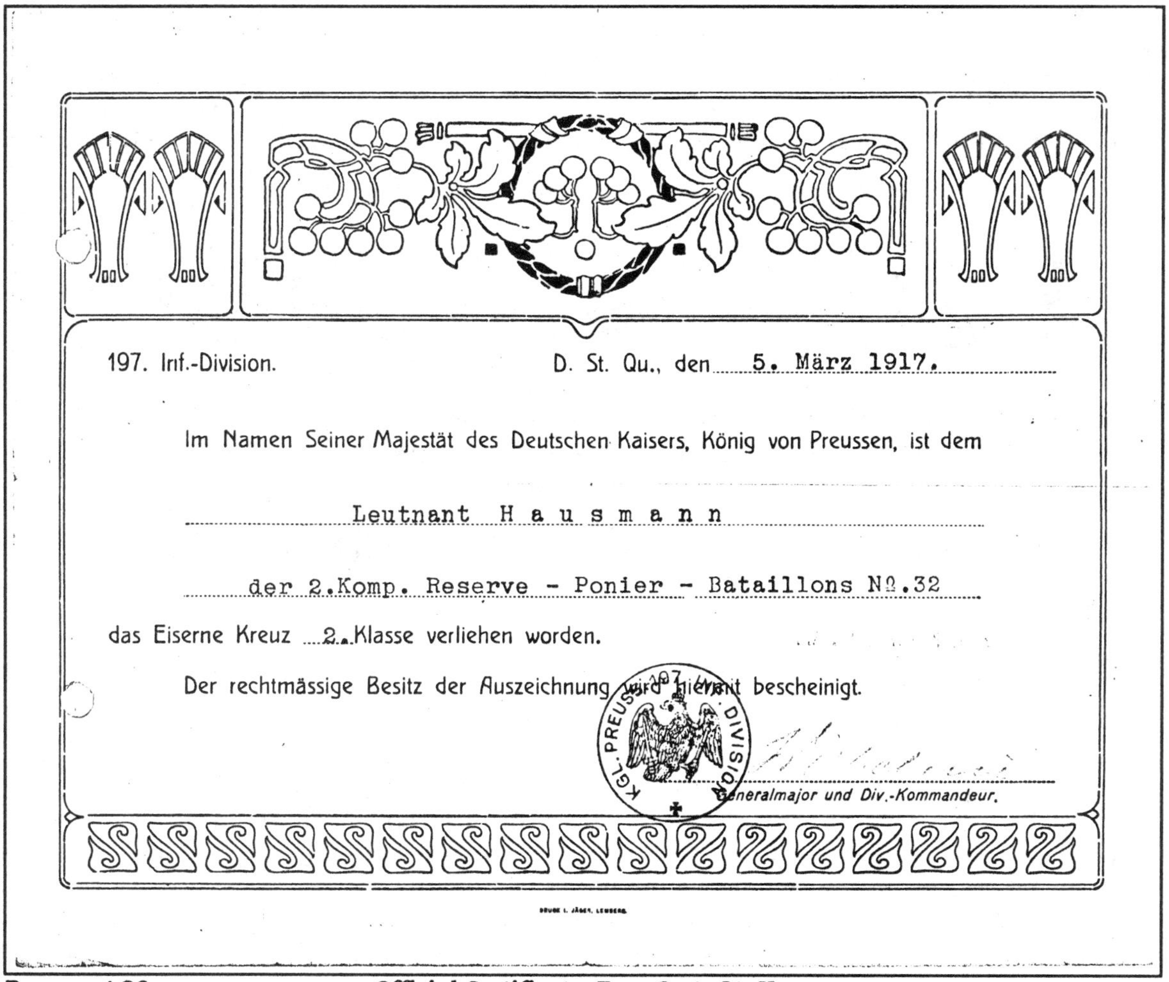

197. Inf.-Division.   D. St. Qu., den __5. März 1917.__

Im Namen Seiner Majestät des Deutschen Kaisers, König von Preussen, ist dem

__Leutnant Hausmann__

der 2.Komp. Reserve - Ponier - Bataillons № 32

das Eiserne Kreuz __2. Klasse__ verliehen worden.

Der rechtmässige Besitz der Auszeichnung wird hiermit bescheinigt.

Generalmajor und Div.-Kommandeur.

| Document 39 | *Official Certificate, Type 9, to Lt. Hausmann* |

The document is unusual in the decorative style and measures 20.5 cm. wide x 17.0 cm. high. It was issued from the divisional headquarters on 5 March 1917. It is signed by the divisional commander in purple indelible pencil; to the left of the signature is the purple ink official stamp of the 197th Infantry Division. Along the left margin are the punched holes indicating that the certificate was a part of the military record of Lt. Hausmann.

The 197th Infantry Division was formed in August 1916 on the eastern front. It was a part of the 2nd Austrian Army and the 197th Infantry Division occupying the Zborov sector, northwest of Tarnopol, in August 1916. While in this sector the division saw action during the Russian Broussailov offensive.

In September 1916, the division was in the front line to the northeast of Zalosce, to the north of Zborov, and later in the vicinity of Zloczov. The 197th Infantry Division stayed in the Zloczov sector until July 1917. It successfully checked the Russian offensive of 1 July 1917. The division participated in the German counteroffensive of 19 July 1917 and advanced by way of Zborov up to Husjatin by August 1917 where the division was relieved and placed in reserve. It was reassigned to the front line at the beginning of September at Hlesczava in the region of Prembovla. From there it was transferred to the western front.

The division held the quiet Chemin des Dames sector until the Aisne offensive of 27 May 1918. It was heavily engaged on an active front for two months in 1918 during which it suffered so many casualties that the division was disbanded in late October 1918. The remaining troops of the 197th Infantry Division were reassigned to other regiments.

✠ ✠ ✠

The document shown below is a Preliminary Authorization Certificate, Type 1, *(Vorläufiges Besitzzeugnis)* named to Corporal *(Unteroffizier)* **OBERST**, who was serving when decorated with the Iron Cross 2nd Class on 6 July 1918, in the 26th Railroad Construction Company on the Russian front.

Document 40   *Preliminary Authorization Certificate, Type 1, to Unteroffizier Oberst*

The decorative document is printed in black ink and measures 21.0 cm. wide x 16.5 cm. high. It was signed in ink by an official of the Railroad Service in **Kiev** (Kiew), Russia, on 10 August 1918 at the headquarters of the Railroad Construction Unit. Below the date is the purple ink official stamp of the unit in Kiev. The railroad construction companies were responsible for maintenance of the rail lines, rail bridges, et cetra, as well as the construction of new lines needed for supplies and troops.

✠ ✠ ✠

The document shown below is an Authorization Certificate, Type 6, *(Besitzurkunde)* to Reserve Second Lieutenant *(Leutnant d. Reserve)* **GERHARD KLOTH**, who was serving in the 4th Reserve Re-

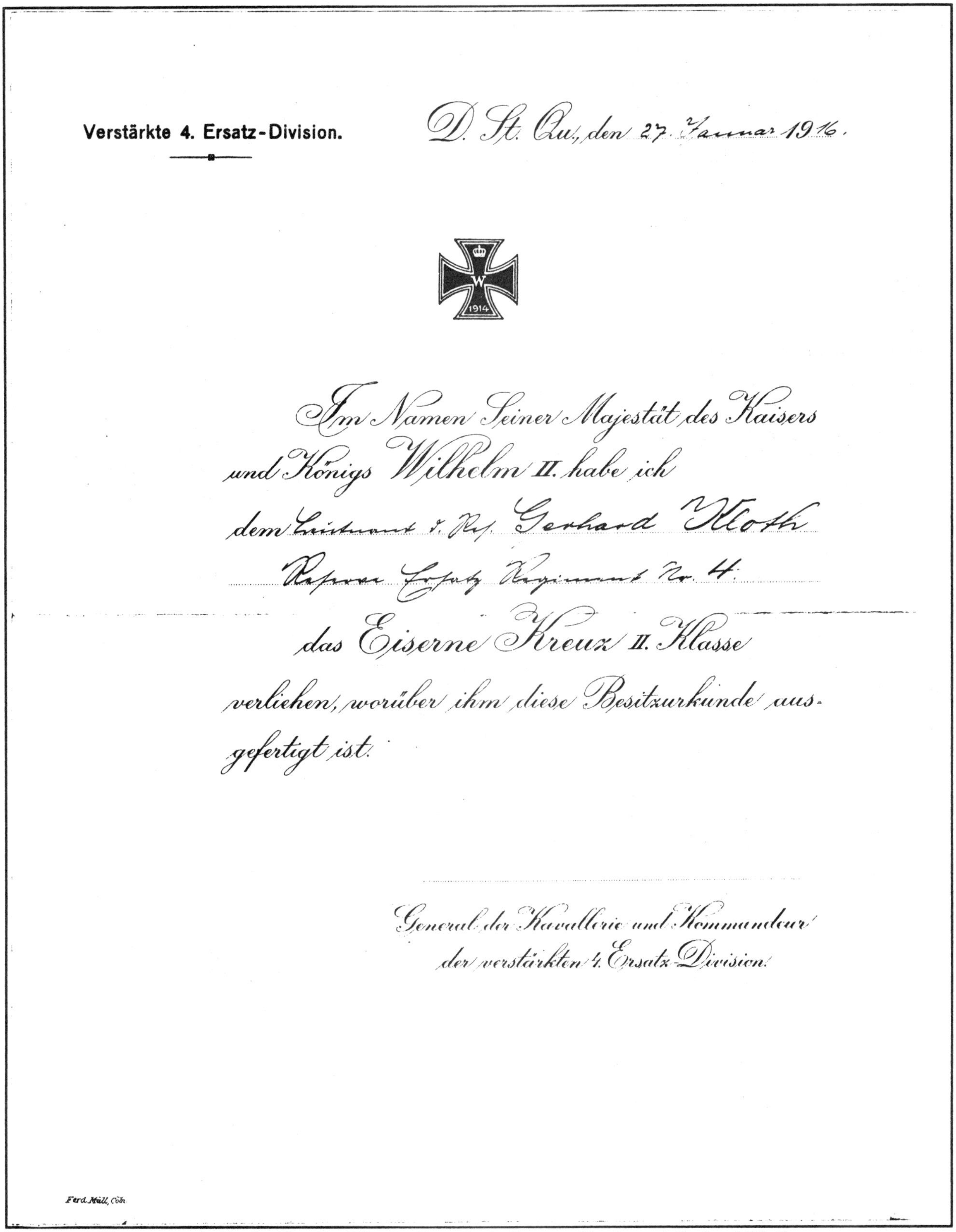

Verstärkte 4. Ersatz-Division.

D. St. Qu., den 27. Januar 1916.

Im Namen Seiner Majestät des Kaisers und Königs Wilhelm II. habe ich

dem Leutnant d. Rs. Gerhard Kloth

Reserve Ersatz Regiment Nr. 4

das Eiserne Kreuz II. Klasse

verliehen, worüber ihm diese Besitzurkunde aus-

gefertigt ist.

General der Kavallerie und Kommandeur der verstärkten 4. Ersatz Division.

Ferd. Müll, Cöln

Document 41   ***Authorization Certificate, Type 6, to Reserve Lieutenant Gerhard Kloth***

placement *(Ersatz)* Regiment, 2nd Reserve Replacement Brigade, Reinforced 4th Replacement Division *(Verstärkte 4. Ersatz Division)*.

The document, having apparently been framed and displayed on a sunny wall, is badly faded. The ink has become brown in color and the signature block and official stamp are so faded that they are barely distinguishable. Unfortunately, they do not show on the reproduced document. The document measures 22.2 cm. wide x 28.2 cm. high. It is similar to Example 42 on the following page. It was signed and dated on 27 January 1916 at the divisional staff headquarters. Note that the commanding general was a General of Cavalry (General der Kavallerie).

The 5th Replacement Infantry Division was organized in the fall of 1915 and given the name "Basedow" Division. The 4th Replacement Division was assigned to the 5th Replacement Division in 1916 and formed part of the Army Corps Wrede by the end of 1915. From January until October 1916 the div-ision remained in Belgium in the Yser area, later moving southwest of Ypres. However, the 4th Reserve Replacement Regiment was transferred to the 206th Infantry Division at the beginning of September 1916. The 206th Infantry Division containing the 4th Reserve Replacement Regiment was assigned to the Somme where it was engaged in four separate actions in the areas of Péronne, La Maisonnette, and in the vicinity of Marchelepot; during these engagements the division suffered heavy losses. It appears that Leutnant Kloth was decorated with the Iron Cross 2nd Class for his leadership and bravery in action during the time the division was assigned in the region of the Yser.

✠ ✠ ✠

The document shown on the following page is an Authorization Certificate, Type 6, (Besitz-urkunde) to Private (Wehrmann) **WILLI VASEL** who, when awarded the Iron Cross 2nd Class, was serving in the 1st Machine Gun Company, 74th Landwehr Infantry Regiment, 5th Replacement (Ersatz) Infantry Division.

The document measures 22.2 cm. wide x 28.0 cm. high, and appears to have been trimmed. It was signed on 31 July 1917 at Division Staff Headquarters by the commanding general of the 5th Replacement Infantry Division. To the left of the signature block is the purple ink official stamp of the 5th Replacement Division.

The document was apparently framed and as a result the original black ink has become brownish. Both the signature and the divisional stamp are badly faded but are readable.

The 5th Replacement Infantry Division was organized in the fall of 1915 and originally called the "Basedow" Division. The 74th Landwehr Infantry Division, formerly with the 26th Reserve Corps, was later attached to the 5th Infantry Division.

Moving to January 1917, the division was sent to the front line at the Illukst sector in the area of Dvinsk in Courland. The division remained in Courland for a year, after which it was reassigned

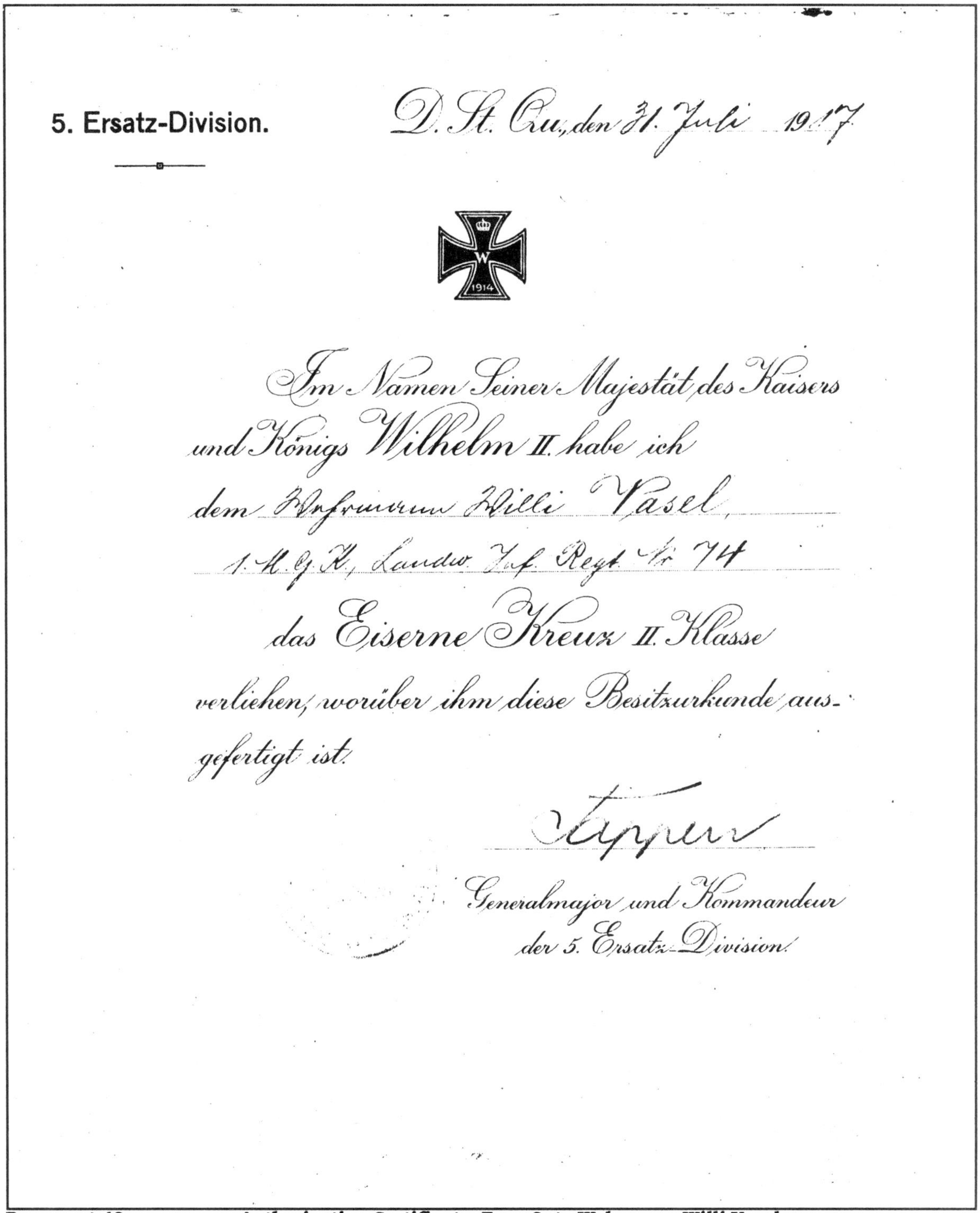

---

5. Ersatz-Division.

D. St. Qu, den 31. Juli 1917

Im Namen Seiner Majestät des Kaisers und Königs Wilhelm II. habe ich

dem Wehrmann Willi Vasel,

1. M. G. K., Landw. Inf. Regt. Nr. 74

das Eiserne Kreuz II. Klasse

verliehen, worüber ihm diese Besitzurkunde aus-
gefertigt ist.

[signature]

Generalmajor und Kommandeur
der 5. Ersatz-Division.

Document 42   *Authorization Certificate, Type 6, to Wehrmann Willi Vasel*

---

to the areas of Lake Stenten and Kchtchava. The areas where the division was assigned were essentially quiet sectors and action consisted primarily of clashes between patrols. It appears that possibly during one of the patrol actions Wehrmann Willi Vasel demonstrated bravery and was awarded the Iron Cross 2nd Class

✠ ✠ ✠

The document on the facing page is an Authorization Certificate, Type 4, *(Besitz-Zeugnis)* named to Private *(Grenadier)* **PAUL ORTH** who was serving, at the time of being decorated with the Iron Cross 2nd Class, in the Machine Gun Section, 8th Life *(Leib)* Grenadier Regiment *(King Friedrich Wilhelm III, 1st Brandenburg)*, 10th Infantry Brigade, 5th Infantry Division.

The document, which is very large, measures 20.4 cm. wide x 33.3 cm. high. It is dated 11 July 1918 and the recipient's name, date, and the title of the regimental commander are written in blue ink. The signature is written with a purple indelible pencil. To the left is the purple ink official stamp of the Prussian Life Grenadier Regiment.

In 1914 the 5th Infantry Division along with the 6th Infantry Division formed the 3rd Army Corps. At the beginning of the war, the divisions were part of the 1st Army *(von Kluck)*. The division entered Belgium on the 14th of August 1914 and passed through Louvain on August 19. The 5th Infantry Division took part in the battle at Charleroi and also the battle of the Marne in the area of Sancy and Cerneux on 6 September 1914. The 5th Infantry Division fought in the battles between the Aisne and the Marne rivers in September and, after the front stabilized between the Aisne and the Oise rivers near Vailly and Soissons the front quieted down for a while. On 13 January 1915, the division was engaged at the battle of Soissons. After 10 June 1915, the 5th Infantry Division was no longer a part of the 1st Army. On 1 July 1915 it was assigned to the area by Douai and around July 14th held the sector before Arras. On 25 September 1915, the division took part in the attacks in the Champagne sector.

In December the division was relieved and returned to Belgium; by December 25 the division was resting in the region of Hirson-Avesnes. In February 1916, the division was in the region of Spincourt and by the end of the month it was assigned to the Verdun sector. The division engaged the enemy near Herbebois on 23 February 1916. The division attacked Douaumont on 26 February 1916 where it suffered heavy casualties. It was again engaged in action from March 8-15 and from April 22 until the end of May in the Verdun area. July found the division at the Somme front in the area of Longueval and Bois Delville. By the middle of August, the division had been transferred to Champagne in the sector of Auberive until it was relieved on 12 October 1916. By December 1916, the 5th Infantry Division had again been assigned to the Verdun area in the region of Vaux. The division was withdrawn from the Verdun front about 25 December 1916 and sent to the region of Mulhouse. It stayed in Upper Alsace in the area of Mulhouse and Serrette until 20 April 1917. During this period, the division was used mainly for the building of defensive positions on the French front and along the Swiss frontier.

In July 1917, the 5th Infantry Division was sent to the eastern front and was in the region of Zbrucz until the beginning of September. Around October 1917, the division was sent from Galicia to Italy and by the beginning of January 1918 was relieved from the Italian front and reassigned back to France.

On January 20th 1918, the division went into the front line near Butte du Mesnil. During the year of 1918 on the night of June 26th the division entered the front line southeast of Lizy. In the offensive the division advanced by way of Chavignon, Malmaison, Uregny, into the region of Pommiers to Mercin and Pernant east of Ambleny. The division was relieved on July 7th and the last elements of the division were withdrawn from the front lines by 13 June 1918.

It appears that Grenadier Paul Orth, according to the date indicated on his document, was decorated "for outstanding bravery before the enemy" *(für hervorragende Tapferkeit vor dem feinde)* during the January offensive. The 5th Infantry Division remained on the western front until the end of the war.

✠ ✠ ✠

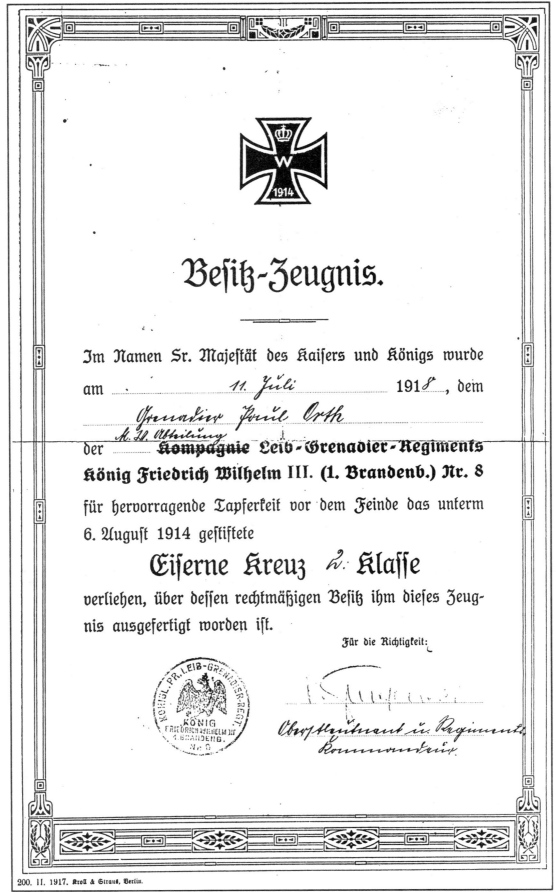

Besitz-Zeugnis.

Im Namen Sr. Majestät des Kaisers und Königs wurde

am _____ *11. Juli* _____ 191*8*, dem

Grenadier Paul Orth

M. H. Abteilung

der _____ ~~Kompagnie~~ **Leib-Grenadier-Regiments**

König Friedrich Wilhelm III. (1. Brandenb.) Nr. 8

für hervorragende Tapferkeit vor dem Feinde das unterm

6. August 1914 gestiftete

Eiserne Kreuz *2.* **Klasse**

verliehen, über dessen rechtmäßigen Besitz ihm dieses Zeugnis ausgefertigt worden ist.

Für die Richtigkeit:

[signature]

Oberstleutnant u. Regiments
Kommandeur

200. II. 1917. Kroll & Strauß, Berlin.

Document 43   *Authorization Certificate, Type 4, to Grenadier Paul Orth*

The document shown below is an Authorization Certificate, Type 4, *(Besitz-Zeugnis)* named to Reserve Private *(Reservist)* **GEORG NEUMANN**, serving in the 3rd Company, 190th Infantry Regiment, 4th Guards Brigade, 220th Infantry Division.

The colorful and decorative document printed on heavy card stock measures 21.5 cm. wide x 16.0 cm. high. The inner border, the "B" and "Z" in Besitz-Zeugnis are printed in red. The document was signed in the field *(Im Felde)* on 2 November 1917 by the regimental commander using a purple indelible pencil. In the lower left under the date is the purple ink official stamp of the 190th Infantry Regiment.

Document 44   *Authorization Certificate, Type 4, to Reservist Georg Neumann*

The 220th Infantry Division was formed at the end of 1916. In April 1917, the 190th Infantry Regiment joined the division and replaced the 207th Reserve Infantry Regiment. By the end of April 1917, the 220th Infantry Division was relieved from the Arras front and sent to rest in the area of Montagne du Nord, then on to Belgium. The division returned to its old sector in Artois on 29 May 1917 and remained there until 6 July 1917. After a rest and refitting in the vicinity of Douai northwest of Lens, and from the beginning of July until the middle of August, the 220th Infantry Division was engaged near Lens from 16 to 22 August 1917. At the beginning of October, the division was sent to Belgium. On the 12th of October 1917 the 220th Infantry Division went back into the front line east of Zonnebeke. Around October 15 the division was sent to rest in the vicinity of Bruges. Upon return to the front line, it was engaged on the Cambrai sector south of Crèvecoeur during the German offensive at the end of November 1917. It seems that Reservist Private Neumann was decorated for bravery in action during this period.

During 1918 the 220th Infantry Division remained on the western front until the end of the war.

✠ ✠ ✠

The document shown below is a Preliminary Identification Certificate, Type 2, *(Vorläufiger Ausweis)* named to Private First Class *(Gefreiten)* **PAUL HOPPE,** who was serving in the 410th Signal Command, Telephone Section , 10th Reserve Infantry Division, when decorated with the Iron Cross 2nd Class on 16 October 1918.

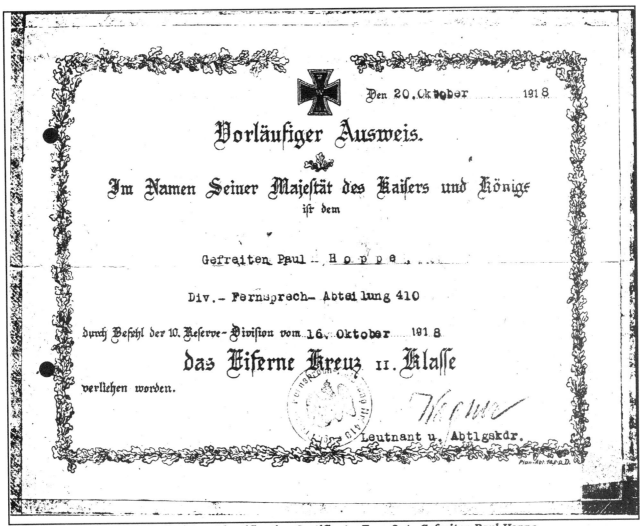

Document 45   *Preliminary Identification Certificate, Type 2, to Gefreiten Paul Hoppe*

The document has had white tape added to the edges and measures 21.7 cm. wide x 17.2 cm. high. The document was signed with a purple indelible pencil by Lt. Wagner, the section commander, on 20 October 1918. The award was authorized on 16 October 1918 through the authority of the 10th Reserve Infantry Division. To the left of the signature is the purple ink official stamp of the 410th Telephone Section. It is interesting that the typed information, such as, name, unit, and dates, are all in purple color similar to that of a duplicator. In the left margin are the two punched holes indicating that this document was part of the military record of Gefreiten Hoppe.

In August of 1918, the division, having rested three weeks at Asfeld, returned to the Vesle front on 28 August near Chalon sur Vesle and was engaged until 18 September 1918. On 18 September 1918, the division was sent to Laon and entered the front line south of Laon at Ferme-Colombe by the 22nd. The division appears to have been constantly in action until 1 November 1918, and possibly until the armistice on the 11th. According to US Army intelligence reports the division fought hard in most of the offensives of the year and when on the defensive put up a hard, steady fight *for two months without relief.*

✠ ✠ ✠

Vorläufiges Besitz=Zeugnis

Im Namen
Seiner Majestät des Kaisers

ist dem

Musketier Jakob Jung

4. Komp. 2. Unt. Els. Inf. Regt. Nr. 137

das Eiserne Kreuz II. Klasse von 1914

verliehen.

Verfügung der 108. Inf. Div vom 29. Aug. 1917

Im Felde , den 1. Septb. 1917

Schlemmer

Leutnant d. R. u. Komp. Führer.

Feldbruckerei Degener.

Document 46   *Preliminary Authorization Certificate, Type 1, to Musketier Jakob Jung*

The document shown on the preceding page is a Preliminary Authorization Certificate, Type 1, *(Vorläufiges Besitz-Zeugnis)* named to Private *(Musketier)* **JAKOB JUNG**, serving in the 4th Company, 1st Battalion, 137th Infantry Regiment *(2nd Lower Alsace)*, 5th Infantry Brigade, 108th Infantry Division, when decorated with the Iron cross 2nd Class on the 29th of August 1917.

The large document measures 21.0 cm. wide x 32.0 cm. high. It was signed in black ink by the company commander in the field *(Im Felde)* on 1 September 1917. The award was authorized by an order from the 108th Infantry Division on 29 August 1917. In the lower left hand corner is the purple ink official stamp of the 1st Battalion of the 137th Infantry Regiment. The document was printed by the field printing section of the Bug Army as seen below the border on the left side.

The 108th Infantry Division was formed during the summer of 1915. The 137th Infantry Regiment was taken from the 31st Infantry Division. The division was called the "Beckmann" Division in honor of its commanding general before it was assigned to be the 108th Infantry Division.

The division was on the eastern front and in June 1916 it was reassigned to Volhynia and opposed the Russian offensive in the vicinity of Svinioukhi. Here during the major Russian attack, the division suffered heavy casualties. On June 16th, the 1st Battalion of the 137th Infantry Regiment, lost 24 officers and 978 men in action. It is most likely that Musketier Jung was recognized for bravery in action during this engagement and recommended for the Iron Cross 2nd Class. The division stayed in this sector until mid-December 1917.

The division was reassigned to the western front where it remained until it was disbanded in August 1918 and the remaining soldiers reassigned to other units.

The document shown below is a Preliminary Identification Certificate, Type 2, *(Vorläufiger Ausweis)* named to Reserve Second Lieutenant *(Leutnant der Reserve)* **GUSTAV MÖLLER**, serving in the 3rd Battery, 32nd Field Artillery Regiment, 40th Artillery Command, 40th Infantry Division, XIXth Army Corps. Lt. Möller was born in Fauluck in Schleswig-Holstein and was 29 years old when awarded the Iron Cross 2nd Class.

Vorlaeufiger Ausweis.

Dem Leutnant d.Res. Gustav M ö l l e r

de s 3. Feldartillerie - Regiments Nr. 32

geboren am 25. 3. 1885 in Faulück, Schleswig-Holstein

wurde von Seiner Exzellenz dem kommandierenden General des XIX. A. K. im Namen Seiner Majestaet des Kaisers u. Koenigs das

Eiserne Kreuz II. Klasse

verliehen.

Im Felde, den 29. Oktober 1914

Oberstleutnant u. Regiments-Kommandeur.

Document 47   *Preliminary Identification Certificate, Type 2, to Lt. Gustav Möller*

The plain printed document measures 21.5 cm. wide x 16.5 cm. high. It was signed in the field *(Im Felde)* on 29 October 1914 by the regimental commander in black ink. To the left of the signature is the purple ink official stamp of the Saxon 32nd Field Artillery Regiment. In the left margin are the two punched holes which indicate the document was a part of the military file of Lt. Möller.

The 40th Infantry Division (4th Saxon) formed, with the 24th Infantry Division (2nd Saxon), the XIXth Army Corps. The division entered the north of Luxemburg on 13 August 1914 and by the 18th, was in Belgium. It crossed the Meuse on 23 August above Dinant and entered France by way of Fumay. The division was engaged at Chesnois on August 30th and advancing on reached Semide on September 1st, Somme Py on the 2nd and on 4 September 1914 reached Châlons. The division took part in the battle of the Marne west of Vitry le François. After the battle, the division retired to Souain.

At the beginning of October, the XIXth Army Corps was transferred to Lille. Attacked by British troops, the division was forced back to a line between Ploegsteert woods and Grenier woods. It appears that during the British attack Lt. Möller displayed outstanding command and leadership and was recommended for the Iron Cross 2nd Class.

✠ ✠ ✠

The document shown below is a Preliminary Authorization Certificate, Type 1, *(Vorläufiges Besitzzeugnis)* named to Sergeant *(Sergeant)* **EUGEN SCHILDHORN** serving in the 4th Company, 1st Battalion 424th Infantry Regiment, 70th Landwehr Brigade, 11th Landwehr Infantry Division.

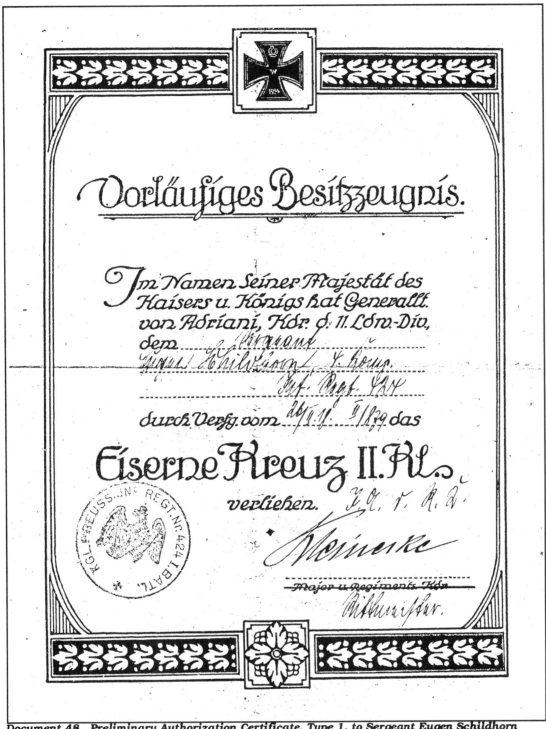

Document 48 Preliminary Authorization Certificate, Type 1, to Sergeant Eugen Schildhorn

The rather attractive document measures 16.4 cm. wide x 21.0 cm. high. It was signed by a Rittmeister (cavalry captain) in purple ink as is the recipient's name and unit, on 26 January 1918 through the authority of orders from the 11th Landwehr Infantry Division. To the left of the signature is the purple ink official stamp of the 1st Battalion, 424th Infantry Regiment.

The 424th Infantry Regiment joined the 11th Landwehr Division on the eastern front at the end of 1916. The division remained in the Vichnev-Krevo sector during the entire year of 1917.

The 11th Landwehr Infantry Division, which was still in the south of Krevo in January 1918, marched to the east in February 1918. It was during February that Sergeant Schildhorn was recommended for the Iron Cross 2nd Class.

The division fought in the Ukraine and by 30 April 1918 it was assigned the sector between Kiev and Koursk. By the middle of July the division was identified as being south of Moscow. During this time men were taken from this division and sent as replacements to the western front. The division spent the entire war on the eastern front.

✠ ✠ ✠

The Document shown below is an Authorization Certificate, Type 4, *(Besitz-Zeugnis)* named to Corporal *(Unteroffizier)* **WILHELM GABLER**, 100th Mortar *(Minenwerfer)* Company, 13th Engineer *(Pionier)* Battalion, Bavarian Replacement *(Ersatz)* Infantry Division.*

Document 49   *Authorization Certificate, Type 4, to Unteroffizier Wilhelm Gabler*

The attractive document measures 21.8 cm. wide x 18.2 cm. high. It was signed in black ink by the battalion commander for the 13th Bavarian Engineer Battalion. Note that the "Bavarian Replacement Division" has been struck through and replaced with the Engineers title. To the left of the signature is the purple ink official stamp of the Staff of the 13th Bavarian Engineer Battalion. Along the botton edge is indicated that the document was printed in Metz.

✠ ✠ ✠

---

* see page 7 for information relating to the Bavarian Replacement Infantry Division.

The document shown below is a Preliminary Authorization Certificate, Type 1, *(Vorläufiges Besitzzeugnis)* named to Private *(Musketier)* **ERICH WERZ** serving at the time he was awarded the Iron Cross 2nd Class in the 12th Company, 3rd Battalion, 15th Reserve Infantry Regiment, 38th Reserve Infantry Brigade, 2nd Guard Reserve Infantry Division.

Vorläufiges Besitzzeugnis.

Der Musk. Erich Werz von der 12. Komp. R.I.R. 15

hat im Namen Sr. Majestät des Kaisers und Königs das Eiserne Kreuz II. Klasse

verliehen erhalten.

den 24. April 1918

H. Noack Nachfl., Düsseldorf. Hauptmann u. Kommandeur III/R.I.R. 15.

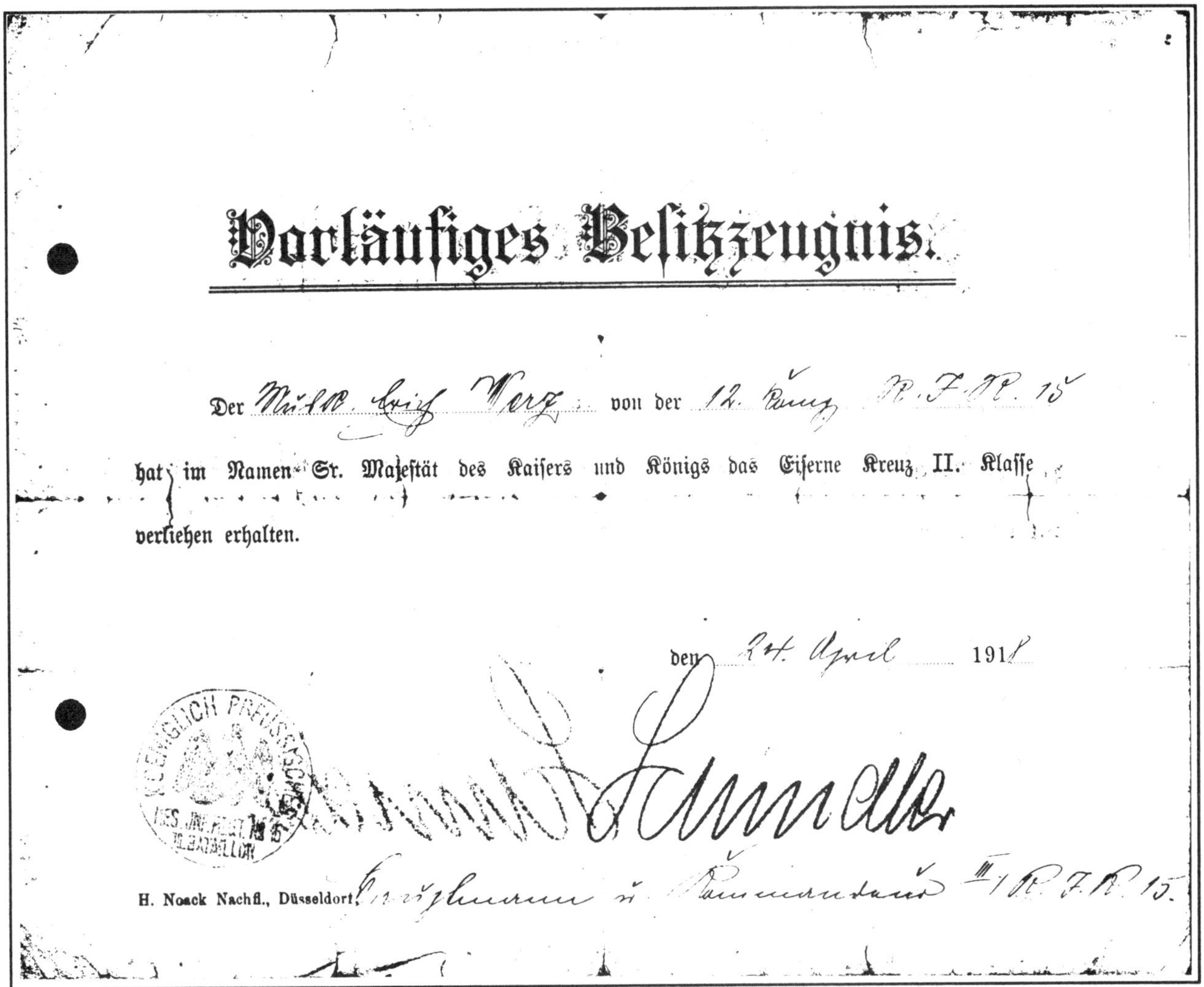

Document 50 ***Preliminary Authorization Certificate, Type 1, to Musketier Erich Werz***

The document measures 21.3 cm. wide x 17.0 cm. high. It was signed on 24 April 1918 by the regimental commander in indelible purple pencil. To the left of the signature is the purple ink official stamp of the 3rd Battalion of the 15th Reserve Infantry Regiment. Directly below the stamp is the name of the printer. The document shows the two punched holes in the left margin indicating it was for a time a part of the military record of Private Werz. However, the document has been folded and shows that it had been carried in a wallet for a considerable period of time. Note that the pencil signature has been mirrored.

Moving to the period when Musketier Werz received the Iron Cross 2nd Class, the division, on 21 March 1918, reinforced the Cambrai front near St. Léger, engaging and suffering heavy losses until the 26th of March when it was relieved. The division returned to the front line west of Neuville-Vitasse on 3 April 1918. On April 29th, the division was relieved by the extension of the fronts of neighboring divisions. It was during the time that Musketier Werz was in this sector that he was recommended for and received the Iron Cross 2nd Class.

The division remained on the western front until the end of the war on 11 November 1918.

✠ ✠ ✠

The document shown below is a Preliminary Authorization Certificate, Type 1, *(Vorläufiges Besitzzeugnis)* named to Corporal *(Unteroffizier)* **MAX OTTO ARMIN KORN,** who was serving in the 7th Company, 474th Saxon Infantry Regiment, 246th Infantry Brigade, 241st Infantry Division.

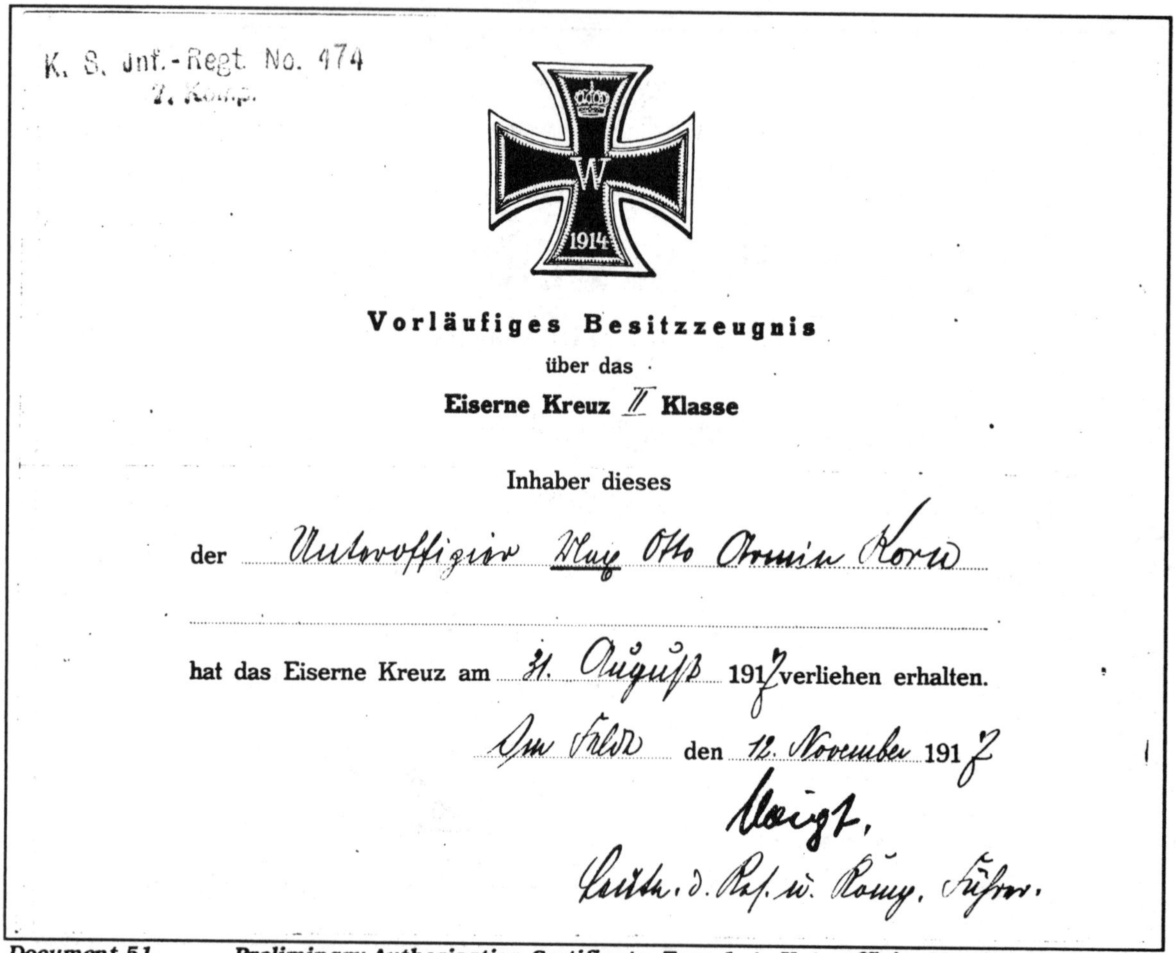

K. S. Jnf.-Regt. No. 474
7. Komp.

Vorläufiges Besitzzeugnis

über das ·

Eiserne Kreuz *II* **Klasse**

Inhaber dieses

der _Unteroffizier Max Otto Armin Korn_

hat das Eiserne Kreuz am _31. August_ 1917 verliehen erhalten.

Im Felde den _12. November_ 1917

Voigt,

Leutn. d. Res. u. Komp. Führer.

Document 51   Preliminary Authorization Certificate, Type 1, to Unteroffizier Max Korn

The document is printed in black ink and measures 20.4 cm. wide x 16.2 cm. high. In the upper left-hand corner is the purple ink block stamp of the 7th Company, 474th Saxon Infantry Regiment. The information entered was written in black ink. The document is signed in the field *(Im Felde)* by the company commander who was a Reserve Lieutenant, using a purple indelible pencil and dated 12 November 1917. The certificate shows Unteroffizier Korn was authorized the Iron Cross 2nd Class on 31 August 1917 three months previously.

The 241st Infantry Division was formed at the beginning of 1917 and was composed entirely of Saxons. On 1 March 1917 the division was sent to Brest-Litovsk. In April it was assigned the sector of Bostavy near Lake Narotch where it remained until the middle of June 1917. The division was relieved by the 21st Infantry Division and on 17 June 1917 sent to Galicia southwest of Brzezany, arriving there on the 22nd of June. At the beginning of July the division went into the front line in this region and took part in the German counteroffensive against the Russians at the end of July, advancing to south of Skala by the beginning of August. The division then took up a sector on the Zbruch *(Zbrucz)* river in the Ukraine. After this time the 241st Infantry Division occupied various sectors on the Galician front. The division was assigned to the eastern front from the time of its formation until February 1918 when it was transferred to the western front. It appears that Unteroffizier Max Korn was awarded the Iron Cross 2nd Class for bravery in action in Galicia.

✠ ✠ ✠

The document shown below is a Preliminary Authorization Certificate, Type 1, *(Vorläufiges Besitzzeugnis)* named to Private First Class *(Gefreite)* **HERMANN MÜLLER**, serving in the 11th Company, 3rd Infantry Battalion, 377th Infantry Regiment, 180th Infantry Brigade, 10th Landwehr Infantry Division.

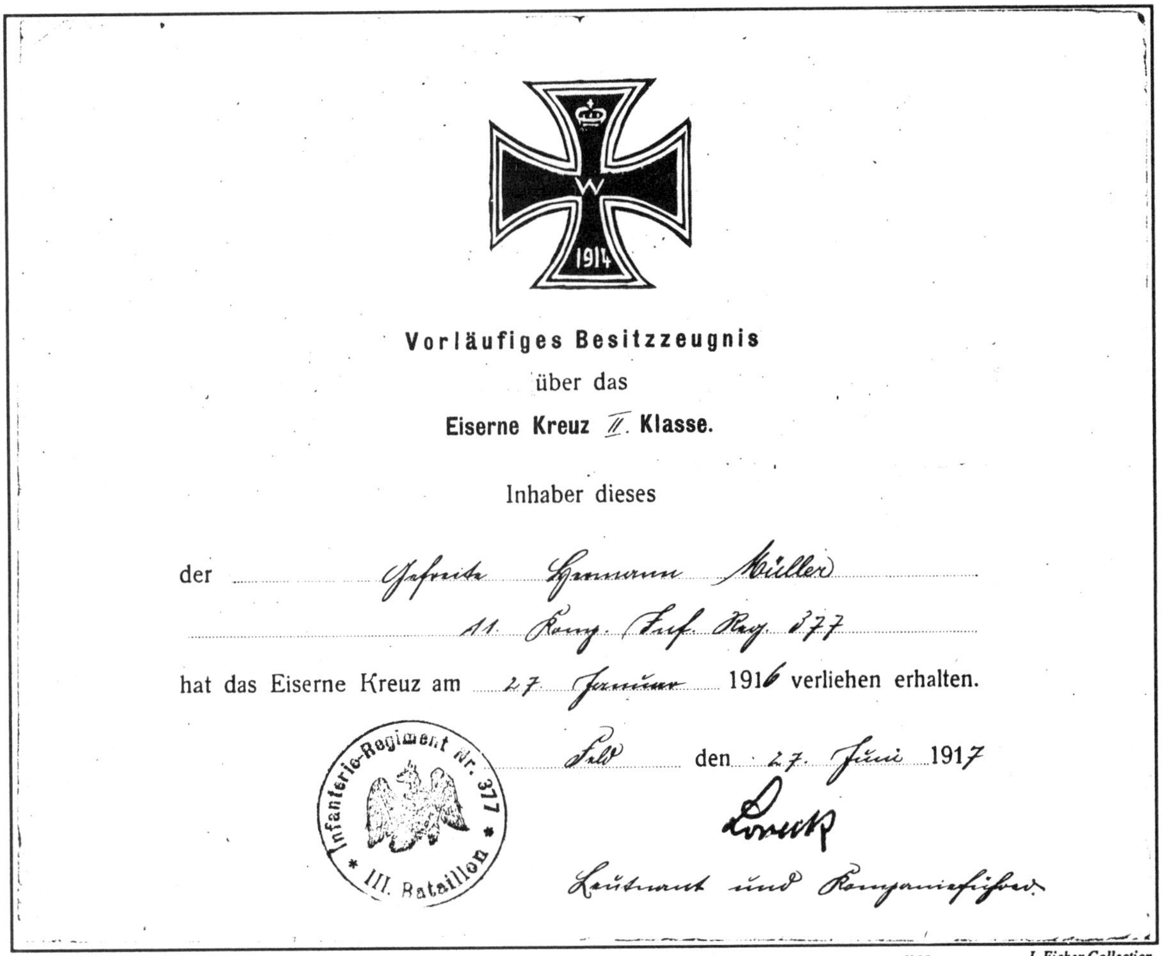

Document 52   ***Preliminary Authorization, Type 1, to Gefreite Hermann Müller***   *J. Eicher Collection*

The document measures 20.4 cm. wide x 16.2 cm. high. It shows that Gefreite Müller was awarded the Iron Cross 2nd Class on 27 January 1916 and the certificate was issued on 27 June 1917. It was signed by the company commander in black ink. To the left is the purple ink official stamp of the 377th Infantry Regiment.

Until 1915 the 10th Landwehr Infantry Division was named the 1st Landwehr Infantry Division. Units of the division were sent to Königsberg as early as August 1914 to constitute its war garrison. This division, at first engaged in Eastern Prussia, took part in the campaign in Poland which began during the first part of 1915. Toward the end of July 1915, the division took part in the offensive against the Russian forces, forced the passage of the Narev river, which resulted in a German success. The division advanced east of Vilna to the region of Zileiki by September 1915. After the front was stabilized, the division established itself between Spiagla and Lake Svir south of Lake Narotch. The division remained on the front near Lake Svir until July 1916. While in this sector Gefreite Müller was cited for bravery in action and decorated with the Iron Cross 2nd Class.

✠ ✠ ✠

The document shown below is a Preliminary Authorization Certificate, Type 1, *(Vorläufiges Besitzzeugnis)* named to Officer Candidate *(Fähnrich)* **HANS RATHKE**, serving in the 1st Company, 1st Battalion, 166th Infantry Regiment *(Hessen-Homburg)*, 31st Infantry Division.

Document 53 *Preliminary Authorization Certificate, Type 1, to Fähnrich Hans Rathke*

The document measures 20.2 cm. wide x 16.3 cm. high. It was signed in the field *(Im Felde)* with a purple indelible pencil by the company commander on 15 November 1916. To the left of the signature is the purple ink official stamp of the 1st Battalion, 166th Infantry Regiment.

Upon mobilization the 31st Infantry Division along with the 42nd Infantry Division constituted the 21st Army Corps, 6th Army. On January 1915 the 31st Infantry Division left the Somme for the eastern front and arrived at Tilset several days later. It concentrated in East Prussia at the beginning of February and was part of the Hindenburg Army. From 29 March to 24 April 1915, the division took part in the battles in the vicinity of Kalwariia-Marianpol. At the end of April the division was withdrawn from the front for rest and replacements. From the time of the division's arrival in Russia until April 10th, the 1st Battalion of the 166th Infantry Regiment lost 17 officers and 1,022 men. The 1st Company, where Fähnrich Rathke was assigned, lost 5 officers and 336 soldiers.

At the end of July, the division again occupied the front at Marianpol. During August and September the 31st Infantry division took part in the offensive at Vilna. On 19 August 1915 it advanced to Kovno and reached Vilna by the end of September. The division was relieved from the front on 6 October 1915 and on 24 October returned to the front in the Postawy-Lake Narotch area. While in this sector Officer Candidate Rathke displayed leadership and bravery in action and was recommended to receive the Iron cross 2nd Class. It remained in this sector until reassigned to the western front in December 1917.

✠ ✠ ✠

The document shown below is a Preliminary Authorization Certificate, Type 1, *(Vorläufiges Besitzzeugnis)* named to Artilleryman *(Kanonier)* **KONRAD PAUL FABER**, serving in the 12th Battery, IVth Section, 10th Field Artillery Regiment *(von Scharnhorst, 1st Hannover)*, 20th Artillery Brigade, 20th Infantry Division.

Document 54   *Preliminary Authorization Certificate, Type 1, to Kanonier Konrad Faber*

The document measures 20.7 cm. wide x 16.3 cm. high. It was signed in the field *(Im Felde)* on 27 May 1918 by the battery commander using a purple indelible pencil. In the lower left corner is the purple ink official stamp of the 10th Field Artillery Regiment. The document shows that Kanonier Faber was awarded the Iron Cross 2nd Class on 21 May 1918.

At the outbreak of the war the 20th Infantry Division entered Belgium on 11 August 1914. It was engaged at Charleroi, at Guise, and also at St. Quentin. The division took part in the battle of the Marne from 6-9 September 1914, after which it retired by way of Neufchâtel sur Aisne to the northwest of Rheims. The division took up its position between Aisne and the Brimont. It remained on the western front for the entire period and was engaged in several major actions.

Shown here are two more examples of look-alike documents. When you compare the four documents, 51, 52, 53, and the one above, you will note that they are very similar but each one is uniquely different. This fact should indicate to the document collector the need to examine very carefully all documents because what may look the same just might not actually be the same.

✠ ✠ ✠

The document shown below is a Preliminary Identification Certificate, Type 2, *(Vorläufiger Ausweis)* named to Light Infantryman *(Jäger)* **FRANZ**, serving in the 2nd Company, 18th Reserve Light Infantry *(Jäger)* Battalion, 5th Jäger Regiment, 2nd Jäger Brigade, 200th Infantry Division. From 1914 until 1916 the 18th Reserve Jäger Battalion served in the 46th Reserve Division and in 1916 was reassigned to the 200th Infantry Division.

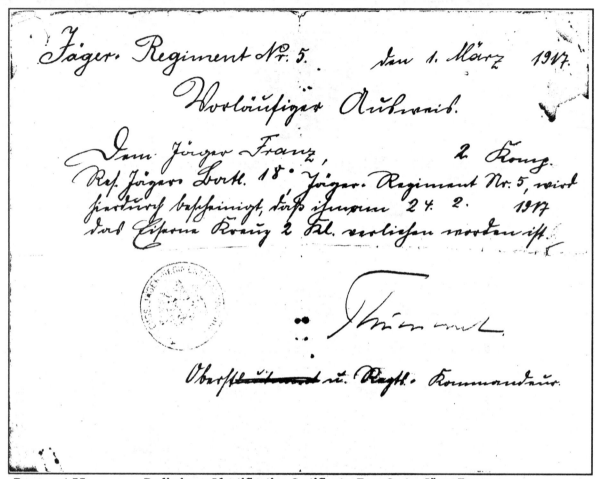

Document 55   *Preliminary Identification Certificate, Type 2, to Jäger Franz*

The stained document measures 21.0 cm. wide x 16.4 cm. high, and appears to be a printed form made from a duplicator mimeograph utilizing black ink. Blank space is left for the company, battalion numbers and date to be added at a later time. The document was signed on 1 March 1917 by the regimental commander using a purple indelible pencil. In the lower left is the blue ink official stamp of the headquarters of the 5th Jäger Regiment. The document indicates that Jäger Franz was awarded the Iron Cross 2nd Class on 24 February 1917. It has been folded and appears to have been carried by the recipient as identification.

The 200th Infantry Division was formed in July 1916 in Galicia. The 5th Jäger Regiment was composed of the 17th, 18th, and 23rd Reserve Jäger Battalions. The 200th Infantry Division together with the 1st Infantry Division formed the Carpathian Corps. The 200th Infantry Division took part in the counteroffensive in the Carpathian mountains against the Russian forces. On 1 September 1916 the division occupied a sector to the north of Mont Omnatik in Bukovina. The 200th Infantry Division stayed in the same area of the Carpathians south of Mt. Pnevié-Mt. Tomnatik until July 1917. It was during this time when Jäger Franz was cited for bravery and awarded the Iron Cross 2nd Class. The division took part in the offensive waged in Bukovina and took a position north of the Sereth. It was kept in this sector until September 1917. At the end of September the 200th Infantry Division was sent to the Italian front.

It arrived in the area of Laibach and rested for about 15 days. The division took positions on the Italian front 22 October 1917 and on the 24th of October engaged in the offensive on the Isonzo front.

The division advanced by way of Cividale and Udine where it fought against the retreating Italian rear guards. It reached Codroipo around 3 November 1917 and Quero on the Piave river by November 23rd. After a short period of rest the division was again assigned to the Mont Tomba region in December 1917.

In 1918 the 200th Infantry Division was withdrawn from the Italian front and reassigned to the western front where it remained until 11 November 1918.

✠ ✠ ✠

Comrades

The document shown below is an Identification Certificate, Type 4, *(Ausweis)* named to Dr. **von BAYER-EHRENBERG**, who was serving as a Civil Commissoner for the area of Verviers, Belgium.

Gouvernement Lüttich
Abt. IIa G. Nr. 90 G.

Lüttich, den **15. März** 1916.

Ausweis.

Im Namen Seiner Majestät des Kaisers hat der Herr Generalgouverneur in Belgien dem

Zivilkommissar für den Kreis Verviers   Dr. von Bayer- Ehrenberg

am 24.1.1916 das Eiserne Kreuz 2. Klasse verliehen.

Von Seiten des Gouvernements

Der Chef des Stabes

Oberst im Generalstab.

Document 56   *Identification Certificate, Type 5, to Dr. von Bayer-Ehrenberg*

The document was issued by the Occupation Government at Liege *(Lüttich)*, Belgium. It measures 21.2 cm. wide x 16.8 cm. high, and was signed at the governmental headquarters in Liege on 15 March 1916. The document shows that Dr. von Bayer-Ehrenberg was awarded the Iron Cross 2nd Class on 24 January 1916. It was signed in black ink by Colonel von Griesheim of the General Staff. To the left is the purple ink official stamp of the Occupation Government in Liege, Belgium.

✠ ✠ ✠

The document shown on the following page is an Authorization Certificate, Type 3, *(Besitz-Zeugnis)* named to Private *(Musketeer)* **KARL KNÜDEL**, 4th Company, 15th Engineer *(Pionier)* Battalion *(1st Alsace)*, 99th Infantry Regiment, 60th Brigade, 30th Infantry Division.

The document is a large format type measuring 19.6 cm. wide x 30.2 cm. high. It was signed in the field *(Im Felde)* by a Captain *(Hauptmann)* of the 15th Pionier Battalion with a purple indelible pencil. To the left of the signature is the purple ink official stamp of that unit. What is special about this document is that it shows a likeness of Emperor Wilhelm II. The document shows that the award was authorized on 21 June 1917 and that the words *"habe ich"* (I have) have been scratched out and replaced with the words *"wurde heute""* (have today), i.e., the award was made on the same day, 21 June 1917.

Beſitz=Zeugnis.

Im Namen
Seiner Majeſtät des Kaiſers

wurde heute
~~habe ich~~

dem Musketier Karl Knüdel, Inf.-Regt. Nr. 99,

= 4. Kompagnie =

das Eiſerne Kreuz II. Klaſſe von 1914 verliehen.

Im Felde, den 21. Juni 1917.

Hauptmann.

Nr.............. der Ordensliſte des A.=O.=K.

M. 1002. — Straßburger Druckerei u. Verlagsanſtalt. — 67.

Document 57   Authorization Certificate, Type 4, to Musketeer Karl Knüdel

At the beginning of the war, the 30th Infantry Division was a part of the 7th Army (von Heeringen). Entraining on 8 August 1914, the division was sent to Upper Alsace, where it was engaged until the 13th of August. It was transferred from that area to south of Sarreburg and crossed the French border after a series of engagements on 20 August 1914. The division advanced by way of Raon l'Étape across the Meurthe. At the beginning of September , the division was concentrated near Avricourt before going to Tergnier. It engaged in several actions in that area from middle September to mid-October.The next engagement of the 30th Infantry Division was southeast of Ypres, an area in which it remained for almost 15 months, from October, 1914 until January, 1916.

Toward the end of January, 1916, elements of the 30th Infantry Division were transferred to Verdun to take part in the February offensive. The division went into action on the front of Maucourt-Warcq on 24 February 1916. It remained in this sector until 11 July 1916 when the 99th Infantry Regiment took part in a new offensive. Around the end of September, 1916, the division was relieved and sent to rest in the Cambrai area. A short time afterward it returned to the Somme front at Sailly Saillisel and remained there for one month. Relieved at the end of November, 1916, the division was sent back to the Verdun front. After a rest near Dun sur Neuse, it went back into the front line in the vicinity the Mort Homme, where it took no part in any offensive or defensive engagements.

On 1 March 1917, the division went into the front line in the sector east of Auberive and was still there at the time of the spring offensive in Champagne. At the beginning of May, the division was attacked by the British but was able to check their advance and occupied their assigned sector until the middle of August, 1917. It appears that Musketier Knüdel was cited for bravery during this time.

On 25 August 1917, the 30th Infantry Division was again transferred to the Meuse area and occupied the trenches in the vicinity of Forges-Bethincourt. On 24 October 1917, the division was relieved. The British assault at Cambrai on 20 November required the division to be recalled to the front. It was sent into the front line on 23 November 1917, where it remained until 10 December 1917. After a rest in the Sedan area, the division was sent to the Champagne front northwest of Auberive, around the middle of January, 1918.

According to reports of the time by the US Army Intelligence Service, the division was classified as a first class division and was well commanded. During 1918 the 30th Infantry Division remained on the western front until the end of the war.

✠ ✠ ✠

The document shown below is an Official Certificate, Type 8, named to Reserve 2nd Lieutenant *(Leutnant der Reserve)* **HOFFMANN**, 30th Railroad Construction *(Eisenbahn Bau)* Company.

Oberkommando der Heeresgruppe
v. Mackensen.

H.-Qu., den *8. März 1916*

Im Namen Seiner Majestät des Deutschen Kaisers, Königs von Preußen ist dem

Leutnant d. R. Hoffmann,

Eisenbahn - Bau - Kompagnie 30,

das Eiserne Kreuz *2.* Klasse verliehen worden.

Der rechtmäßige Besitz der Auszeichnung wird hierdurch bescheinigt.

Der Oberbefehlshaber:

v. *Mackensen,*

Generalfeldmarschall.

Document 58   ***Official Certificate, Type 4, to Leutnant Hoffmann***

The document is printed in black ink and measures 20.7 cm. wide x 16.5 cm. high. It was issued on 8 March 1916 from the High Command Headquarters of Army Group von Mackenson. The document was signed in ink by General Field Marshal (GFM) von Mackensen. To the left of his signature is the purple ink official stamp of the High Command of Army Group von Mackensen.

Army Group von Mackensen was formed 18 September 1915 and disbanded on 30 July 1916. The Group was named after and commanded by GFM August von Mackensen, pictured at right. The Army Group was stationed on the eastern front and engaged in the defeat of the Russian forces. The Army Group von Mackensen also operated in Serbia and Macedonia.

Generalfeldmarschall von Mackensen

✠ ✠ ✠

VORLÆUFIGER AUSWEIS

DER KOMMANDIERENDE GENERAL DES

IX. RESERVEKORPS HAT IM NAMEN SEINER

MAJESTÆT DES KAISERS UND KŒNIGS DEM

Dru.- Gefreiten Johann Kräusel

VON DER *2.* KOMP. INFANTERIE - REGIMENT 394

DAS

EISERNE KREUZ

II. KLASSE

VERLIEHEN, WORUEBER IHM DIESER VORLÆUFIGE

AUSWEIS AUSGEFERTIGT WIRD.

REGTS.-STABSQUARTIER, DEN *14. 10. 1916.*

MAJOR UND REGIMENTSKOMMANDEUR

KORPSDRUCKEREI IX. R.-K.

Document 59   *Preliminary Identification Certificate, Type 2, to Sanitäts Gefreiten Johann Kräusel*

The document shown on the facing page is a Preliminary Identification Certificate, Type 2, *(Vorläufiger Ausweis)* named to Medical Orderly *(Sanitäts Gefreiten)* **JOHANN KRÄUSEL**, serving in the 2nd Company, 394th Infantry Regiment, 2nd Reserve Replacement *(Ersatz)* Brigade, 206th Infantry Division.

The document is rather large, measuring 25.0 cm. wide x 32.2 cm. high. It was signed by Major Mansfeld, the regiment commander, using a purple indelible pencil on 14 October 1916 at regimental headquarters. It is interesting that the document does not show a regimental stamp. The document was printed by the IXth Corps printers.

The 206th Infantry Division was organized in Belgium at the beginning of 1916. In October, 1916, the division was sent to the Somme where it was engaged in four different major actions. The actions took place in the regions of Péronne, La Maisonnette, and in the vicinity of Marchelepot. It was during one of these engagements that Sanitäts Gefreiten Kräusel was cited and rewarded with the Iron Cross 2nd Class. The division was relieved on 25 November 1916; it was sent to Alsace, taking over the sector of Ban de Sapt until the beginning of January 1917. The division was later sent to rest in the region of Château Salins and returned to the front around the middle of February 1917, assigned to the sector between the forest of Bezange and Leintrey. The division remained there until 20 April 1917. It was then sent to Laonnois, where it was assigned to a sector near Mont Cornet from 22 April until 30 April. Then the division was sent to Laon, staying there from 30 April to 4 May, 1917. Relieved on 10 June 1917, the division was sent to Lorraine at Blamont-Sarrebourg for a rest of four weeks. At the end of July, 1917, the division took over the sector of Hill 304-Pommerieux, where it was engaged during the French attack on 20 August 1917, and suffered heavy losses. Relieved two days after this attack, the division was sent to receive replacements and rest behind the Rheims front until the middle of September. It then held the Derru-Cernay sector where there were no engagements of consequence from the middle of September until 24 November 1917. On 28 November 1917, the division was sent to the St. Quentin front.

The division remained on the western front until the end of the war and took part in several major actions.

Medical orderly in action

✠ ✠ ✠

Stellvertretendes Generalkommando

   X. Armeekorps.   Hannover, den 12. August 1916.

Abt. IIa Nr. 64654

An

den Königlichen Leutnant der Landw.

Herrn Pohlmann, Hochwohlgeboren,

hier.

Seine Majestät der Kaiser und König haben die Gnade gehabt, Euer Hochwohlgeboren nach Schreiben des Chefs des Militärkabinetts vom 7.8.1916 für Kriegsverdienste in der Heimat

das Eiserne Kreuz 2. Klasse

zu verleihen.

Euer Hochwohlgeboren gebe ich hiervon unter Übersendung der Dekoration und Beifügung eines Besitzzeugnisses Kenntnis.

Der kommandierende General.

[signature]

General der Infanterie.

Document 60   *Transmittal Letter, Type 8, to Leutnant Pohlmann*

✠ ✠ ✠

The document shown on the preceding page is a Letter of Transmittal, Type 8, sent to Reserve 2nd Lieutenant *(Leutnant der Landwehr)* **POHLMANN.**

The Transmittal Letter was sent from the delegated representative of the General Headquarters of the Xth Army Corps advising Lt. Pohlmann that he was recommended on 7 August 1916 to receive the Iron Cross 2nd Class for war merit *(Kriegsverdienste)* in Germany proper *(Heimat)*. Note that Lt. Pohlmann is addressed as "Honorable Sir" *(Hochwohlgeboren)*, however, since this letter is coming from a higher headquarters it is just a formal salutation. It advises the officer that the decoration and the additional preliminary certificate *(Besitzzeugnis)* is being sent to him.

The document is mimeographed except for the name of the recipient and measures 20.9 cm. wide x 30.2 cm. high. It is signed in ink by a General of Infantry and dated 12 August 1916 in Hanover.

✠ ✠ ✠

The document shown below is a Preliminary Identification Certificate, Type 2, *(Vorläufiger Ausweis)* named to Reserve Private First Class *(Unteroffizier der Reserve)* **NÖKEL.**

Document 61   *Preliminary Identification Certificate, Type 2, to Unteroffizier d. Reserve Nökel*

The document measures 20.8 cm. wide x 16.5 cm. high, and appears to be mimeographed using black ink. It shows that Sgt. Nökel was awarded the Iron Cross 2nd Class on 8 March 1916. It was signed in black ink at Headquarters of Army Group "Falkenhausen" on 14 March 1916 by the adjutant. To the left of the signature is the purple ink official stamp of Army Group "Falkenhausen."

✠ ✠ ✠

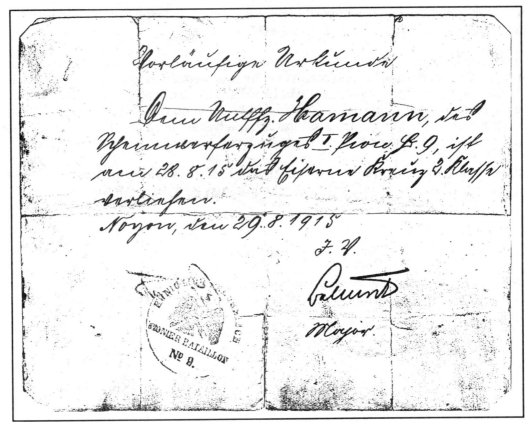

Document 62   *Authorization Certificate, Type 3, to Unteroffizier Hamann*

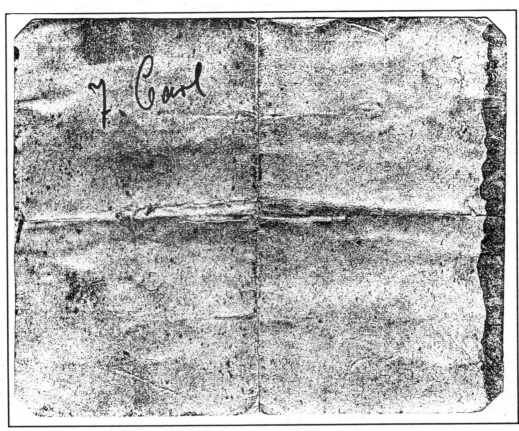

Document 63   *Back of the Authorization Certificate to Unteroffizier Hamann*

The document shown on the facing page is an Authorization Certificate, Type 3, *(Vorläufige Urkunde)* named to Corporal *(Unteroffizier)* **HAMANN**, serving in the Searchlight Section *(Scheinwerfer Zuges)* I. Engineer *(Pionier)* Battalion No. 9, 17th or 18th Infantry Division, 9th Army Corps, 1st Army (von Kluck).

The document is interesting in that it was made to be carried by the recipient as an identification to wear the Iron Cross 2nd Class. The document is all hand-written on heavy cream colored stock and had a darker outer cover. It measures 13.3 x 10.5 cm. It has the purple ink official stamp of the 9th Pionier Battalion and was signed in purple indelible pencil by a major of the unit on 29 August 1915. It shows that Unteroffizier Hamann was awarded the Iron Cross 2nd Class on 28 August 1915.

Some units of the I. Pionier Battalion No. 9 were assigned to the 17th Infantry Division until 1916. Other units of this battalion were assigned to the 18th Infantry Division from 1915 through 1917. It is almost impossible to determine to which division the Search Light Section and Unteroffizier Hamann were assigned.

☩ ☩ ☩

The document shown below is a Preliminary Authorization Certificate, Type 1,*(Vorläufiges Besitzzeugnis)* named to Private *(Musketier)* **WALTHER KARL ALFRED WICHMANN,** serving in the 2nd Home Guard *(Landwehr)* Infantry Battalion (Altona IX/15).

```
          V o r l ä u f i g e s  B e s i t z z e u g n i s .
          ---------------------------------------------------------

Dem  M u s k e t i e r

des  2. Landsturm - Infanterie - Bataillons  A L T O N A  IX/15


W a l t h e r   Karl  Alfred  W i c h m a n n

geboren  am  19. 3. 1897  zu   H a m b u r g ,

wird hiermit bescheinigt, dass derselbe

     Inhaber des Eisernen Kreuzes II.Klasse

ist.  Diese Bescheinigung gilt als vorläufiges Besitzzeugnis.

          E d i n g e n , den 10. D e z e m b e r  1917.

          Kommando des 2. Landsturm-Inf.-Bataillons  A L T O N A


               Major  und  Kommandeur .
```

Document 64   Preliminary Authorization Certificate, Type 1, to Musketier Walther Wichmann

The document measures 20.8 cm. wide x 16.5 cm. high, and is entirely typewritten. It shows that Musketier Wichmann, 20 years old at the time, was awarded the Iron Cross 2nd Class on 10 December 1917. The document was signed with a purple indelible pencil and then re-signed in black ink by the battalion commander. To the left of the signature block is the purple ink official stamp of the 2nd Land-sturm Infantry Battalion "Altona."

✠ ✠ ✠

The attractive document shown below is a Preliminary Authorization Certificate, Type 1, *(Vorläufiges Besitzzeugnis)* named to Private *(Soldat)* **AUGUST JENSSEN**, serving in the 102nd Württemberg Electric Generator *(Starkstrom)* Company.

Document 65   *Preliminary Authorization Certificate, Type 1, to Private August Jenssen*

The document is printed in black ink and measures 21.7 cm. wide x 17.8 cm. high. This document is very interesting for two very unusual reasons: one, the unit itself is unique in that it provided the electric generators that provided the power for searchlight units. Two, the document is not signed. In the bottom middle of the document is the purple ink official stamp of the 102nd Starkstrom Company; it was dated 4 April 1918 in the field *(Im Felde)*, which authorized the Iron Cross 2nd Class to Pvt. Jenssen on this date.

✠ ✠ ✠

The document shown below is an Official Certificate, Type 9, named to Private *(Musketier)* **DÖRNER**, serving at the time in the 385th Landwehr Infantry Regiment, 19th Landwehr Infantry Division, when he was awarded the Iron Cross 2nd Class on 22 September 1917.

Document 66   *Official Certificate, Type 9, to Musketier Gottfried Dörner*

The decorative document measures 20.5 cm. wide x 16.5 cm. high. The award was authorized on 22 September 1917 at the 19th Landwehr Division Staff Headquarters and bears the facsimile signature of Prince Heinrich XXX of the Principality of Reuss, a Major General and divisional commander. In the lower left hand corner is a purple ink official stamp of the 19th Landwehr Infantry Division.

The 19th Landwehr Infantry Division was formed at Cortemarck on 29 September 1916 through the combination of the 383rd, 385th, and 388th Landwehr Infantry Regiments. These regiments were composed of Home Guard *(Landsturm)* battalions made up mostly of older men and others not too physically fit. In early October 1916, the 19th Landwehr Division was assigned to the Dixmude-Steenstraat sector where the division remained for over a year.

The document shown on the following page is a Military Service Certificate *(Militär Dienstzeitbescheinigung)* of Gottfried Dörner. This document, dated 9 May 1938, shows the military service, assignments, engagements, decorations, and discharge. From this document we see that Dörner was born in Aachen on 5 November 1894 and that he was 21 years old when he entered the army. He was 23 years old when he received the Iron Cross 2nd Class.

Gottfried Dörner entered the army on 12 January 1915 and was assigned to the Recruit Depot II, Replacement *(Ersatz)* Battalion, 1st Guard *(Garde)* Infantry Regiment. By the 16th of June 1915 Dörner was assigned to the 6th Company, 1st Guard Infantry Regiment. On 11 August 1915 he was

Zentralnachweiseamt
für Kriegerverluste und Kriegergräber

Büro für Kriegsstammrollen
Nr. St VII 236 D 38.

Berlin SW 68, den 9. Mai 1938.
Lindenstraße 37
Fernsprecher 17 51 46

Bei Rücksendung ist diese
Bescheinigung beizufügen

Militär-Dienstzeitbescheinigung*)

über den **Musketier Gottfried Dörner,**

geboren am 5.11.1894 in Aachen.

1. Dienstverhältnisse: keine.
   a) vor dem Kriege:

   b) nach Eintritt der Mobilmachung:
   12.1.1915 z. Rek. Depot II.Ers.Batl. 1. Garde-Rgt. z.FB.,
   16.6.1915 z. 6. Komp. 1. Garde-Rgt. z.FB.,
   11.8.1915 erkrankt und dem Lazarett überwiesen,
   5.1.1916 z. 5. Komp. I.Ers.Batl. 1. Garde-Rgt. z.FB.,
   5.7.1916 z. 7. Komp. " " " ",
   13.7.1916 z. 3. Komp. " " " ",
   Entlassen: Fortsetzung umseitig:

2. Gefechtshandlungen seiner Truppenteile unter anderen (bzw. Aufenthalt im Kriegsgebiet):

(Anordnungsgemäß erfolgt für jedes Jahr nur Angabe einer Kampfhandlung oder eines zweimonatigen Aufenthalts)

1914:
1915: 17.-22.6. Schlacht bei Lemberg,
1916: 29.9.-31.12. Stellungskämpfe an der Yser,
1917: 1.1.-26.5. Stellungskämpfe an der Yser,
1918: 18.2.-4.3. Kämpfe zur Befreiung von Liv= und Estland,

3. Beförderungen: //
4. Orden: Eis.Kreuz zweiter Klasse 22.9.1917.
5. Bemerkungen: //

Vorstehende Angaben stimmen mit der Kriegs-Stammrolle Bd. Nr. 3583/58 überein.

Im Auftrag

*) Militärpässe werden bestimmungsgemäß nicht mehr ausgestellt.

Vordr. 86a.

Document 67   *Page 1 of the Military Service Record of Musketier Gottfried Dörner*

in the hospital suffering from a sickness although not having been wounded. By January 5, 1916, he was assigned to the 5th Company, I. Replacement *(Ersatz)* Battalion, 1st Guard Infantry Regiment. He saw his first action from the 17th until the 22nd of June 1916 at Lemberg on the eastern front. On 5 August 1916, Musketier Dörner was reassigned to the 7th Company, but on the 13th of August he was again reassigned to the 3rd Company, I. Replacement *(Ersatz)* Battalion, 1st Guard Infantry Regiment.

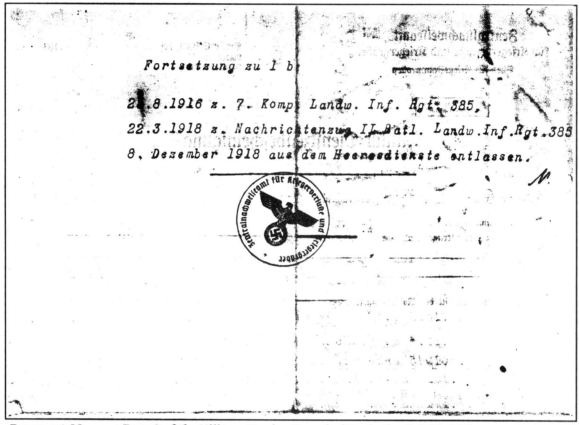

Document 68   ***Page 2 of the Military Service Record of Musketier Gottfried Dörner***

On August 25th he was back in the 7th Company, 385th Landwehr Infantry Regiment. He saw action in the Yser sector of the western front from 29 September until 31 December 1916. From 1 January until 26 May 1917, he was engaged in the trench fighting in the Yser sector with the 385th Landwehr Infantry Regiment. On 22 September 1917, Musketier Dörner received the Iron Cross 2nd Class for bravery in action on the Yser front.

His unit was transferred to the eastern front where between 18 February and 4 March 1918, he took part in several engagements during the "liberation" of Latvia and Estonia from the Russians. On 22 March 1918 he was transferred to the Communications Section of the II. Battalion, 385th Landwehr Infantry Regiment. Musketier Gottfried Dörner was discharged from the army on 8 December 1918.

✠ ✠ ✠

The document shown on the facing page is the Preliminary Authorization-Identification Certificate, Type 2, *(Verläufiger Besitz-Ausweis)* to Private *(Schütze)* **RUDOLF HUNDERTMARK**, who was serving in the 3rd Machine Gun Company, 219th Reserve Infantry Regiment, 47th Reserve Infantry Division when awarded the Iron Cross 2nd Class on 30 April 1918.

The large document measures 21.0 cm. wide x 32.6 cm. high. It was signed on 6 July 1918 and authorized the Iron Cross 2nd Class to Pvt. Hundertmark on 30 April 1918. In the lower left hand corner is the registration number (2839), and the document is signed in pencil by the regimental commander. Below the signature block is the purple ink official stamp of the 219th Reserve Infantry Regiment.

The 47th Reserve Infantry Division was formed between August and October 1914. It was a part of the 24th Reserve Corps and was concentrated in the vicinity of Metz about 20 October 1914. The division was sent to Woevre south of Etain on 26 October 1914. It went into action at Magnaville on the 31st and at Maucourt from 6 until 11 November 1918. On 23 November 1914, the 47th Infantry Division was sent to the eastern front. It arrived in the vicinity of Kracow at the beginning of December and went into action on the Dunajec river west of Tarnow on 8 December 1914. Moving to the year 1916, the 47th Reserve Infantry Division remained in the sector of Lipsk-Baranovitchi during the fall of 1916 until May of 1917. From 10 July until 9 August 1916, Hundertmark's regiment was in the front line trenches at Baranovitchi.

In May 1917 the division was transferred back to the western front. From 8 June through 7 July 1917, Hundertmark was in action at Chemin des Dames. Now moving to the year 1918, the division was engaged in the Somme offensive on 21-22 March 1918, at St Quentin, near Tergnier and participated in the offensive until 25 March 1918. It was reengaged on 1 April southwest of Lassigny and held that sector until 2 May 1918 when the division was relieved by the 206th Infantry Division.

It appears that Pvt. Hundertmark was wounded in action during this offensive, displayed bravery and was recognized by being awarded the Iron Cross 2nd Class. The division was then transferred and moved on 6 May 1918 to the St. Quentin area. From 27 May 1918 onward it followed up the advance behind the 113th Infantry Division and finally relieved that division on 1 June 1918 near Viersy. The 47th Reserve Infantry Division was relieved from the front on 20 June 1918. The division was returned to the front after a short rest. At this time it suffered again heavy losses on the front and on about 27 July 1918 the division was withdrawn for rest and refitting. The division was dissolved at Mainbresson on 30 June 1918. The 219th Reserve Infantry Regiment was drafted into the 158th Infantry Regiment.

✠ ✠ ✠

VORLÄUFIGER BESITZ-AUSWEIS

Im Namen Seiner Majestät des Kaisers und Königs

hat der Herr Divisions-Kommandeur Generalmajor Freiherr von Eichendorff

dem Schützen (aktiv) Rudolf Hundertmark

der 3. Masch. Gew. Kompagnie Res.-Infanterie-Regts. Nr. 219

am 30. April 1918

das

Eiserne Kreuz II. Klasse

verliehen.

Regiments-Stabsquartier, den 6. Juli 1918.

[illegible]

Major und Regiments-Kommandeur.

KÖNIGL. PREUSSISCHES RES. INF. REGT. 219

Lfd. Nr. 2839.

Document 69 *Preliminary Authorization Certificate, Type 1, to Schütze Rudolf Hundertmark*

On the following pages are excerpts from Rudolf Hundertmark's Military Pass book *(Militärpaß)* which trace his military career during World War I. The document shown to the below right, actual size, is page 1 of the Military Pass Book.

Part 1. of the first page shows that he was born on 7 December 1894 in Holzminden and a citizen of Prussia.

Part 2. shows that he was a baker by profession.

Parts 3. and 4. show Hundertmark was single and was a member of the evangelical church.

Part 5. shows that he entered the army on 15 May 1915 at the age of 21.

Part 6. shows he was assigned to the Ist Recruit Depot, IInd Replacement *(Ersatz)* Battalion, 159th Infantry Regiment.

Pages 2, 3, 8, and 9 of the Military Pass Book of Rudolph Hundertmark are seen, reduced in size, on the following page.

On page 2 *(Document 71)* under "Unit Assignment *(Versetzungen)* Section" entries of unit assignment are shown. By 19 August 1915, Hundertmark was serving in a unit in the field. However, by 24 September 1915, he was assigned to the 10th Company, 219th Reserve Infantry Regiment. Hundertmark served in the 10th Company until 21 December 1917 when he was transferred to the 3rd Machine Gun Company of the 219th Reserve Infantry Regiment.

Document 70   Military Pass Book of Rudolf Hundertmark

On page 3 under Part 9 "Orders and Awards *(Orden und Ehrenzeichen)* Section" we see that Rudolf Hundertmark was awarded the Iron Cross 2nd Class on 30 April 1918.

Also on page 3 note that Part 10 "Campaigns, Wounds *(Feldzüge, Verwundungen)* Section" refers the reader to pages 8 and 9 *(S.Seite 8-9)*.

On pages 8 and 9, seen on the following page *(Document 72)*, in the "Personal Notice *(Personalnotizen)* Section" we see the official battles *(Gefechte)* listed in which Hundertmark saw action. The reader will notice entries for the battle of Baranovitchi on the Russian front and Chemin des Dames and St. Quentin on the western front.

Note: The entries in the Military Pass Book of Rudolph Hundertmark have the purple ink stamp of the 2nd Battalion of the 158th Infantry Regiment which indicates the entries were made __after__ the 16th of August 1918.

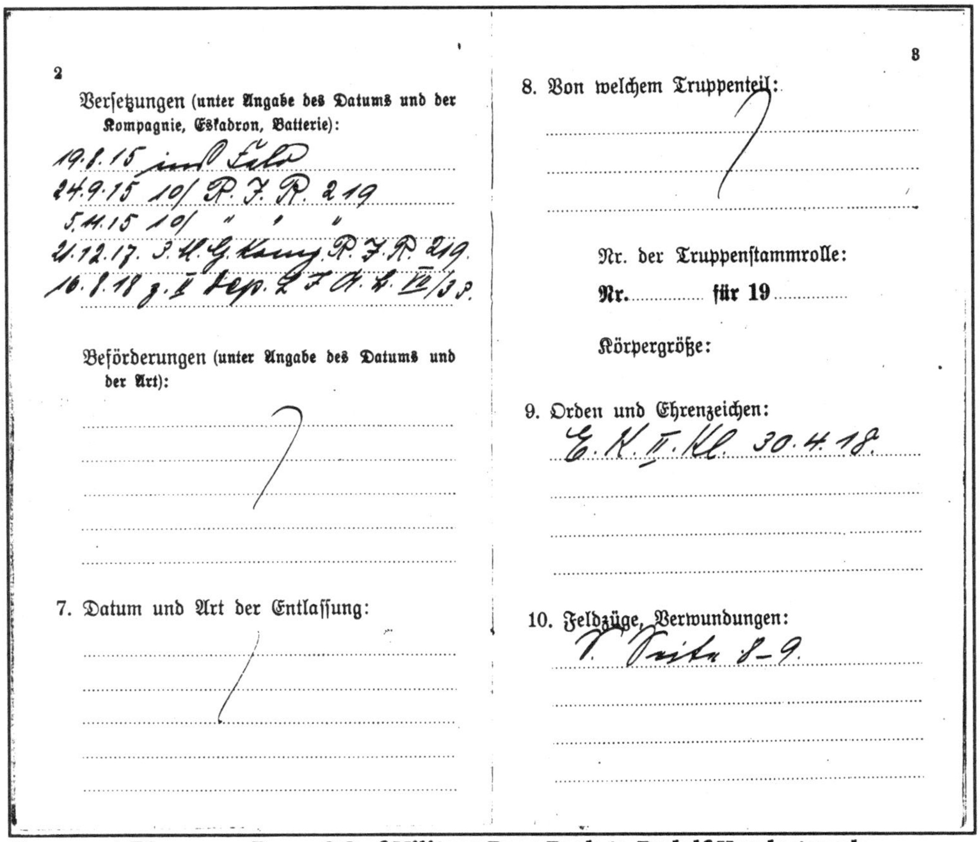

2

Verſetzungen (unter Angabe des Datums und der
Kompagnie, Eskadron, Batterie):

19.8.15 ins Feld

24.9.15 10/ R. J. R. 219

5.4.15 10/ „ „ „

21.12.17 J. H. G. Komp. R. J. R. 219

10.1.18 z. 2. Kop. L. J. A. VII/33.

Beförderungen (unter Angabe des Datums und
der Art):

7. Datum und Art der Entlaſſung:

8

8. Von welchem Truppenteil:

Nr. der Truppenstammrolle:

Nr. .... **für 19** ....

Körpergröße:

9. Orden und Ehrenzeichen:

E. K. II. Kl. 30.4.18

10. Feldzüge, Verwundungen:

V. Frkr. 8—9

Document 71   Pages 2-3 of Military Pass Book to Rudolf Hundertmark

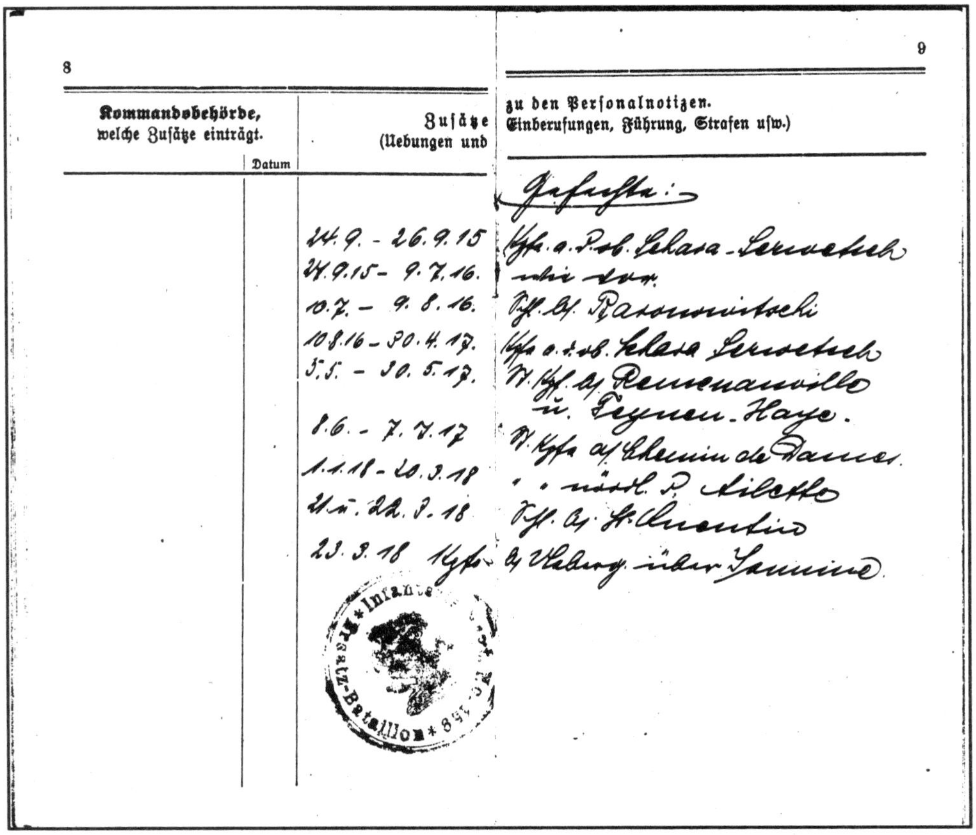

8

Kommandobehörde, welche Zuſätze einträgt.		Zuſätze (Uebungen und
	Datum	

9

zu den Perſonalnotizen.
(Einberufungen, Führung, Strafen uſw.)

Gefechte:

24.9. - 26.9.15

24.9.15 - 9.7.16.

10.7. - 9.8.16.

10.8.16 - 30.4.17.

5.5. - 30.5.17.

1.6. - 7.7.17

1.1.18 - 20.3.18

21. u. 22.3.18

23.3.18

Document 72   Pages 8-9 of Military Pass Book to Rudolf Hundertmark

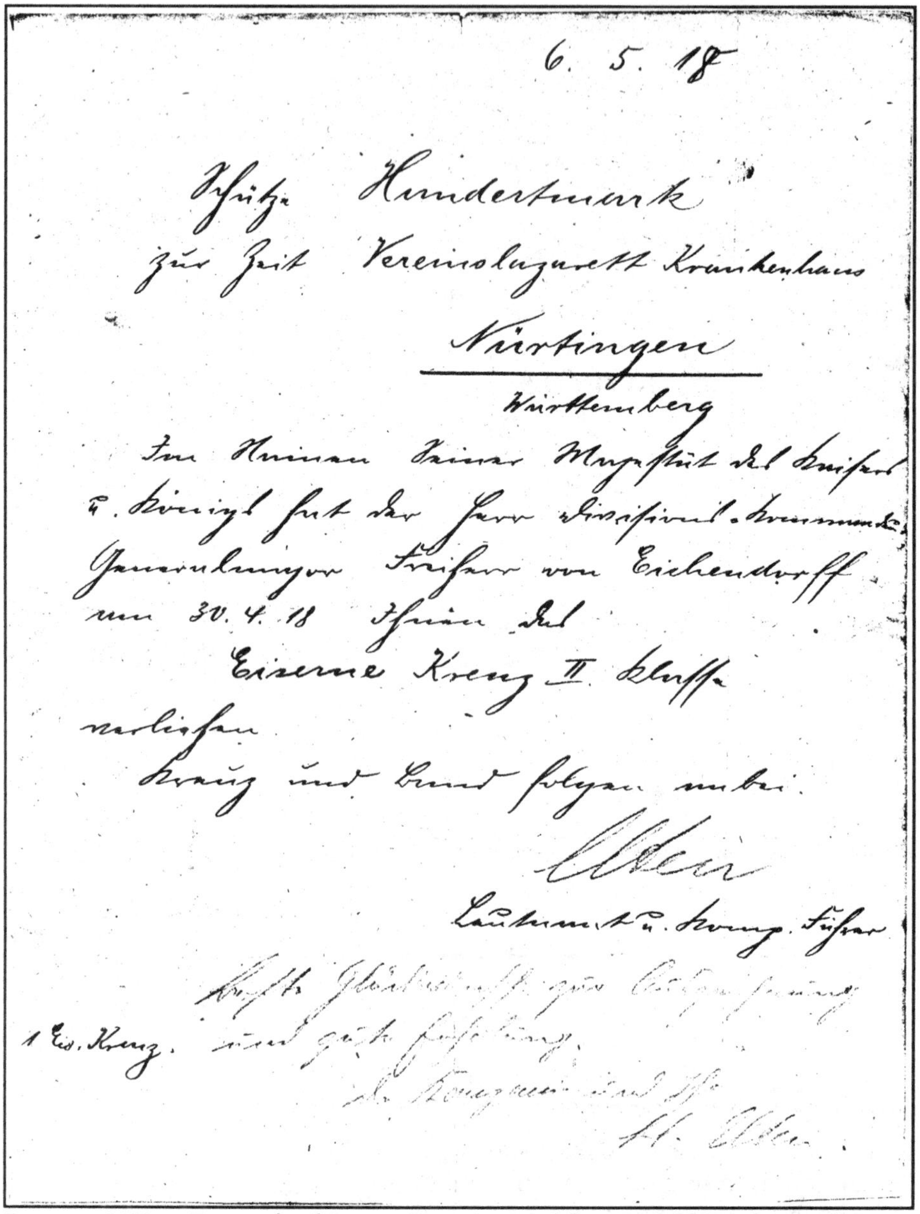

6. 5. 18

Schütz Hundertmark

zur Zeit Vereinslazarett Krankenhaus

Nürtingen

Württemberg

[handwritten German text]

Eiserne Kreuz II. Klasse

[handwritten German text]

1 Eis. Kreuz.

Shown at left is a Transmittal Letter, Type 8, sent to Pvt. Hundertmark from his company commander. Pvt. Hundertmark was recuperating in a hospital from wounds received in action when he was advised he had been awarded the Iron Cross 2nd Class on 30 April 1918.

In the lower left hand corner is the notation that an Iron Cross 2nd Class had been sent along with the letter.

At the bottom of the letter is a personal message, written in pencil, by the company commander, wishing Hundertmark good luck and a quick recovery.

Document 73   Transmittal Letter, Type 8, to Schütze Rudolf Hundertmark

To the right is a 1929 German Passport photo taken of Rudolf Hundertmark when he immigrated to the United States.

Rudolf Hundertmark
Document 74

✠ ✠ ✠

All Rudolf Hundertmark documents are from the J. Eicher Collection

The document shown below is an Identification Certificate, Type 5, *(Ausweis)* named to Private *(Infantrist)* **LUDWIG BRAUNBECK** who was serving in the 4th Company, 1st Bavarian Infantry Regiment *(König)*, 1st Bavarian Infantry Brigade, 1st Bavarian Infantry Division.

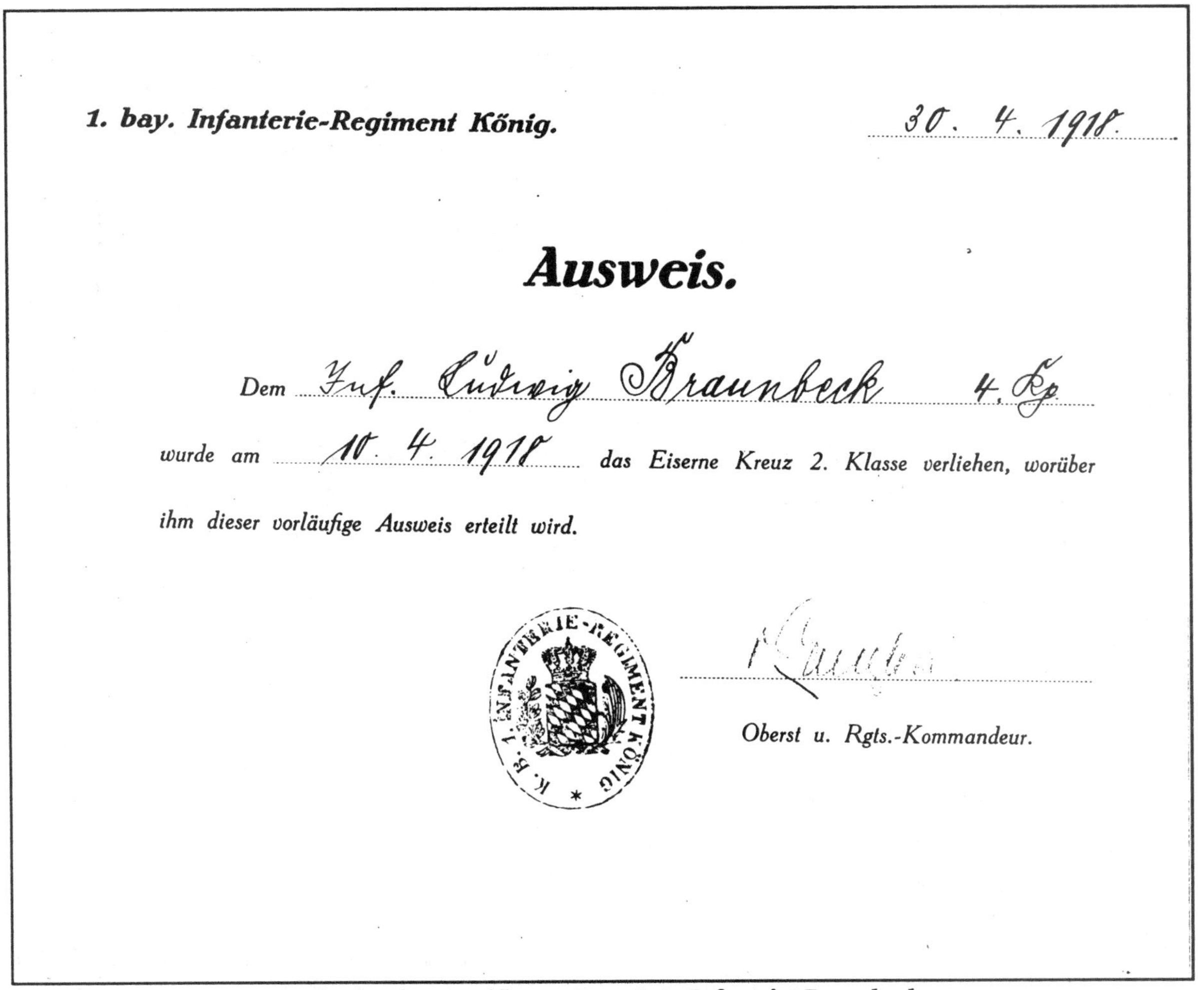

1. bay. Infanterie-Regiment König.   30. 4. 1918.

Ausweis.

Dem *Inf. Ludwig Braunbeck* 4. Kp

wurde am _10. 4. 1918_ das Eiserne Kreuz 2. Klasse verliehen, worüber

ihm dieser vorläufige Ausweis erteilt wird.

Oberst u. Rgts.-Kommandeur.

Document 75   *Authorization Certificate, Type 5, to Infantrist Braunbeck*

The document measures 20.4 wide x 16.3 cm. high. It was signed on 30 April 1918 at regimental headquarters and is signed by the commanding officer with a purple indelible pencil. The document showed that Private Braunbeck was authorized the Iron Cross 2nd Class on 10 April 1918. To the left of the signature block is the purple ink stamp of the 1st Bavarian Infantry Regiment *(König)*.

Moving to 1918 on the opening day of the 1918 March offensive, the division reinforced the front south of St. Quentin. It was withdrawn the next day. On 23 March 1918, the division returned into the front line north of Chauny. Around the 30th the division was relieved from the front. It was while in this sector that Private Braunbeck was cited for bravery. On 6 April 1918 the division relieved the 3rd Bavarian Infantry Division west of Lassigny. It was in turn relieved by the 3rd Bavarian Infantry Division on 12 April 1918. Having suffered a great many casualties during the engagements on the Somme in the early years of the war, the division was taken to a quiet sector in Champagne, relieving the 52nd Reserve Infantry Division on 1 May 1918 north of Souain. About 30 June 1918 the division was relieved from the front by the 30th Infantry Division. The division reinforced the front near Souain on 15 July 1918 and was withdrawn from the front on 31 July 1918. The division next entered the front line northeast of Soissons on 11 August 1918. It was relieved by the Light Infantry *(Jäger)* Division about August 19th and moved to the west taking over the Cuts sector northeast Noyon on 20 August 1918. It was withdrawn on the 22nd of August. On 31 August 1918 the division was found at Folenbray, northwest of Coucy-le-Chateau and was taken out of that sector September 12th. About 27 September 1918 the division took over the Manre sector southeast of Vouziers, where it remained, engaging in several actions, until the war was over.

✠ ✠ ✠

The document shown below is an Authorization Certificate, Type 4, *(Besitzzeugnis)* named to Militia Captain *(Hauptmann der Landwehr)* **BAHN.** He was serving at the time he was decorated with the Iron Cross 2nd Class in the 2nd Company, 17th Brigade Replacement *(Ersatz)* Battalion *(formerly the 23rd Landwehr Infantry Regiment)*, 4th Landwehr Infantry Division.

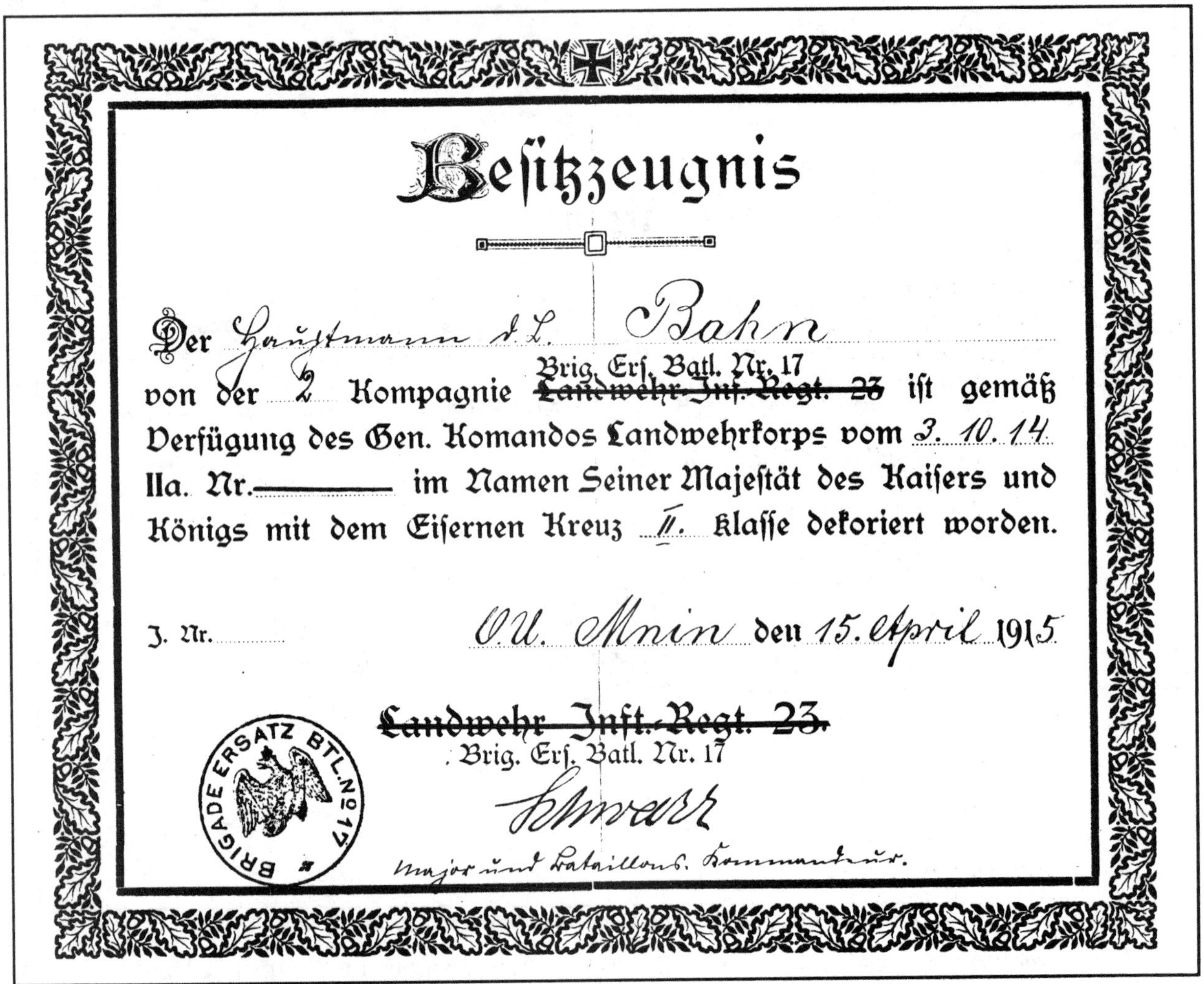

Besitzzeugnis

Der Hauptmann d.L. Bahn

von der 2. Kompagnie ~~Landwehr-Inf.-Regt. 23~~ Brig. Erf. Batl. Nr. 17 ist gemäß Verfügung des Gen. Komandos Landwehrkorps vom 3. 10. 14 IIa. Nr._____ im Namen Seiner Majestät des Kaisers und Königs mit dem Eisernen Kreuz II. Klasse dekoriert worden.

J. Nr._____ O.U. Mnin den 15. April 1915.

~~Landwehr-Inf.-Regt. 23.~~ Brig. Erf. Batl. Nr. 17

Major und Bataillons-Kommandeur.

| Document 76 | *Authorization Certificate, Type 4, to Hauptmann Bahn* |

The decorative document measures 23.4 cm. wide x 19.2 cm. high. The 23rd Landwehr Infantry Regiment has been lined through to show the unit's new classification. Inside the decorative border is a red inner border. The "B" in Bestizzeugnis and the "D" in Der are printed in red. The document was signed on 15 April 1915 at the unit headquarters in Mnin by the battalion commander in ink. To the left is the purple ink official stamp of the 17th Brigade Ersatz Battalion. It shows that Captain Bahn was awarded the Iron Cross 2nd Class on 2 October 1914.

At the beginning of the war the 4th Landwehr Infantry Division, with the 3rd Landwehr Infantry Division, formed the 2nd Landwehr Corps, which was engaged on the eastern front. At the beginning of September 1914 the 4th Landwehr Infantry Division took part in the battle of Tarnovka. They followed the campaign at Warsaw and the retreat of the Russian forces with an enveloping action of the Russians at Lodz. It was during these actions that Captain Bahn was cited for leadership and bravery in action and received the Iron Cross 2nd Class. In December 1914 the division was located between the Vistula river and Pilica. The 4th Landwehr Infantry Division remained on the Russian front for the entire war.

✠ ✠ ✠

The document shown below is an Identification Certificate, Type 5, *(Ausweis)* named to Driver *(Kraftfahrer)* **WILHELM HAGEMANN** serving in the 7th Army Telephone *(Fernsprech)* Section, 7th Army.

VORLÄUFIGER-AUSWEIS.

Dass dem Kraftfahrer Wilhelm H a g e m a n n

von der Armee Fernsprech Abteilung Nr. 7

am 8/. November   1918 von dem Oberbefehlshaber der 7. Armee im

Namen seiner Majestät des Kaisers und Königs das E i s e r n e

K r e u z II.Klasse verliehen worden ist, wird hiermit bescheinigt.

Armee - Hauptquartier, den 5. Dezember 1918.

Hauptmann und Abteilungs -

Kommandeur.

Document 77   Identification Certificate, Type 5, to Kraftfahrer Wilhelm Hagemann

The document is a typed and printed form which served as both a Preliminary Identification *(Vorläufiger Ausweis)* Certificate and as an Identification *(Ausweis)* Certificate. By striking out the *"Vorläufiger"* it becomes identification only. The document shows that Driver Hagemann was awarded the Iron Cross 2nd Class on 8 November 1918, three days before the armistice. However, the certificate was not issued until 5 December 1918, after the war had ended. It measures 21.2 cm. wide x 16.5 cm. high, and was signed in pencil by the section commander. To the left of the signature is the purple ink official stamp of the 7th Army Telephone Section.

✠ ✠ ✠

Telephone section at work

Document named to Medical Corpsman Kaiser

The document shown on the facing page is a Privately Purchased Certificate, Type 10, *(Besitzzeugnis)* named to Medical Corporal *(Sanitäts Unteroffizier)* **KAISER**, serving in the 170th Machine Gun Company.

The extremely large and decorative document measures 27.5 cm. wide x 40.5 cm. high. What is very intriguing about this document is that no unit, other than the company, is shown. There is no date other than the "1914/15" and no official stamp. However, the signature of the commanding general is written in black ink. The very beautiful document, does not say anything about the recipient other than his being a medic, and an awardee of the Iron Cross 2nd Class. This is the third document identical to this one the author has seen. An unsolved mystery!

✠ ✠ ✠

9. INFANTERIE-REGT. WREDE.

BESITZ-ZEUGNIS.

Dem   Vizefeldwebel

                             Georg B u d i o n

Kgl. 9. Infanterie-Regiments

6.   Kompagnie

geboren am: 3. April 1892 zu Damm

Bezirksamt: Aschaffenburg

Regierungs-Bez.:   Unterfranken

Bundesstaat: Bayern

wurde im Namen

SEINER MAJESTÆT DES KAISERS

durch Se. Exz. den Herrn kommandierenden General k. b. II. Armee-Korps

am: 25. Dezember 1915

das

Eiserne Kreuz 2. Klasse

verliehen.

Wredehof,   1. Juni   1916.

KGL. BAYER. 9. INFANTERIE-REGIMENT WREDE.

Oberleutnant und Regiments-Kommandeur.

Felddruckerei Vendinbrück.

Document 79   *Authorization Certificate, Type 4, to Vizefeldwebel Georg Budion*

The document shown on the facing page is an Authorization Certificate, Type 4, *(Besitz-Zeugnis)* named to Assistant Sergeant Major *(Vizefeldwebel)* **GEORG BUDION**, serving in the 6th Company, 7th Bavarian Brigade, 9th Infantry Regiment *(Wrede)*, 4th Bavarian Infantry Division, 2nd Bavarian Army Corps.

The large document measures 20.7 cm. wide x 31.8 cm. high. It was printed by the military printers in Vendinbrück. It is unusual as it shows in the upper left-hand corner the ribbon for the Iron Cross. The certificate was signed at the regimental headquarters in Wredehof on 1 June 1916 by the regimental commander in purple indelible pencil. To the left of the signature is the oval purple official stamp of the 9th Bavarian Infantry Regiment. It shows that Vizefeldwebel Budion was awarded the Iron Cross 2nd Class for bravery on 25 December 1915, when he was 23 years old. It must have been an outstanding Christmas present for him.

Crown Prince Rupprecht of Bavaria

At the mobilization of 1914 the 4th Bavarian Infantry Division, with the 3rd Bavarian Infantry Division, formed the 2nd Bavarian Army Corps. Assembled on the 18th of August 1914, in the area of the Metz-Strassburg area along with the 2nd Bavarian Army Corps, these divisions constituted the 6th Army under the command of Crown Prince Rupprecht of Bavaria, shown at right.

On 20 August 1914, the division fought its first battle west of Morhange. The division captured the fort of Manonviller and advanced to Mortagne south of Luniville. The division held this position until 11 September 1914 when it was relieved. On September 18th the division left Metz for Namur from where it was assigned north of Péronne, arriving in that area on 25 September 1914. The division was engaged on the front from September 26 through the middle of October 1914 in the region north of the Somme. During the third and fourth weeks of October beginning on the 23rd, the division went to Flanders south of Ypres. It was assigned the sector of Wytschaete from 14 November to 15 October 1914 and was in defensive positions.

On September 26, 1915, some units of the division saw action on the Loos-Hulluch front at the time of the British major assault. In the counterattack, the Bavarians retook "Ditch #8" from the British and inflicted heavy losses on them. It is very probable that Vizefeldwebel was cited for leadership and bravery during the British attacks or on related patrol activities. In November, the division was in the region of Loos south of Hulluch, where it stayed until August 16th. In this sector the division carried on mine warfare. About the end of April 1916, the division lost 1,100 men while attempting a gas attack.

Toward the end of August of 1916 the division was again assigned to the Somme area. It was engaged between Martinpuich and Longueval, where it took part in several heavy actions for possession of the Bois Haut *(High Forest)*. From 16 October 1916 to 17 June 1917 the division was sent to Flanders and held the sector northeast of Armentières.

Official records of the US Army Intelligence Service show that the 4th Bavarian Infantry Division was of the best quality and had a very high morale.

✠ ✠ ✠

**Der kommandierende General
des XXVI. Reservekorps.**

K.H.Qu. Roulers,
den 2. März 1915.

**Im Namen Seiner Majestät des Deutschen Kaisers
und Königs von Preußen Wilhelm II. habe ich dem**

Gefreiten **Gassert**

von der 12. Komp Res. Inf. Regt. 233

geboren am 21. Juli 1893 zu Waltershausen.

**für mutiges und tapferes Verhalten in den Kämpfen
östlich der Yser das Eiserne Kreuz II. Klasse verliehen.**

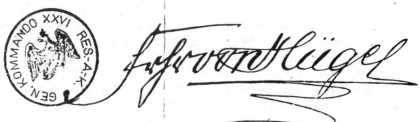

General der Infanterie.

The document shown on the preceding page is an Official Certificate, Type 9, named to Private First Class *(Gefrieten)* **GASSERT** serving in the 12th Company, 233rd Reserve Infantry Regiment, 101st Reserve Infantry Brigade, 51st Reserve Infantry Division, XXVIth Reserve Army Corps.

The document is a large format measuring 21.1 cm. wide x 28.2 cm. high. It was signed at the XXVIth Reserve Corps Headquarters at Roulers on 2 March 1915. The document is signed in ink by General Freiherr von Hügel,* commander of the XXVIth Reserve Army Corps. To the left of the signature is the stamp of the XXVIth Reserve Corps in black ink.

It is interesting that the document awarding the Iron Cross 2nd Class to Gefreiten Gessert, who was 22 years old at the time, states that he displayed "courageous and brave behaviour in action east of the Yser" *(für mutiges und tapferes Verhalten in den Kämpfen östlich der Yser).*

The 51st Reserve Infantry Division along with the 52nd Reserve Infantry Division was created between August and October 1914 and together formed the XXVIth Reserve Army Corps. The division went into action northeast of Ypres in the middle of October 1914. It was engaged in the front line at Cortemarck-Moorslede on October 22nd. The division reached Langemarck on 24 October and finally took up its front line position near Poelcappelle. The division remained in the area northeast of Ypres during the entire year of 1915 until September 1916. It appears that Gefreiten Gessert was cited to receive the Iron Cross 2nd Class during this period on the front. In September 1916, the division transferred the 233rd Reserve Infantry Regiment to 195th Infantry Division. The 195th Infantry Division was created in order to provide defense against the Russian advance in Galicia.

✠ ✠ ✠

The document shown on the following page is an Official Certificate, Type 9, named to Home Guard Private *(Landsturmmann)* **RUDNER**, serving in the 1st Company of the 14th Prisoner-of-War Labor Battalion *(Kriegsgefangenen - Arbeits - Batallions Nr. 14).* attached to the 52nd Infantry Division.

This document is almost identical to the Gassert document on the facing page except for some text. It is a large format measuring 21.1 cm. wide x 28.2 cm. high. It is signed at the XXVIth Reserve Corps Headquarters at Savigny on 7 May 1917. The document is signed in black ink by General Freiherr von Hügel,* commander of the XXVIth Reserve Army Corps. To the left of the signature is the stamp of the XXVIth Reserve Corps in black ink.

From 1915 until the end of the war the 52nd Infantry Division was assigned to the western front and took part in many major actions and was highly rated as a fighting division by the US Army Intelligence records.

Landsturmmann Rudner was in all probability an older man who could have possibly served in the 1870-71 Franco-German War and had been assigned to the Home Guard until recalled for duty where he was assigned as a guard in the Labor battalion. The big question is what Landsturmmann Rudner did to be recommended and awarded the Iron Cross 2nd Class for "courageous and brave behaviour" *(für mutiges und tapferes Verhalten).*

Also of interest is that according to captured German documents dated 4 June 1917, three Labor POW companies were attached to the 52nd Infantry Division.

✠ ✠ ✠

---

* General of Infantry Frhr. Otto von Hügel, Commanding General, XXVI. Reserve Corps. was awarded the Prussian Pour le Mérite Order on 28 August 1916. The citation reads:

> "... in recognition of outstanding leadership... during the campaigns in Flanders...
> The XXVI Reserve Corps... captured over 6,000 enemy weapons and 60 artillery
> pieces..."

"The History of the Prussian Pour le Mérite Order, 1888-1918," Volume III, W.E. Hamelman, p. 462, entry 149.

Der Kommandierende General
des XXVI. Reservekorps.

K.H.Qu., Savigny,

den 7. Mai 1917.

Im Namen Seiner Majestät des Deutschen Kaisers
und Königs von Preußen Wilhelm II. habe ich dem

Landsturmmann Rudner

der 1. Kompagnie

des Kriegsgefangenen - Arbeits - Bataillons Nr. 14

für mutiges und tapferes Verhalten das Eiserne
Kreuz II. Klasse verliehen.

GEN. KOMMANDO XXVI. RES-A-K.

Frhr. von Hügel

General der Infanterie.

Document 81 ***Official Certificate, Type 9, to Landsturmmann Rudner***

The document shown below is a Preliminary Identification Certificate, Type 2, *(Vorläufiger Ausweis)* named to Private First Class *(Gefreiten)* **FRANZ CLAES** serving in the 210th Mortar Company, 310th Engineer *(Pionier)* Battalion, 10th Reserve Infantry Division.

The document measures 21.0 cm. wide x 16.5 cm. high. The rather poorly printed certificate is dated 21 March 1917 but you will notice that in the upper right hand corner there is an incomplete date. The name of the recipient, unit and date are written in black ink. The document is signed by a captain using a purple indelible pencil. To the left of the signature is the purple ink official stamp of the Engineer Command of the 10th Reserve Infantry Division.

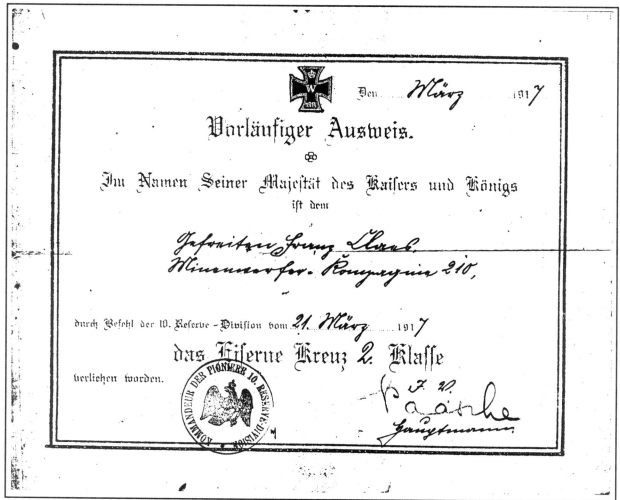

Document 82   *Preliminary Identification Certificate, Type 2, to Gefreiten Franz Claes*

The 10th Reserve Infantry Division has been on the western front since 1914. Moving ahead to the year 1917, we find the division in February 1917 in a rest area in the region of Sedan. At the beginning of March 1917, the division went into the line in the area of Berry au Bac in the sector Hill 108 to Spigneul. It was relieved at the beginning of the major French offensive on 16 April 1917. The division suffered heavy losses resulting from the French artillery bombardment preceding the attack.

From the date on the document it appears that Gefreiten Claes received his Iron Cross 2nd Class during this period when the division was sustaining the French artillery bombardment.

The division remained on the western front until the end of the war. It was rated in US Army Intelligence service as a first class fighting division.

✠ ✠ ✠

The document shown on the following page is an Official Certificate, Type 9, named to Private (Musketier) **SINNING**, who was serving in the 81st Reserve Infantry Regiment, 42nd Reserve Infantry Brigade, 21st Reserve Infantry Division when decorated with the Iron Cross 2nd Class.

The exceptionally beautiful document is printed on heavy stock and measures 22.0 cm. wide x 33.0 cm. high. It was signed in the field *(Im Felde)* on 3 December 1916. The document is signed by the regimental commander in pencil. On the signature is the purple ink official stamp of the 81st Reserve Infantry Regiment. It awards the Iron Cross 2nd Class to Musketier Sinning for "demonstrated bravery before the enemy" *(für Bewiesne Tapferkeit vor dem Feinde).*

At the outbreak of World War I the 21st Reserve Infantry Division formed, along with the 25th Reserve Infantry Division, the 18th Reserve Army Corps. The corps was a part of the 4th Army under the command of Prince Albrecht of Württemberg. On 10-12 August 1914 the division passed to the north of Luxemburg and entered Belgium by Martelange. After an engagement on 22 August 1914 at Neufchateau the 21st Reserve Infantry Division reached Carignan on August 25th. The division saw action at Mouzon on August 28th, crossed the Meuse at that point and from there, by way of Grandpré, skirting Argonne to the west, it arrived at the Marne-Rhine Canal on 6 September 1914. At the battle of the Marne, the division went into action in the Saulx sector, which was in the vicinity of Mognéville, from 7 to 10 September 1914.

From January to December 1915, the division was in the sector of Ville sûr Tourbe. During September 1915, it took part in several of the Champagne battles.

From January until June of 1916 the division occupied the Massiges sector. After a rest in the Briey area from the end of June until 15 July 1916, the division was sent to Verdun in the Fumin Wood sector where it saw heavy action from 15 through 25 July and remained there until the beginning of September 1916. At that time the division was returned to its sector at Ville sûr Tourbe. A short time afterwards the division transferred the 81st Reserve Infantry Regiment to the 222nd Infantry Division which was then being formed.

The 222nd Infantry Division was formed on 11 September 1916, behind the front north of Verdun. The division took two of its regiments from existing divisions. The 81st Reserve Infantry Regiment came from the 21st Reserve Infantry Division. From 15 September to 24 October 1916, the 222nd Infantry Division rested in Alsace near Rouffach. On 25 October 1916 the division was transferred to the vicinity of Cambrai. On November the 5th it went into action on the Somme front near Lesboeufs and remained on the front until December 7-8, 1916. It appears that when Musketier Sinning was cited for bravery and awarded the Iron Cross 2nd Class, his regiment was a part of the 222nd Infantry Division.

After a few days of rest the division was sent into the area of Laonnois. The 222nd Infantry Division took over the sector of Ville aux Bois southeast of Craonne which it occupied until 15 February 1917. On 16 March 1917, the division was engaged east of Soissons on the Vregny-Combe Plateau. From there the division counterattacked on 21 March north of Missy sur Aisne. The division withdrew in the direction of Laffaux Mill - Jouy - Aizy at the beginning of April and engaged in other actions on this front from 18 to 21 April 1917. The division, having established its position between Laffaux Mill and Malmaison Farm, was again engaged in heavy action on 5 and 6 May 1917. It was withdrawn from the Aisne front on 13 May 1917 and sent to rest in the area Marle-Vervins and was reorganized.

The 222nd Infantry Division remained on the western front until the end of the war.

✠ ✠ ✠

DEM MUSK · SINNING ·
RES · J · RES · 81 ·

JST FÜR BEWIESENE TAPFERKEIT
VOR DEM FEINDE DAS
EISERNE KREUZ · II · KL ·
VERLIEHEN WORDEN ·
JM FELDE DEN : 3 · 12 · 16 ·

MAJ OBERST & RES · KOMMANDEUR ·

Document 83   *Official Certificate, Type 9, to Musketier Sinning*

The document shown below is very interesting. It is a Confirmation of Bestowal Certificate, Type 7, *(Verleihungs Bestätigung)* named to Reserve 1st Lieutenant *(Oberleutnant der Reserve)* **MARSEEN** (or possibly Narseen) serving in the Replacement *(Ersatz)* Battalion, 61st Landwehr Infantry Regiment, 85th Landwehr Infantry Division.

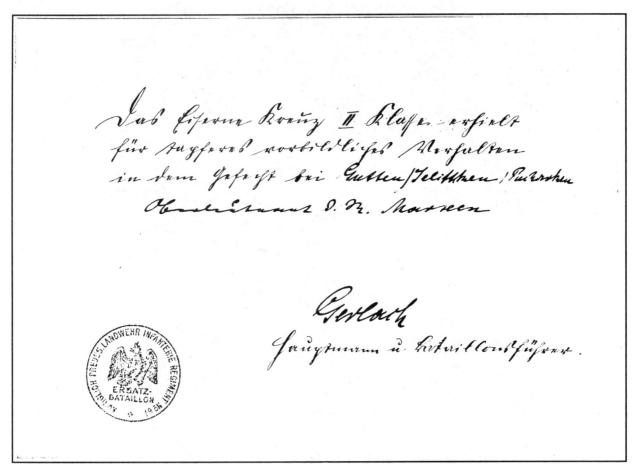

Document 84   *Identification Certificate, Type 7, to 1st Lieutenant Marseen*

The document, which bears no date, is handwritten except for the recipient's name and the battle which, unfortunately, is unreadable, in which he displayed leadership and bravery and was awarded the Iron Cross 2nd Class. It appears from the different inks and pens used that possibly the battalion commander filled in the recipient's name and engagement. The document measures 20.8 cm. wide x 15.5 cm. high. In the lower left-hand corner is the purple ink official stamp of the Replacement *(Ersatz)* Battalion, 61st Landwehr Infantry Regiment. It appears the document had been prepared in advance stating that the named soldier was awarded the Iron Cross 2nd Class "for brave and exemplary behavior" *(für tapferes vorbildliches Verhalten)*. It is an interesting and unusual type of document.

The 85th Landwehr Infantry Division was formed at the beginning of World War I and operated primarily on the eastern front. Until July 1915, the division was engaged in Poland in the region of Prasnysz. In July the division took part in the offensive against the Russians, advancing by mid-July to the west of Pultusk. They besieged Novo-Georgievsk and, by the beginning of August were on the Bug river. By the end of August the division was near Bielsk. The 61st Landwehr Infantry Regiment entered Warsaw on 2 August 1915 and remained there during the month of September. With the stabilization of the eastern front the 85th Landwehr Infantry Division occupied the Vichnev sector south of Krevo on the Little Berezina river. The division remained on the Vichnev-Deliatitchi front for more than two years from September 1915 until October 1917.

In September 1917 the 85th Landwehr Infantry Division transferred the 61st Landwehr Infantry Regiment to the 217th Infantry Division then being organized.

✠ ✠ ✠

The document shown below is an Authorization Certificate, Type 4, *(Bestizzeugnis)* named to Driver *(Kraftfahrer)* **KARL DITTERT**, serving in the XXVIth Reserve Corps. No other unit designation appears on the document.

Document 85   *Authorization Certificate, Type 4, to Kraftfahrer Karl Dittert*

The plain document is handwritten and measures 21.0 cm. wide x 16.5 cm. high. The document shows that Driver Dittert was awarded the Iron Cross 2nd Class on 14 November 1918, three days after the war was over. It was signed on 16 November 1918 at Corps headquarters by a Leutnant Niescher with a purple indelible pencil. At the bottom is the purple ink official stamp of the XXVIth Reserve Army Corps. The document appears to have been carried by the recipient.

The 51st Reserve Infantry Division along with the 52nd Reserve Infantry Division was created between August and October 1914 and together formed the XXVIth Reserve Army Corps. There is no way to know if Driver Dittert was assigned to either division or whether he was in other units attached to these divisions. However, at the time of the authorization of the award, it appears that Dittert was serving on the western front.

✠ ✠ ✠

The document shown below is a Preliminary Identification Certificate, Type 2, *(Verläufiger Ausweis)* named to Reservist Replacement *(Ersatz Reservisten)* **THOMAS SMURAWA** who was serving in the 1st Company, Machine Gun Sharpshooters, 56th Detachment, attached to Army Group Metz.

Document 86   *Preliminary Identification Certificate, Type 2, to Ersatz Reservisten Thomas Smurawa*

The document measures 17.0 cm. wide x 20.0 cm. high. The document is most interesting since it is not signed nor does it show a date. However, it appears to have been in the military record of Reservist Smurawa as shown by the two punched holes in the left margin, and also appears to have been folded and carried by him for quite some time after receiving it possibly after the war. The issuing authority was the Governor of Metz, General of Infantry Adolf von Oven* and to the left of the authority block is the purple ink stamp of the Metz Group *(Gruppe Metz)*.

Along with the Smurawa Iron Cross document is a Wound Badge certificate *(Verwundeten-Abzeichen)* showing that Reservist Smurawa was wounded in action on 19 May 1918, while serving in the 1st Company, Machine Gun Sharpshooters, 56th Detachment. We can only assume that he was wounded during the action in which he was cited for the Iron Cross 2nd Class. If that is the case, then Smurawa was recommended for the Iron Cross during May 1918.

---

*   General von Oven was awarded the Prussian Pour le Mérite Order on 22 September 1918. The citation reads in part:

> "...in recognition of excellent administrative abilities while serving as Governor of Metz..."

"The History of the Prussian Pour le Mérite Order , 1888-1918, " Volume III, W.E. Hamelman, p. 608, entry 699

The wound document shown below named to Private *(Schützen)* **Thomas Smurawa** measures 22.4 cm. wide x 18.4 cm high. The oak leaf motif border is printed in green. It is signed by the detachment commander with a purple indelible pencil. Directly between the signature and the date is the blue ink official stamp of the 56th Machine Gun Sharpshooter Detachment.

Document 87   *Wound Certificate to Schützen Smurawa*

The document is dated 19 May 1918. In the left margin are the two punched holes indicating the document had been a part of the military record of Private Smurawa. It also appears to have been carried by Smurawa for a long period after the war.

✠ ✠ ✠

The document shown at right is an Authorization Certificate, Type 4, named to Reserve Corporal *(Unteroffizier der Reserve)* **EUGEN HOFBAUER** serving in the 1st Heavy Cavalry *(Schweren Reiter)* Regiment "Prinz Karl von Bayern," 1st Bavarian Cavalry Brigade, Bavarian Cavalry Division.

The document is rather large and measures 21.1 cm. wide x 32.0 cm. high. It shows that Corporal Hofbauer was awarded the Iron Cross 2nd Class on 17 May 1915. The document is signed in black ink by Lt. General von Hellingroth who commanded the Bavarian Cavalry Division from 6 March 1915 until 14 December 1916. To the left of the signature is stamped, in blue ink, the official seal of the Bavarian Cavalry Division.

During the time when Reserve Unteroffizier Hofbauer was decorated with the Iron Cross, the 1st Bavarian Heavy Cavalry Regiment was commanded by Lt. Colonel Ritter von Scherf.

Document 88   Authorization Certificate, Type 4, to Unteroffizier Hofbauer

The Bavarian Cavalry Division was active from the beginning of the war on the western front until the beginning of 1918. Units of the division were transferred to Russia and used on police duties in the Ukraine, and other units were sent to Rumania in the spring of 1918. A part of the division was serving in the Crimea in early summer of 1918.

✠ ✠ ✠

Note: The unusual form of the Iron Cross shows "Mit Gott für König und Vaterland" *(With God for King and Fatherland).*

The document shown below is a Preliminary Identification Certificate, Type 2, *(Verläufiger Ausweis)* named to Territorial Reserve Second Lieutenant *(Leutnant der Landwehr)* **ARNOLD** serving

Document 89   *Preliminary Identification Certificate, Type 2, to Second Lieutenant Arnold*

in the Munitions Column, 9th Reserve Foot Artillery Battery , 9th Landwehr Field Artillery Regiment, 9th Landwehr Infantry Division.

The decorative document measures 17.0 cm. wide x 21.0 cm. high. It is signed by Lt. Col. Müller, the artillery unit commander, and to the left of the signature is the blue ink official stamp of the 9th Landwehr Artillery Regiment. The document shows that Lt. Arnold was authorized the Iron Cross 2nd Class on 5 May 1916.

From the time of its organization, the 9th Landwehr Infantry Division was assigned to the Argonne front. From the beginning of 1915 the division held the sector near the Aisne river, north of Ville sur Tourbe and north of Vienne le Chateau. During 1916 the division held the sector north of Vienne le Chateau, from the region of Rouvroy to the ravine of Fontaine aux Charnes. During 1917 the division, still in the Argonne, held the sector north of Vienne le Chateau.

In 1918, the division continued to secure the sector in the Argonne woods until the American attack on 26 September 1918. It was engaged during the opening days of the offensive and withdrew on the 28th of September. The shattered elements were reformed and reentered the front line on the extreme right flank of the 4th French Army in the vicinity of the Aisne river. The last sector held by the 9th Landwehr Infantry Division was at Villers sur le Mont until 10 November 1918.

✠ ✠ ✠

The document shown on the following page is a Preliminary Authorization Certificate, Type 1, *(Vorläufiges Besitz-Zeugnis)* named to Private *(Musketier)* **OTTO DEGÜNTHER**, serving in the 11th Company, 224th Reserve Infantry Regiment, 96th Reserve Infantry Brigade, 48th Reserve Infantry Division, until 1917 when the 224th Reserve Infantry Regiment was transferred to the 61st Reserve Infantry Brigade, 215th Infantry Division. It was while his regiment was attached to the 215th Infantry Division that Private Degünther was decorated with the Iron Cross 2nd Class.

What makes this document so very unique is the illustration. Shown below is a photo of the Quadriga with the figure of the Winged Goddess of Victory which adorns the Brandenburg Gate in Berlin. It is obvious that the illustration shown on the document, seen on the following page, was inspired from this photograph. The photo is on page 2 of the ***Volksbücher der Geschichte*** Series number 123 entitled *"Das Eiserne Kreuz."* These booklets were published during the early war years of the First World War.

The attractive and large document measures 22.0 cm. wide x 34.0 cm high. It was signed on 11 August 1918 in the field *(Im Felde)* by Rittmeister Müller, the Regimental Adjutant, with a purple indelible pencil, which is unable to be seen on the photocopy. To the left of the signature block is the blue stamp of the 224th Reserve Infantry Regiment. On the lower left border is the imprint of the Field Printer of the Army of the Bug *(Felddruckerei Bugarmee).*

Exhibit 2   **Berlin Brandenburg Gate Quadriga with Goddess of Victory**

Vorläufiges Besitz-Zeugnis.

Im Namen Seiner Majestät des Kaisers

[handwritten text]

das **Eiserne Kreuz II. Klasse**

verliehen.

[handwritten] , den 11. Aug. 1918.

Rittmeister.

Document 90   *Preliminary Authorization Certificate, Type 1, to Musketier Otto Degünther*

The 48th Reserve Infantry Division was formed during August and October 1914. During the middle of October, the division was sent to the area between Armentières and La Basée. On 1 November 1914 the division held the front line at Neuve Chapelle. By the middle of November, some elements of the division were sent further north, west of Wytschaete. At the end of November the 48th Reserve Division left the western front for Russia. On 3 December 1914, the division was in Poland in the vicinity of Kalisch. It was then made a part of the Xth German Army and fought west of the Rawka, near Warsaw, at the end of December.

In 1915 elements of the division fought in the Carpathians, southwest of Beskides. The division was assigned to the German Army of the South (von Linsingen) and was opposed to the Russians in the vicinity of the Uzsok Ridge from February through May 1915. The division took part in the spring and summer offensive of 1915. It marched to Halicz in May, crossed the Dniester river in the middle of June, advanced to Brzezany-Tarnopol and was on the Zlota-Lipa by the end of July 1915. One of the regiments of the division, the 224th Reserve Infantry Regiment was renewed several times resulting from its high losses from August to October 1915. When the offensive was resumed in October and November 1915, the 48th Reserve Infantry Division progressed from the Zlota-Lipa as far as the Stripa river.

In 1916 the 48th Reserve Infantry Division was retained at the Stripa, west of Tarnapol, during the winter and spring. It was in this sector at the time of the Russian attack called "Broussilovs Offensive" from June until September 1916. In the beginning of October, the division went into action with the von Falkenheim Army against Rumania and fought in the vicinity of Hermannstadt, then at Préoéal in November 1916. It then left the Transylvanian front and went to eastern Galicia, where it was part of the von Bothmer Army. The division took up its position between Brzezan and the Dniester.

At the beginning of 1917 the 224th Reserve Infantry Regiment left the 48th Reserve Infantry Division and was transferred to the 215th Infantry Division which was at the time in the process of reorganization. During 1917, the 215th Infantry Division occupied, in Vohynia, the sector located east of Gorokhov.

Early in the year 1918 the 215th Infantry Division was still in Russia holding a sector near Kiev during March 1918 and in the Kharkov region in April 1918. Early in May, the division had advanced to the Sea of Azov. It was during this time that Private Degünther was decorated for bravery in action with the Iron Cross 2nd Class.

Early in September all unmarried men less than 35 years of age were sent to the western front which probably explains the many reports of the division having been sent to France in intelligience records. Whereas, in all probability the division never left the Ukraine.

✠ ✠ ✠

The document shown on the following page is a Preliminary Identification Certificate, Type I, *(Verläufiger Ausweis)* named to 1st Sergeant of Artillery *(Wachtmeister)* **BERGSTÄDT**, who was serving in the 3rd Battery, 17th Reserve Field Artillery Regiment, 17th Reserve Infantry Division.

The large document measures 21.0 cm. wide x 29.5 cm. high. It was signed at the regimental headquarters on 25 February 1916 by the regiment commander in black ink. To the left of the signature is the purple ink stamp of the 17th Reserve Field Artillery Regiment.

The 17th Reserve Infantry Division along with the 18th Reserve Infantry Division formed the 9th Reserve Corps. During the early part of August 1914, the division was used to guard the coast of Schleswig-Holstein. Sent to the western front, the division reached Termonde on 4 September 1914 and remained outside of Antwerp. On 9 September 1914 it was transferred to the Valenciennes area and

Vorlaeufiger Ausweis.

Der Kommandierende General des IX. Reservekorps hat im Namen Seiner Majestaet des Kaisers und Koenigs dem

Wachtmeister Bergstädt

von der 3. Batterie des Reserve-Feld-Artillerie-Regiments 17 das

EISERNE KREUZ II. KLASSE

verliehen, worueber ihm dieser vorlaeufige Ausweis ausgefertigt wird.

Regts. St. Qu., den 25. Februar 1916.

Korpsdruckerei des IX. Res.-Korps.

Document 91   Preliminary Identification Certificate, Type 2, to Wachtmeister Bergstädt
J. Eicher Collection

then on to the Aisne. The division was at Chauney by the 13th of September and went into action on the right bank of the Oisne, south of Noyan. On 7 October 1914 it was sent to the vicinity of Roye where it was heavily engaged. Around the middle of November the division occupied the front between the Avreand Roye. On 20 December 1914 the division was in the front line between Ribécourt and Thiescourt.

On 6 February 1915 the division left its position along the banks of the Oise to return to the area south of of the Avre, between Lassigny and Roye. It remained in this sector until October 1915. By mid-October the 17th Reserve Infantry Division was withdrawn from the front south of Roye and assigned to Artois, near Lens.

The division remained in Artois until the battle of the Somme. During February 1917 the division launched several attacks. It was during one of these engagements that Wachtmeister Bergstädt was recognized for his bravery in action and rewarded with the Iron Cross 2nd Class.

The division remained on the western front holding various sectors and engaging in many actions and major battles until 3 November 1918 when it was finally taken out of the line.

✠ ✠ ✠

The document shown below is a Preliminary Identification Certificate, Type 2, (*Vorläufiger Ausweis*) named to Private (*Schützen*) **EMIL STÖSSEL** serving in the 1st Machine Gun Company, Lehr Infantry Regiment, 6th Guard Infantry Brigade, 3rd Guard Infantry Division, Army Group *"Kronprinz."*

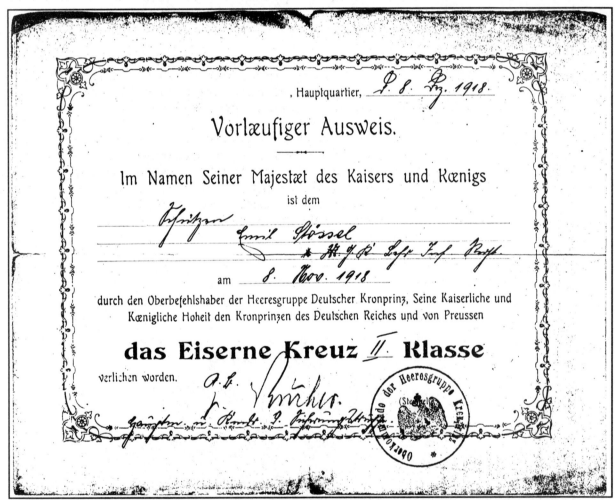

Document 92   *Preliminary Identification Certificate, Type 2, to Schützen Emil Stössel*

The badly printed document measures 20.6 cm. wide x 16.3 cm. high. The certificate shows that Schützen Stössel was authorized the Iron Cross 2nd Class on 8 November 1918 but the document was not issued until 8 December 1918, a month after the war had ended. It is signed in purple indelible pencil by a captain and commander of the 9th Security (*Sicherung*) Section. To the right is the purple ink official stamp of the High Command of the Army Group *"Kronprinz."* It appears to have been folded and carried by Schützen Stössel.

In August 1914 the 3rd Guard Infantry Division was first directed to the western front and was first engaged below Namur. By the 27th of August 1914, the division was reassigned to Silesia and took part in the invasion of southern Poland.

In April 1916, the 3rd Guard Infantry Division was sent back to the western front where it occupied a sector in Champagne and took part in no major actions.

Moving ahead to 1918 we find that on 10 January the division returned to the front line in a sector southwest of Cambrai. It was relieved from the front on 12 February 1918 and rested in the area of Hem-Lenglet. The division returned to the front line on 19 March 1918 between Inchy-en-Artois and Pronville and took part in the German advance between the 21st and 24th of March. However, the division suffered heavy losses on the 22nd in the fighting north of Beaumetz, passing to the second line on 24 March 1918. The division returned to the offensive and participated in the actions around Bucquoy and Hebuterne from 26 March until 3 April 1918. Being relieved from the Somme front around 4 April 1918, the division rested until the 18th of April.

The division was engaged on the Lys, northeast of Estaires, after 18 April 1918, then north of Kemmel from 30 April until 5 May 1918. During these actions the division again suffered heavy losses. After resting the division was assigned to the Chateau Salins sector. While in this quiet sector the division received replacements. When it left the line on 24 June 1918, the division was up to strength and comparatively fresh.

In the offensive of 15 July 1918, the division engaged east of Rheims in the region of des Monts. Between the 15th and 31st the division again suffered heavy losses. The division held the line in Champagne north of St. Hilaire-le-Grand from 15 August until 18 September 1918.

From 27 September to 5 October 1918, the division was engaged in several actions between Somme-Py and Manre. Acting as a rear guard, the division covered the German retreat from Machault to Voziers. Sent by truck to Romagne, it entered the front line on 12 October 1918 opposing the American troops. In this sector the division fought vigorously, making perhaps the stiffest resistance encountered in the American offensive. It was probably during these actions that Private Stössel was cited for bravery in action and recommended for the Iron cross 2nd Class. On 7 November 1918 the division was holding the line southeast of Mezieres.

The document shown below is a Preliminary Authorization Certificate, Type 1 *(Vorläufiges Besitz -Zeugnis)* named to Private *(Musketier)* **GUSTAV HACKENBERG** serving in the 6th Company, 143rd Infantry Regiment, 60th Infantry Brigade, 30th Infantry Division.

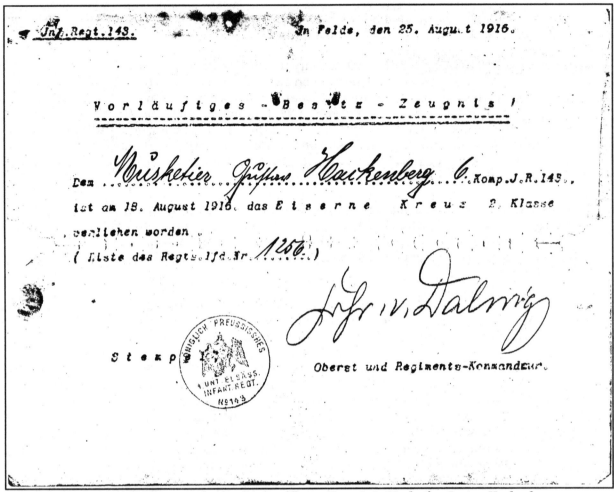

Document 93   Preliminary Authorization Certificate, Type 1, to Musketier Gustav Hackenberg

The plain typed document measures 21.0 cm wide x 16.3 cm. high. The text was produced on a mimeograph duplicator having the usual purple color. The name of the recipient, company number and Regimental Awards List number (1256) are written in blue ink. The document is signed in purple indelible pencil by the regimental commander and to the left of the signature is the purple ink official stamp of the 143rd Lower Alsace Infantry Regiment. It is dated 25 August 1916 and was given in the field (Im Felde). Note that along the middle horizontal crease are small holes which indicate that this certificate had been sewn either by hand or machine to Musketier Hackenberg's soldiers identification booklet. The document is badly stained.

In 1916 when Musketier Hackenberg was awarded the Iron Cross 2nd Class, we find that toward the end of January the elements of the division were transferred to Verdun to take part in the February offensive. On 24 February 1916 the division went into action as part of the German attacking forces on the Maucourt-Warcq front.

The 30th Infantry Division was not relieved after the battles of February and March 1916. On 11 July the 99th and 143rd Infantry Regiments took part in a new offensive. On August 8th the 143rd Infantry Regiment attacked the defenses of Thiaumont and was decimated. It was during this engagement that Musketier Gustav Hackenburg displayed bravery in action and was recommended for the Iron Cross 2nd Class. He was 27 years old at the time. Later he was also wounded in action during June 1918 as shown by the wound badge certificate on the following page.

Shown below is the Authorization Certificate for the Wound Badge awarded to now Corporal *(Unteroffizier)* **Gustav Hackenberg** who was still serving in the 6th Company, 143rd Infantry Regiment, 60th Infantry Brigade, 30th Infantry Division. It appears that he was wounded in June 1918. During that time, the 143rd Infantry Regiment engaged in several intense actions and suffered casualties amounting to 30 percent of its total effectives.

The badly stained document measures 20.8 cm. wide x 16.3 cm. high. It was authorized on 11 June 1918. The document is signed in purple indelible pencil by the regimental commander. To the left of the signature is the purple ink official stamp of the 143rd Infantry Regiment, which is the same stamp as shown on the Iron Cross 2nd Class document.

Document 87   ***Wound Document to Unteroffizier Gustav Hackenberg***

After the war Gustav Hackenberg became a member of the veterans society of the 143rd Infantry Regiment.

In 1941 he was honored by the 143rd Infantry Regiment War Veterans Society being awarded the Silver Honor Badge *(Silberne Ehrenzeichen)* number 231. He was 52 years old at the time.

The document, seen at right measures 21.8 cm. wide x 15.0 cm. high. It is dated 7 March 1941 and the registration number is 231.

✠ ✠ ✠

The document shown below is a Preliminary Authorization Certificate, Type 1, *(Vorläufiges Besitzzeugnis)* named to Reserve Torpedo Machinist Mate *(Torpedo-Maschinistenmaaten der Reserve)* **HEINRICH EGGERS** serving aboard the S.M.S. *Friedrich der Große.*

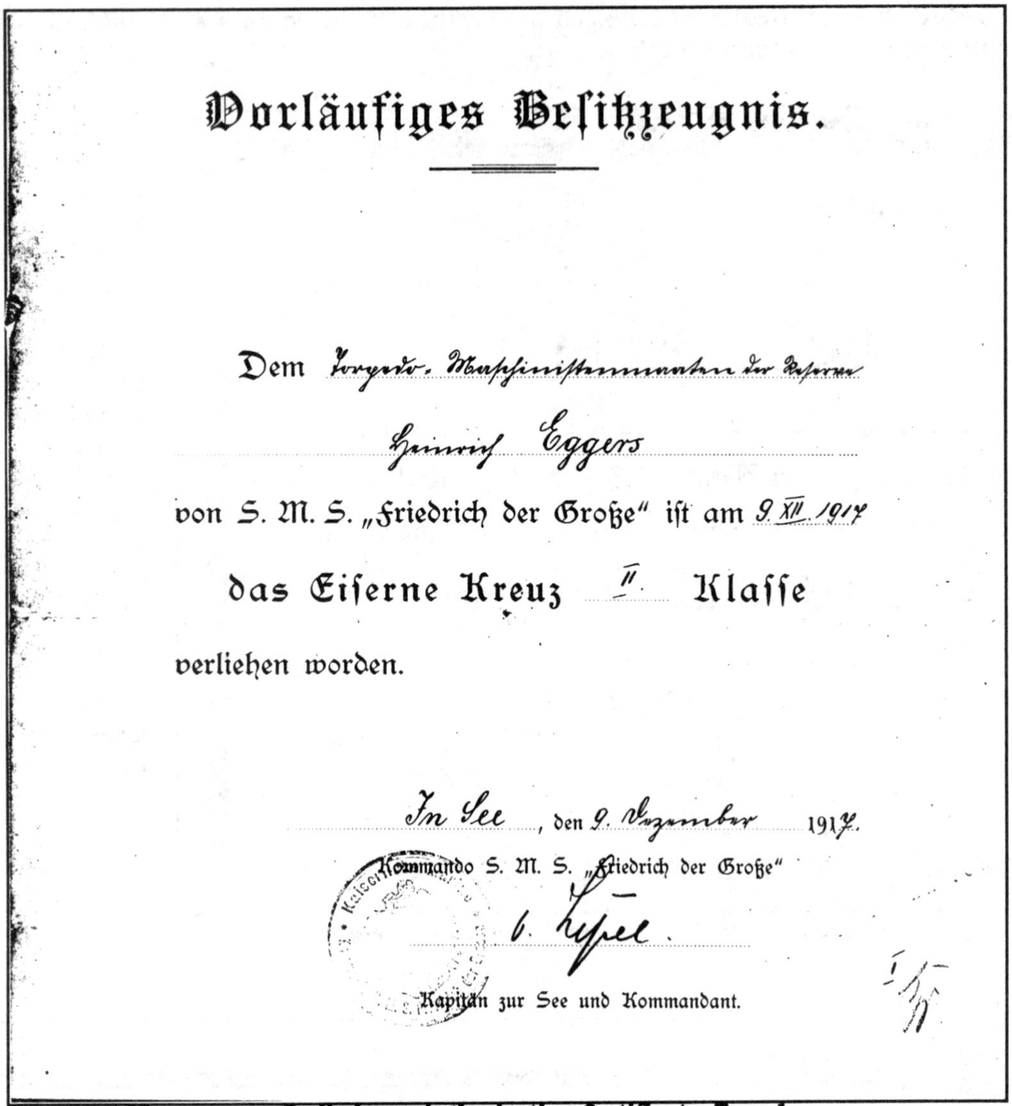

Vorläufiges Besitzzeugnis.

Dem *Torpedo- Maschinistenmaaten der Reserve*

Heinrich Eggers

von S. M. S. „Friedrich der Große" ist am *9 XII 1917*

das Eiserne Kreuz *II* Klasse

verliehen worden.

In See, den *9. Dezember* 1917.

Kommando S. M. S. „Friedrich der Große"

v. Lipee.

Kapitän zur See und Kommandant.

Document 95   ***Preliminary Authorization Certificate, Type 1,***
to Petty Officer Heinrich Eggers

The large format plain document measures 21.0 cm wide x 33.0 cm high. The document authorized Torpedo Machinist Mate Eggers the Iron Cross 2nd Class on 9 December 1917. It was signed in pencil by the Captain and Commander aboard the S.M.S. *Friedrich der Große* at sea* *(In See)* on the same day. To the left of the signature is the purple official stamp of the S.M.S. *Friedrich der Große.*

Heinrich Eggers served aboard a very proud ship, the S.M.S. *Friedrich der Große*; however, there is no way of knowing if he was assigned to this ship on 31 May 1916. It was on this date that the Battle of Jutland began (sometimes called by the Germans, the Battle of the Skagerrak). The *Friedrich der Große* was the flagship of the German High Seas Fleet and under the command of Admiral Reinhard Scheer** who was also the commander-in-chief of the High Seas Fleet.

---

* "At sea" basically meant aboard ship whether in port or at sea.

** Admiral Reinhard Scheer was awarded the Prussian Pour le Mérite on 5 June 1916. The citation reads in part:

"... to acknowledge the German naval victory at the Battle of Jutland on 31 May - 1 June 1916."

"The History of the Prussian Pour le Mérite Order, 1888-1918," Volume III, W.E. Hamelman, p. 453, entry 122.

Eggers also received the Hamburg Hanseatic Cross for Merit. The large and very attractive document, shown below, has the text written in *Sütterlin* script and measures 21.0 cm. wide x 33.0 cm. high. It was authorized, in the name of the "Senate of the Free and Hansa City of Hamburg" *(Der Senat*

Document 96   **Hamburg Merit Cross Certificate to**
                Torpedo Maschinistenmaaten Heinrich Eggers

der freien und Hansestadt Hamburg) on 17 January 1917 and has a facsimile signature of a Senior Senate Civil Administrator. In the upper center is the Great Arms of the City of Hamburg.

Shown to the left is the Preliminary Certificate of Good Conduct *(Vorläufiger Führungszeugnis)* [note the word 'vorläufiger' has been added to the document] for the naval service of Heinrich Eggers.

The document shows that he was born in Hamburg on 23 March 1890 and 23 years old when first joining the Imperial German Navy. He served in the 6th Company, 1st Torpedo Division aboard the S.M.S. *Yorck** until 10 July 1913.

The very large document measures 21.4 cm. wide x 34.0 cm. high. was signed on 11 July 1913 and issued from aboard the S.M.S. Seydlitz while in Danzig Bay *(Danziger Bucht)* .

The document indicates that Torpedoman Eggers' conduct was very good *(sehr gut)*, during his naval service and he had no punishments *(keine Strafen)* and was never under arrest *(keine strengem Arrest)*. Eggers service was registered as number 95 in the Naval Records of 1910.

The S.M.S. *Yorck* was a part of a squadron attached to the Scouting Forces of the High Seas Fleet and the S.M.S. *Seydlitz*** was the flagship.

✠ ✠ ✠

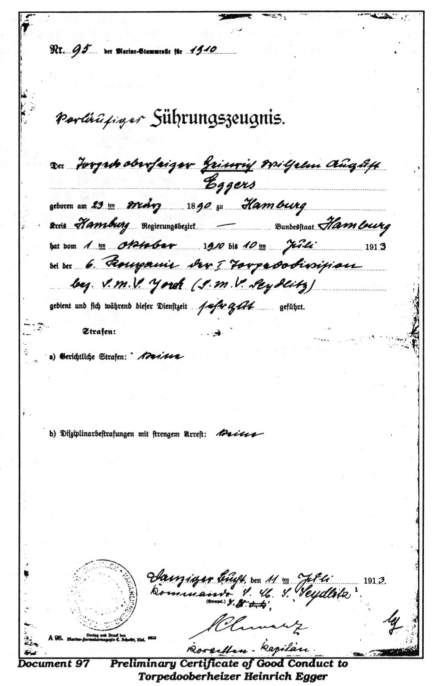

Document 97   *Preliminary Certificate of Good Conduct to Torpedooberheizer Heinrich Egger*

---

* S.M.S. Yorck, an armored cruiser, 9,350 tons, having a crew of 633, struck a mine on 4 November 1914 and sank.

** At the Battle of Jutland the S.M.S. Seydlitz suffered more hits that any other surviving capital ship, reaching harbor with the forecastle awash. The ship was surrendered and interned at Scapa Flow on 24 November 1918 and was scuttled there on 21 June 1919.

The document shown below is a Preliminary Authorization Certificate, Type 1, *(Vorläufiges-Besitzzeugnis)* to Corporal *(Unteroffizier)* **FRITZ SCHRADER** serving in the 19th Army Telephone-Telegraph Unit *(Armee-Fernsprech-Abteilung 19)*.

Document 98   *Preliminary Authorization Certificate, Type 1, to Unteroffizier Fritz Schrader*

The document measures 16.3 cm. wide x 13.0 cm. high. It is hand written and duplicated on a mimeograph in purple ink. The document authorized Corporal Schrader the 2nd Class Iron Cross on 13 June 1916. It was signed in black ink by the unit commander and to the left of the signature is the official purple ink stamp of the 19th Army Telephone Section. The stamp has in the center the Saxon Arms indicating the unit was from the Kingdom of Saxony or one of the Duchies.

✠ ✠ ✠

During 1918 after Schrader had been promoted to Senior Duty Sergeant *(Vizefeldwebel)* he was serving in the 4th Construction Company *(4. Bauzug)* of the 8th Army Telephone - Telegraph Unit *(Armee-fernsprech-abteilung 8)*.

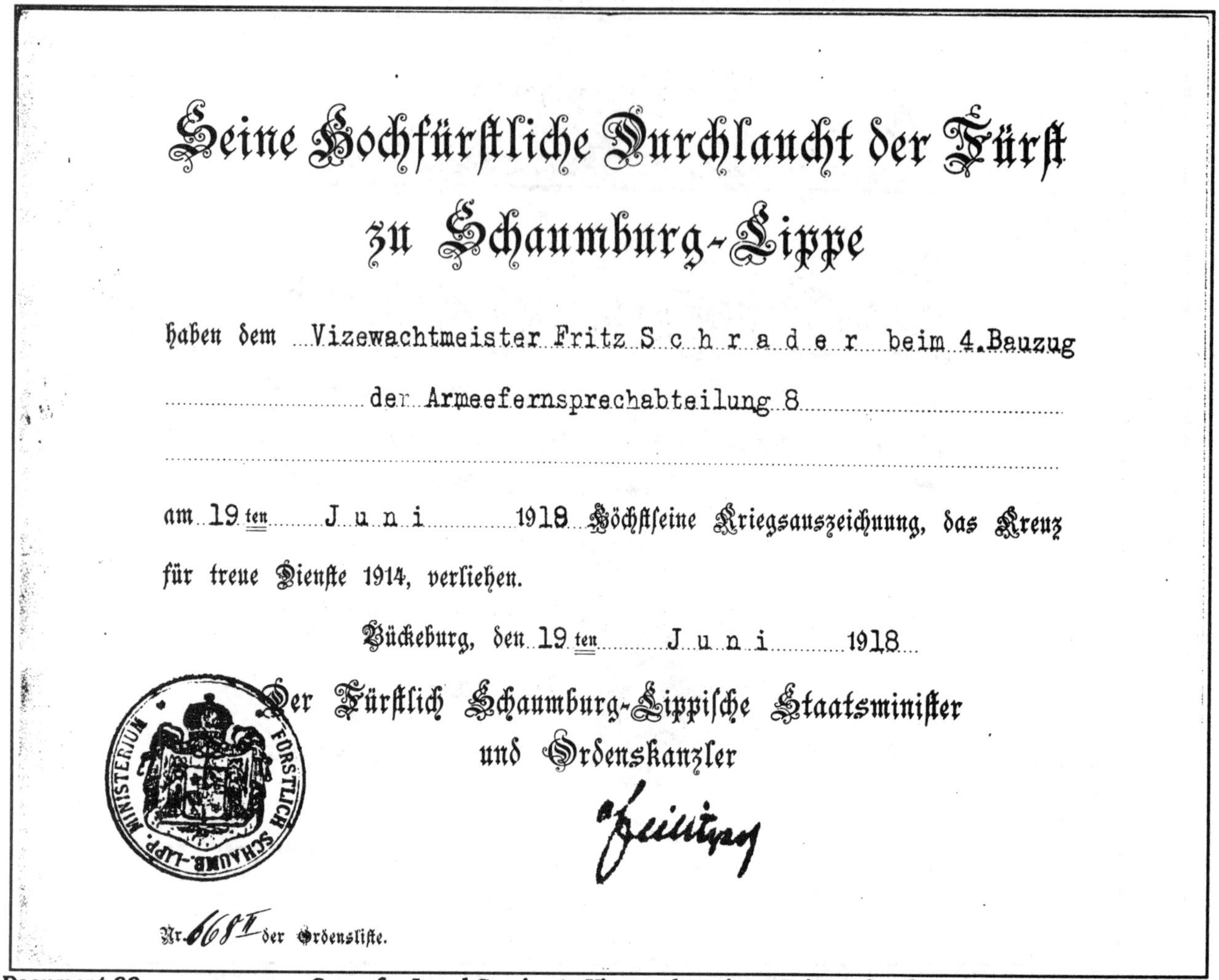

Seine Hochfürstliche Durchlaucht der Fürst
zu Schaumburg-Lippe

haben dem Vizewachtmeister Fritz S c h r a d e r beim 4.Bauzug der Armeefernsprechabteilung 8

am 19 ten J u n i 1918 Höchstseine Kriegsauszeichnung, das Kreuz für treue Dienste 1914, verliehen.

Bückeburg, den 19 ten J u n i 1918

Der Fürstlich Schaumburg-Lippische Staatsminister
und Ordenskanzler

FÜRSTLICH SCHAUMB.-LIPP. MINISTERIUM

Nr. 668 II der Ordensliste.

Document 99 ***Cross for Loyal Service to Vizewachtmeister Fritz Schrader***

Shown above is the certificate for awarding Vizewachtmeister Schrader the 1914 Cross for Loyal Service *(Kreuz für treue Dienste 1914)* from the Principality of Schaumburg-Lippe. The document measures 21.5 cm. wide x 16.8 cm. high. It was authenticated with a black ink signature stamp of the Orders Chancellor of Schaumburg-Lippe. The document shows Schrader was authorized the award on 19 June 1918. To the left of the signature is the blue ink official stamp of the Princely Ministry of Schaumburg-Lippe. Ditectly below the stamp is the registration number, 668 II, of the award on the Awards List *(Ordensliste)*.

✠ ✠ ✠

Vizefeldwebel Schrader also received on 19 July 1918 from the Kingdom of Saxony the Friedrich August Medal in Silver on the ribbon for War Service *(die Friedrich August-Medaille in Silber mit dem Bande für kriegsdienste).*

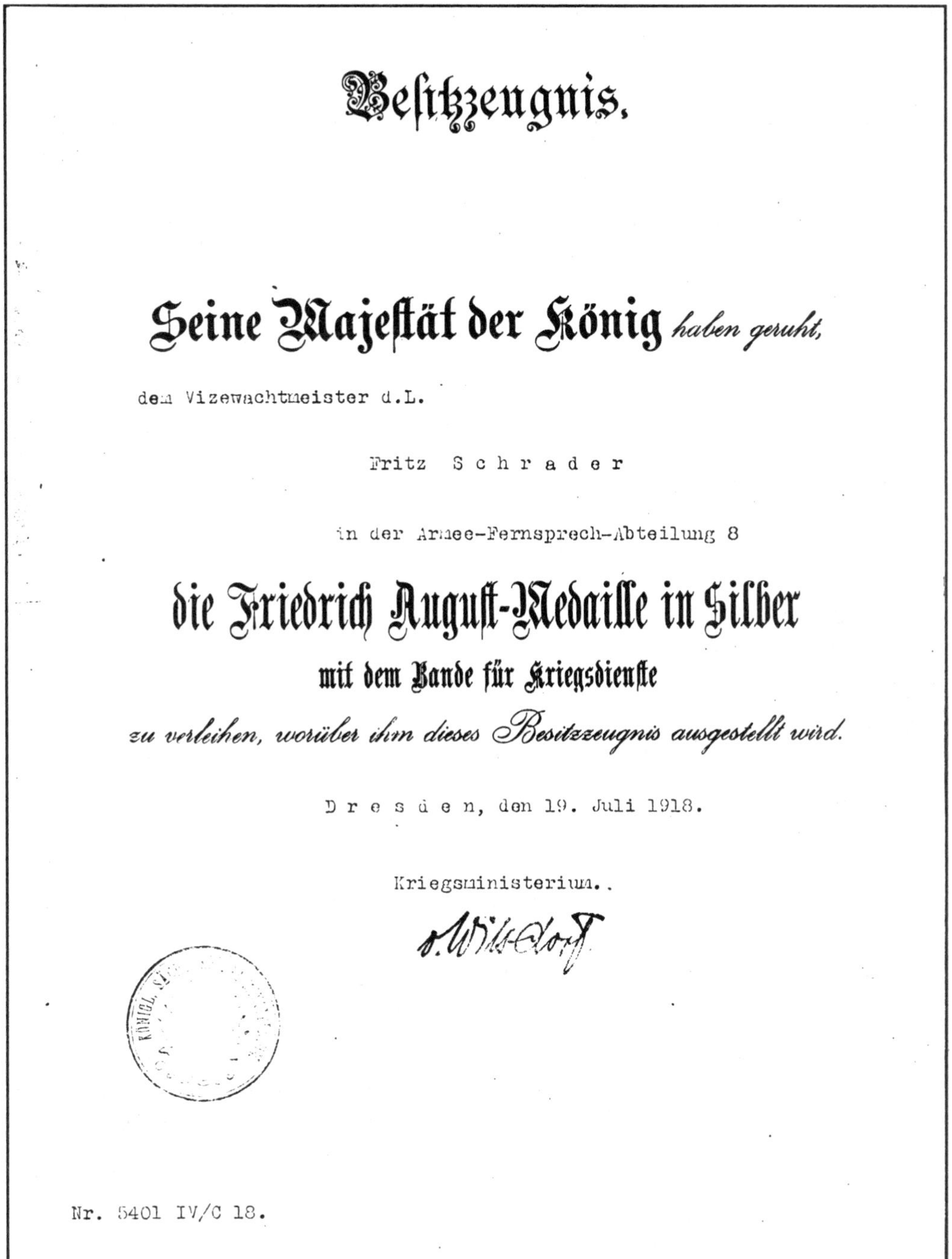

Besitzzeugnis.

Seine Majestät der König haben geruht,

dem Vizewachtmeister d.L.

Fritz S c h r a d e r

in der Armee-Fernsprech-Abteilung 8

die Friedrich August-Medaille in Silber

mit dem Bande für Kriegsdienste

zu verleihen, worüber ihm dieses Besitzzeugnis ausgestellt wird.

D r e s d e n, den 19. Juli 1918.

Kriegsministerium.

Nr. 5401 IV/C 18.

Document 100 ***Friedrich August Medal in Silver on War Ribbon to Vizewachtmeister Fritz Schrader***

The document, shown above, measures 21.1 cm. wide x 32.5 cm. high. It was dated exactly one month later than the Schaumburg-Lippe document and also shows a black ink stamp of the signature of a representative of the Saxon War Ministry. To the left of the signature is the purple ink official stamp of the Royal Saxon War Ministry. Directly below the stamp is the typed registration number for the award as recorded in the Saxon Awards List.

✠ ✠ ✠

The document shown below is a Preliminary Identification Certificate, Type 2, *(Vorläufiger Ausweis)* named to Reserve Second Lieutenant *(Leutnant der Reserve)* **PAUL SCHOMAKER**. When awarded the Iron Cross 2nd Class on 15 September 1917, Lt. Schomaker was serving in the Divisional 449th Telephone Section *(Divisions-Fernsprech-Abteilung 449)*, 449th Signal Command, 49th Reserve Infantry Division.

Vorläufiger Ausweis.

Im Namen Seiner Majestät des Kaisers und Königs

ist dem .....Leutnant.der.Reserve..Paul..S.c.h.o.m.a.k.e.r.

am ...15...September..1917... das **Eiserne Kreuz** ...II.. Kl.

verliehen worden.

Im Felde, den ....21..Maerz..1918..............

Divisions-Fernsprech-Abteilung 449

(L. S.)

Document 101   *Preliminary Identification Certificate, Type 2, to Reserve 2nd Lt. Paul Schomaker*

The plain document measures 21.7 cm. wide x 16.5 cm. high. It is dated 21 March 1918 and indicates the award of the Iron Cross 2nd Class was authorized on 15 September 1917. To the left of the printed unit is the purple ink stamp of the 449th Telephone Section. Note there is no signature. In the left margin are the two punched holes indicating the document was a part of the military records of Lt. Schomaker.

Moving to 1917, the 49th Reserve Infantry Division was sent to rest and be reorganized during June in the vicinity of Tourni-Audenarde. It was returned to the front by the end of June in the Steenstraat-Bixschoote north of Ypres. The division suffered heavy losses during the enemy shelling which preceded the Franco-British attack of 21 July 1917. On July 28th the division was withdrawn from the front.

The division rested and was reorganized during the month of August 1917. In September 1917 the division took over its old Artois sector and was relieved at the end of October. It was during the actions during September on this front that Lt. Schomaker displayed outstanding leadership and was recommended for the Iron Cross 2nd Class.

The division was engaged in several more major engagements and remained on the western front until the end of the war. ✠ ✠ ✠

The document shown below is an Identification Certificate, Type 5, *(Ausweis)* named to Corporal *(Unteroffizier)* **FRIEDRICH HELD** serving as a dispatch rider *(Meldereiter)* in the 8th Company, 242nd Reserve Infantry Regiment, 106th Reserve Infantry Brigade,* 53rd Reserve Infantry Division.

Ausweis.

Dem

Unteroffizier (Meldereiter) Friedrich H e l d .,

Reserve-Infanterie-Regiment 242, ...8..... Kompagnie,

wird hiermit bescheinigt, dass er im Besitze nachstehender Kriegsauszeichnungen ist :

E i s e r n e K r e u z 2.Klasse

O.U. Im Felde , am 4.März 191 6.

Oberstleutnant und Regimentskommandeur.

Document 102   *Identification Certificate, Type 5, to Unteroffizier Friedrich Held*   **J. Eicher Collection**

The printed document is unusual in that it is generic and can show multiple awards. It measures 21.0 cm. wide x 17.0 cm. high. It was issued in the field *(Im Felde)* on 4 March 1916 and signed in black ink by Lt. Colonel Lüddecke, the regimental commander. To the left of the signature is the purple stamp of the 242nd Reserve Infantry Regiment which has the Saxon Arms in the center.. The stamp is very light and cannot be seen on the document reproduced above. Note the two punched holes in the left margin indicating it was a part of the military record of Unteroffizier Held.

Moving to 1915, the 53rd Reserve Infantry Division remained in line north of Ypres during the winter of 1914-15. The division took part in the second battle of Ypres near Frenzenberg and Gravenstafel. In June 1915 it occupied the sector of Wytchaete-St. Éloi and returned northeast of Ypres by mid-July. In early October, the 105th Reserve Infantry Brigade was sent to Champagne to reinforce the lines near Tahure. In November the division was regrouped and sent to rest. The division remained behind the front during the winter of 1915-16 near Roulers. It was during this time Unteroffizier Held was awarded the Iron Cross 2nd Class.

At the end of March 1916, the 53rd Reserve Infantry Division left Flanders and went into the line on both banks of the La Bassée Canal.

✠ ✠ ✠

* The 242nd Reserve Infantry Regiment was assigned to the 105th Reserve Infantry Brigade during 1914-15 and then was assigned to the 106th Reserve Infantry Brigade from 1916 until 1918.

The document shown below is a Preliminary Identification Certificate, Type 2, *(Vorläufiger Ausweis)* named to Senior Duty Sergeant *(Vizefeldwebel)* **ERICH MARTIN**, who was serving in the 59th Artillery Rangefinder Unit *(Art. Messtrupp, 59)*, 59th Field Artillery Regiment, 15th Artillery Command, 15th Infantry Division.

Vorläufiger

Ausweis.

Auf Allerhöchsten Befehl Seiner Majestät des Kaisers
und Königs ist dem

Vizefeldw. M a r t i n, Erich, Art. Messtrupp, 59.

das Eiserne Kreuz zweiter Klasse verliehen worden.

Hauptquartier Schloss - Homburg im A p r i l   191 6.

General der Infanterie.

poppen & Sohn, Freiburg

Document 103   *Preliminary Identification Certificate, Type 2, to Vizefeldwebel Erich Martin*

The document measures 22.2 cm. wide x 19.3 cm. high. It was signed in black ink by General Hans Gaede* at Army Headquarters located at the time in the Schloss Homburg. The award was authorized during April 1916. To the left of the signature is the purple ink official stamp of the Headquarters of the Army Group "Gaede."

From June 1915 until June 1916 the 15th Infantry Division occupied various sectors of the Aisne: Vailly-Pommiers, Nouvron and Ste. Marguerite-Bucy le Long. It was during the time the division was on the Aisne front that Vizefeldwebel Martin was decorated with the Iron Cross 2nd Class.

✠ ✠ ✠

* Infantry General Gaede, Commander-in-Chief, Army Group "Gaede" was awarded the Prussian Pour le Mérite Order on 25 August 1915. The citation reads in part:

> "... for outstanding leadership and distinguished military planning...
> against invading French forces..."

"The History of the Prussian Pour le Mérite Order, 1888-1918," Volume III, William E. Hamelman, p. 436, entry 88, .

The document shown below is an Official Certificate, Type 9, named to Corporal *(Unteroffizier)* **GROLMAN** serving in the 2nd Battery, 23rd Field Artillery Regiment *(2nd Rhine)*, 16th Artillery Brigade, 16th Infantry Division.

Im Namen Seiner Majestät
des Kaisers und Königs

ist durch den Kommandeur der 16. Infanterie-Division

dem *Unteroffizier Grolman* *2.Batterie*

des 2.Rheinischen Feldartillerie Regiments Nr.23

das Eiserne Kreuz II. Klasse

am *27.5* verliehen worden.

J.A.d.R.K.

Major und Abtlgs.-Führer.

Document 104 *Official Certificate, Type 9, to Unteroffizier Grolman*

The attractive document measures 18.7 cm. wide x 11.4 cm. high. In the upper left corner, within a wreath is an Iron Cross suspended from a black and white ribbon. The wreath is composed of oak leaves which are green. Binding the wreath at the bottom and both sides are the German national colors of black, white and red. It is signed in blue ink by the section leader on 27 May 1918. To the left of the signature is the purple ink official stamp of the 23rd Field Artillery Regiment.

Moving to 1918 when Corporal Grolman was decorated with the Iron Cross 2nd Class, the 16th Infantry Division was resting in the Meulebecke area in Belgium until around 1 March 1918. The division returned to the front where it went into action east of Passchendaele until 23 March 1918. It was relieved and placed in reserve in the Tourcoing sector until 4 April 1918. Later the division was in Lille until April 10th.

The division was engaged on 4 April 1918 north of Neuve Chapelle and south of Merville on the 12th. During this major engagement, two regimental commanders were casualties. The division was relieved east of St. Venant on 1 May 1918. Since the division rested for two weeks, it appears that Unteroffizier Grolman displayed leadership and bravery in action during this major battle which resulted in his being recommended for the Iron Cross 2nd Class. The division was engaged in several more major actions and remained on the western front until the end of the war in November 1918.

✠ ✠ ✠

The document seen at the right is a Preliminary Authorization Certificate, Type 1, *(Vorläufiges Besitz-Zeugnis)* named to Corporal *(Unteroffizier)* **JOSEF HÖRMANN** serving in the 8th Company, 11th Bavarian Infantry Regiment, 9th Bavarian Infantry Brigade, 16th Bavarian Infantry Division.

The attractive document measures 15.8 cm. wide x 26.8 cm. high. It shows that Hörmann was born in Tannstein on 12 August 1891 and when awarded the Iron Cross 2nd Class was 26 years old. The document is signed in black ink by the regimental commander on 3 August 1917. To the left of the signature is the purple ink official stamp of the 11th Bavarian Infantry Regiment. Outlining the text of the certificate is a brown border and the decorative "D" in "Das" is also in brown.

The 11th Bavarian Infantry Regiment was with the 6th Bavarian Infantry Division until the end of January 1917 when the regiment was transferred to the newly created 16th Bavarian Infantry Division.

Toward the end of April 1917, the division took over the calm sector of Armentières south of Lys. At the beginning of June the division was sent north of Lys because of a

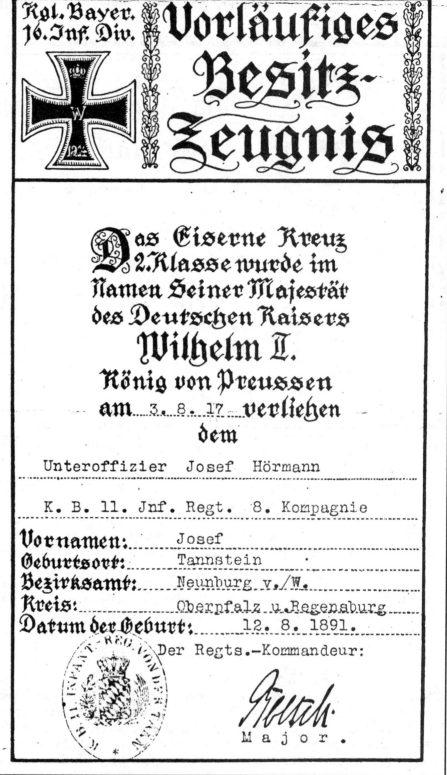

Document 105   *Preliminary Authorization Certificate, Type 1, to Unteroffizier Josef Hörmann*

menace of a strong British attack on the Messines front. During the battle, which commenced on 9 June 1917, the division sent some units to reinforce the 4th Bavarian Infantry Division. It was during this engagement that Unteroffizier Hörmann displayed bravery in action and was subseqently awarded the Iron Cross 2nd Class. On 23 April 1918, Hörmann was promoted to Sergeant *(Sergeanten)*.

The division remained on the western front and fought many action until the end of the war.

The very attractive document shown below is a Certificate of Merit from the City Council of Deggendorf given to Josef Hörmann in recognition of his military service during World War I.

Document 106   *Certificate of Merit awarded Josef Hörmann*

It was awarded on 12 October 1919 and signed in black ink by a Mr. Reuss, the secretary to the mayor of Deggendorf. It was printed on heavy cardboard having a yellow-brown background and measures 21.5 cm. wide x 30.4 cm. high. At the bottom in the center is the purple ink official stamp of the City Council of Deggendorf.

✠ ✠ ✠

The document shown below is an Official Certificate, Type 9, named to War Volunteer Private First Class *(Kriegs-Freiwilliger Gefreiter)* **HELLMUTH WALTHER** serving in the 9th Company, 233rd Reserve Infantry Regiment, 101st Reserve Infantry Brigade, 51st Reserve Infantry Division, XXVIth Reserve Army Corps.

Der Kommandierende General
des XXVI. Reservekorps.

K. H. Qu. Westroosebeke,
den 9. Dezember 1914.

Im Namen Seiner Majestät des Deutschen Kaisers
und Königs von Preußen Wilhelm II. habe ich dem

Kriegs- Freiwilliger Gefreiter Walther

von der 9. ten Kompagnie des Res. Inf. Reg. № 233

geb. am 10. November 1895 zu Zwick Kreis Meiningen

für mutiges und tapferes Verhalten in den Kämpfen östlich
der Yser das Eiserne Kreuz 2. Klasse verliehen.

General der Infanterie

Document 107   *Official Certificate, Type 9, to Gefreiter Walther*   **S. Fore Collection**

The following documents indicate that Gefreiter Walther, who voluntarily enlisted at the beginning of the war *(Kriegs-Freiwilliger)*, was commissioned an officer prior to July 1915.

The document was signed at Reserve Army Corps Headquarters, located at the time, at Westroose-beke, on 9 December 1914. It measures 21.0 cm. wide x 28.0 cm. high. Instead of the usual ink signature, this document has used a purple ink stamp, which is not very distinct and has been stamped twice, for the signature of General Freiherr von Hügel [original signatures seen on pages 102 and 104]. To the left of the stamped signature is the purple ink official stamp of the XXVIth Reserve Army Corps Headquarters. This document also states that Gefreiter Walther was decorated for "courageous and brave behavior in action east of the Yser" *(für mutiges und tapferes Verhalten in den Kämpfen östlich der Yser)*.

The document also shows that Gefreiter Walther was 23 years old at the time he received the Iron Cross 2nd Class. See page 103 for the regimental actions which also apply here.

Shown below is the Authorization Certificate *(Besitzzeugnis)* showing that Reserve Lieutenant Walther, now serving in the 98th Infantry Regiment "Metzer," was wounded in action and entitled to the black wound badge. The document was signed by the regimental commander in pencil. To the left of the signature is the red ink official stamp of the 98th Infantry Regiment.

Document 108   *Black wound badge certificate to Lt. Hellmuth Walther*

The 98th Infantry Regiment was part of the 66th Infantry Brigade of the 33rd Infantry Division. The division took part in the Second Battle of the Marne. From 7 June until 11 July 1918, the division rested south of Soissons. It returned to the Marne front by Braisne. It was held in reserve when on 17-18 of July, the division fell back on Beuvardes and Grisolles and was heavily engaged the following day southeast of Neuilly St. Front. In the severe actions of 21-23 July 1918, the division was pushed back south of Oulchy-le-Château toward Fére en Tardenois. It withdrew until the Vasle was reached and there it was relieved on 31 July 1918. It was during this fighting that Lt. Hellmuth Walther was wounded. The division remained on the western front until the end of the war.

Other awards given to Lt. Hellmuth Walther are from Saxon Duchies. Shown below is a large and very beautiful document from the Duchy of Saxon-Meiningen awarding him the War Merit Cross which actually was a medal. It was authorized on 21 July 1915 and signed in ink by a State Ministry official.

Document 109   Saxon-Meiningen War Merit Cross Certificate to Lt. Hellmuth Walther

To the left of the signature is the official paper seal and below the seal is the registration number, 32,1057 I. The initial in the lower right corner is the mark of the awards registrar.

Shown below is another large and beautiful document from the Duchy of Saxon, Coburg and Gotha awarding Lt. Hellmuth Walther the Knights Cross 2nd Class with Swords (in recognition of outstanding war service) of the Saxon Ernestine House Order.

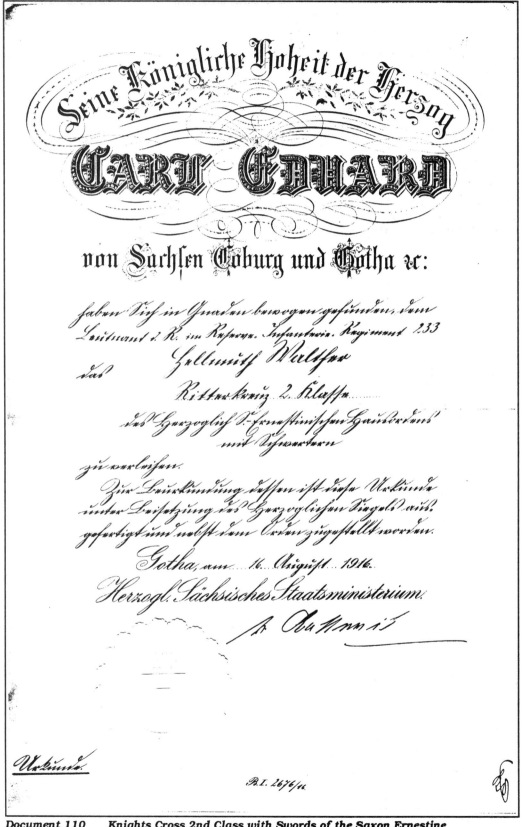

It was signed in black ink by a State Ministry official on 16 August 1916.

The document shows that Lt. Walther was still serving in the 233rd Reserve Infantry Regiment and in all likelihood as a company commander.

Along the lower center edge is the registration number and to the left of the signature is the official paper seal. In the lower right corner is the initial of the Orders registrar for the Duchy of Saxon-Coburg and Gotha.

Both documents measure 21.0 cm. wide x 34.0 cm. high.

✠ ✠ ✠

Document 110   *Knights Cross 2nd Class with Swords of the Saxon Ernestine House Order Document to Lt. Hellmuth Walther*

Notes:

1914 First and Second Class Iron Cross Documents
to the Same Recipient

The following documents are for both classes of the Iron Cross that have been awarded to the same individual. For a collector of Iron Cross documents, it is most desirable to be able to obtain as many documents to the same individual as is possible. In this way, the document collector is sometimes able to trace the military and/or civil career of a person with very interesting results.

The document shown below is a Preliminary Authorization Certificate, Type 1, *(Vorläufiges Besitz-zeugnis)* named to Musketeer *(Musketier)* **PAUL BOROFSKI** serving in the 9th Company, 143rd Infantry Regiment *(4th Alsace)*, 60th Infantry Brigade, 30th Infantry Division, 15th Army Corps.

Document 111   *Preliminary Authorization Certificate, Type 1, to Musketier Paul Borofski*

The document is unusual as it shows **both** awards of the Iron Cross. The document measures 21.5 cm. wide x 17.0 cm. high. It has been printed on a heavy stock paper. The document has been signed by the regiment commander in plain pencil on 15 June 1918 authorizing Musketeer Borofski the Iron cross 1st Class. To the left of the signature is the purple ink official stamp of the 143rd Infantry Regiment. In the left lower corner of the document is the entry showing Borofski was awarded the Iron Cross 2nd Class on 12 October 1916. Below that is again the signature of the regiment commander in plain pencil and also the purple ink stamp of the regiment. It has been folded and appears to have been carried by the recipient.

Toward the end of January 1916 elements of the 30th Infantry Division were transferred to the Verdun area to take part in the February German Offensive. On 24 February 1916 the 15th Army Corps, the western wing of the German attacking forces, went into action on the front of Maucourt-Warcq. The division was relieved by mid-March but remained in the sector. On July 11th the 143rd Infantry Regiment with the 99th Infantry Regiment took part in the new offensive. On 8 August 1916, the 143rd Infantry Regiment attacked the French defenses at Thiaumont and suffered heavy losses. Around the end of September 1916 the division was relieved and sent to rest in the Cambrai area. It returned to the front a short time afterwards, being assigned to the Somme at Sailly Saillisel and remained there one month. During this engagement the 143rd Infantry Regiment lost half of its effectives. It was during this battle that Musketeer Borofski received the Iron Cross 2nd Class.

Moving to 12 June 1918, the division was assigned to reenforced the front line near Courcelles. It suffered heavy losses in the fighting that followed and the division was withdrawn from the front on 22 June 1918. During this fighting Borofski again showed bravery in action and was awarded the Iron Cross 1st Class.

✠ ✠ ✠

The document shown below is a Preliminary Identification Certificate, Type 2, *(Vorläufiger Ausweis)* named to Home Guard Private *(Landsturm)* **GERHARD ADOLF BOGISCH** serving in the 1st Battalion, 395th Infantry Regiment, 9th Reserve Infantry Division.

Den ___13. November___ 191 **7**

Vorlaeufiger Ausweis

Im Namen Seiner Majestaet
:: des Kaisers und Koenigs ::

ist dem

Lastm. Gerhard Adolf Bogisch

durch Tages-Befehl der 9. Reserve-Division vom ___27. Oktober___ 191 **7** das

Eiserne Kreuz 2. Klasse

verliehen worden.

Hauptm. und Batls.-Kdr.

9. Reserve - Division Abt. II b Druckerei

Document 112   *Preliminary Identification Certificate, Type 2, to Private Gerhard Bogisch*

The document measures 20.7 cm. wide x 16.2 cm. high. The award was authorized and published in the divisional daily orders *(Tages Befehl)* on 27 October 1917, however, Private Bogisch did not receive the authorization until 13 November 1917. The document is signed by the battalion commander in black ink and to the left of the signature is the purple ink official stamp of the 1st Battalion, 395th Infantry Regiment.

The 395th Infantry Regiment joined the 9th Reserve Infantry Division during March 1916. The division advanced through Maucourt-Ornes and established a sector north of Vaux. On 9-10 March 1916, three regiments successfully attacked the village and fort at Vaux. Around 12 March, the division was relieved and sent to a rest area near Senon-Amel. On March 20th the division returned to the front lines south of Damploup. It received heavy enemy bombardment which resulted in severe losses. Relieved at the end of April 1916, the 9th Reserve Infantry Division rested and was refitted at Saverne in Alsace where it remained until 12 June 1916. The division arrived on the front on 20 June 1916 at the Souain-Tahure sector in Champagne. The division was engaged in heavy action along its front on the eastern side of Bouchavesnes on 18 October 1916.

In February 1917, the division held the sector north of Ancre in the Somme. Relieved on 10 March, it rested near Cambrai and was returned to the front on 20 March 1917 west of Catelet near Gouzeaucourt. In July 1917, the division returned to the front on the Ypres Road at Menin and on 20 September 1917 engaged in a major battle. The 3rd Company of the 395th Infantry Regiment lost over half of its men. During these engagements Private Bogisch was cited for bravery in action and recommended for the Iron Cross 2nd Class. During 1918 the division was assigned to various sectors but did not engage in any other major battles.

Document 113   *Authorization Certificate, Type 4, to Gerhard Bogisch*

Five and a half years after the end of World War I, Gehard Bogisch, now living in Berlin-Friednau, was awarded the Iron Cross 1st Class on 6 March 1924. The Authorization Certificate *(Besitzzeugnis)* was issued by the Defense Ministry, Army Department, Personnel Section *(Reichswehrministerium, Heersleitung, Personalamt)*. The document measures 20.7 cm. wide x 16.4 cm. high. It was signed by the section chief, Lt. Col. Schemmel, on 6 March 1924. Adjacent to the signature is the official black ink stamp of the Defense Ministry. Below the ministry stamp is the registration number of the award "297 6.2.24." The first three numbers, "297," are the registration and the remaining being the date of 6 February 1924. It is interesting that it took so long to award the 1st Class Iron Cross to Bogisch.

✠ ✠ ✠

The document shown below is a Preliminary Authorization Certificate, Type 1, *(Vorläufiges Besitzzeugnis)* named to Corporal *(Unteroffizier)* **SCHLEIF** serving in the 1st Field Company, 27th Engineer *(Pionier)* Battalion, 31st Infantry Division.

Vorläufiges Besitzzeugnis

über das

Eiserne Kreuz **II.** Klasse.

Inhaber dieses

der *Unteroffizier Schleif*
der 1. Feldkomp. Pionier - Batl N° 27

hat das Eiserne Kreuz am *11. August* 1915 verliehen erhalten.

O. U. den *20 Jan.* 1916

Für die Richtigkeit

Oberleutnant u. Komp. Führer

Document 114   Preliminary Authorization Certificate, Type 1, to Unteroffizier Schleif

The document measures 19.5 cm. wide x 16.0 cm. high. It was signed by the company chief in purple indelible pencil on 20 January 1916; however, the document shows that Corporal Schleif was awarded the Iron Cross 2nd Class on 11 August 1915 almost four months earlier. To the left of the signature is the purple ink official stamp of the 1st Company of the 27th Engineer Battalion.

Moving to the activities of the 31st Infantry Division in 1915, we find that on 25 January 1915 the division left the Somme for the eastern front and detrained at Tilsit. It was concentrated in Eastern Prussia and was a part of the Hindenburg Army. In the month of August 1915, the division took part in the German offensive at Vilna. It advanced to Kovno on August 19th, to Vilna by the end of September, and reached the Smorgoni-Soly area where it established its front. During this offensive Corporal Schleif displayed bravery in action and won his Iron Cross 2nd Class.

The division was relieved on October 6th and after resting and refitting went back into the line on 24 October 1915 holding the Postawy-Lake Narotch area. The 31st Infantry Division remained in the vicinity of Lake Narotch until being reassigned to the western front in December 1917.

From 19 January until 4 February 1918 the division held the Moorslede sector south of the Ypres-Roulers railroad. In April, the division was reassigned to the Messines front. The division was engaged in several fierce and major actions in this area and also south and southwest of Kemmel from 18 April until 24 April 1918 when it passed into a close support role until the 26th of April. The division's losses were large in this major engagement. When relieved in the Kemmel area, the division was sent north of Tourcoing where it rested until 6 May 1918. It returned to the front north of Kemmel on the night of 6-7 May, relieving the German Alpine Corps *(see document 11, page 14)*. The division again suffered heavy losses from the French attack of 21 May. The division was relieved on 24 May 1918 and rested in the Courtrai-Menine area until 15 June 1918. It again saw action in the sector south of Ypres from 15 June until 27 July 1918. Following its arduous service on the Ypres front, the division was moved to a quiet sector in the Woevre area. After engaging US forces in the St. Mihiel salient, the division was assigned back into the line north of Thiavcourt on the 14 October and held the sector until 28 October 1918. The division was again engaged at Imecourt and took part in the final fighting in this area. It was still in the front line on 11 November 1918.

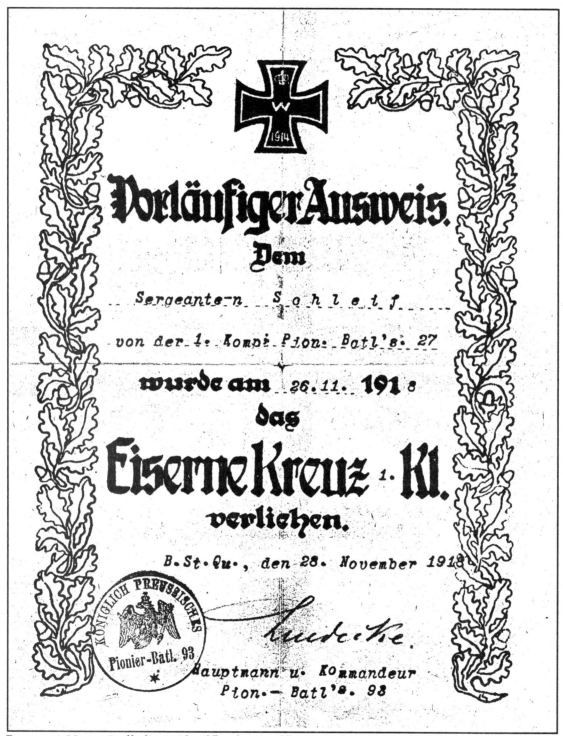

Document 96   *Preliminary Identification Certificate, Type 2, to Sergeant Schleif*

The document, shown above in original size, measures 16.6 cm. wide x 21.0 cm. high. Signed in purple indelible pencil on 28 November 1918 by the commander of the 93rd Engineer *(Pionier)* Battalion showing Sergeant Schlief (his having been promoted by this time) was awarded the Iron Cross 1st Class on 26 November 1918, 15 days after the war had ended. To the left of the signature block is the red ink official stamp of the 93rd Engineer Battalion. However, Sgt. Schleif was still serving in the 1st Company of the 27th Engineer (Pionier) Battalion, the unit now being under the command of the 93rd Engineer Battalion. ✠ ✠ ✠

The document shown below is a Preliminary Identification Certificate, Type 2, *(Vorläufiger Ausweis)* named to Acting Officer Paymaster *(Zahlmeister Stellvertrater)* **HEINRICH EMIL FRIEDRICH BARUSCHKE** serving in the 14th Transport Column of the 2nd Army Supply Service Corps *(Etappen Trains 2. Armee).*

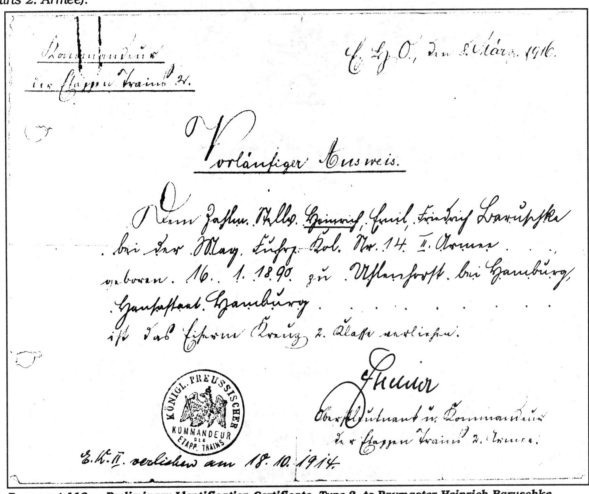

Document 116   Preliminary Identification Certificate, Type 2, to Paymaster Heinrich Baruschke

The plain purple ink duplicated handwritten document measures 21.0 cm wide x 16.5 cm. high. The name of the recipient, unit, date and place of birth were written in black ink. The document appears to have been duplicated on 8 March 1916 and signed in black ink by the commander of the 2nd Army Supply Service Corps. To the left of the signature is the purple ink official stamp of the headquarters of the Supply Service Corps. Note that below the stamp, written in black ink, is the notation that Baruschke had received the Iron Cross 2nd Class on 18 October 1914.

Exhibit 3   Back of Baruschke Certificate

On the left margin are the two holes indicating the document was a part of his military record. It also appears that this document, at a later date, had been folded and carried by the recipient.

Shown at the left is what was written on the back of the document in the middle of a fold. It reads "Identification Iron Cross *(Ausweis eisernes Kreuz).*

The document shown below is an Authorization Certificate, Type 6, *(Urkunde)* named to, now promoted, Assistant Paymaster *(Hilfszahlmeister)* **HEINRICH BARUSCHKE** serving on the staff of the German Military Mission in Turkey *(Stab der Militär Mission f.d. Turkei)*.

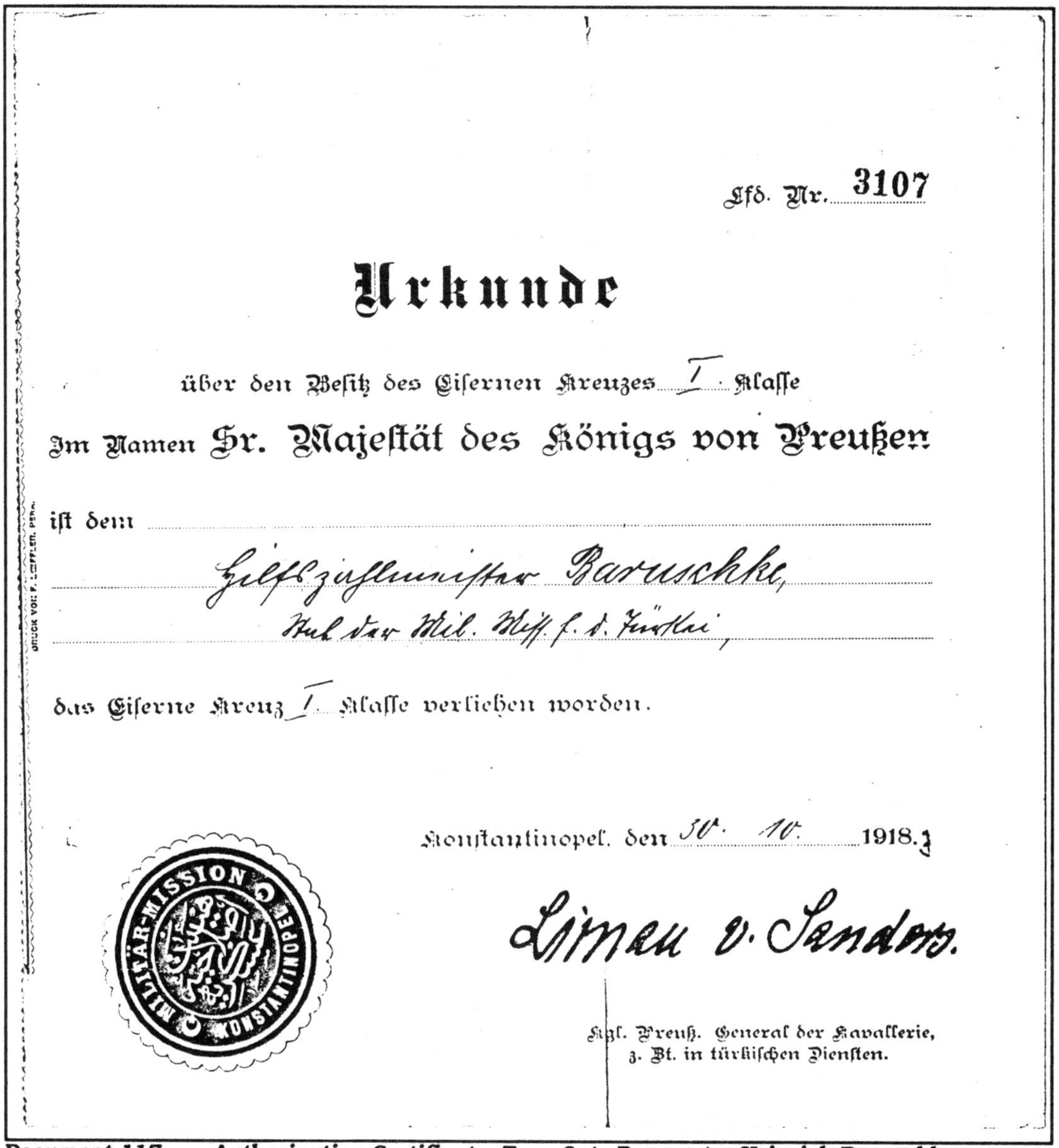
Lfd. Nr. 3107

Urkunde

über den Besitz des Eisernen Kreuzes I. Klasse

Im Namen Sr. Majestät des Königs von Preußen

ist dem

Hilfszahlmeister Baruschke,

Stab der Mil. Miss. f. d. Türkei,

das Eiserne Kreuz I. Klasse verliehen worden.

Konstantinopel, den 30. 10. 1918.

Liman v. Sanders.

Kgl. Preuß. General der Kavallerie,
z. Zt. in türkischen Diensten.

Document 117 ***Authorization Certificate, Type 6, to Paymaster Heinrich Baruschke***

The document, was taken from a forms book *(note the perforated left edge)* and measures 19.0 cm. wide x 19.8 cm high. It has been written in black ink that the award is for the 1st Class, however, this same certificate could be also used for the 2nd Class as well. It was authorized on 30 October 1918 in Constantinople, Turkey. There is a facsimile signature stamp in blue ink of Cavelry General Liman von Sanders, who was serving at the time as German military advisor to the Turkish Army. To the left is a blue paper seal attached to the document. In the upper right hand corner is the registration number 3107. An interesting and seldom seen document.

Baruschke was also awarded the TurkishWar Medal,* on 10 January 1917 and on 30 October 1918, while still in Constantinople, he was decorated with the Turkish Silver Iftichar Medal. Both award documents were issued through the German Military Mission to Turkey and both have the stamped facsimile signature of General Liman von Sanders.

✠ ✠ ✠

---

* The Turkish War Medal is called in German the *"Eiserne Halbmond,"* and so very often mistakenly called the "Gallipoli Star."

The following two documents are named to the same recipient. The document shown below is an Authorization Certificate, Type 4, *(Besitzzeugnis)* named to Lt. Colonel *(Oberstleutnant)* **ERICH FIEDLER.** He was serving in the 60th Landwehr Infantry Regiment, 60th Landwehr Infantry Brigade, 13th Landwehr Infantry Division.

The plain and simple printed document measures 21.5 cm wide x 31.0 cm. high. It was signed at Army High Command "Falkenhausen" on 20 October 1914 when the headquarters was located in Metz.

The document is signed in ink by General Falkenhausen. To the left of the signature is the purple ink official stamp of the High Command of the Army Unit "Falkenhausen."

In the bottom left hand corner is seen the registration number 520 for the Orders List of the Army High Command.

The 13th Landwehr Infantry Division was formed in Lorraine about the middle of May 1915. It was composed, at this time, of the 60th Reserve Landsturm Battalions, (Cassel and Mayence), and of the 60th Landwehr Brigade composed of the 60th Landwehr Regiment and the 61st Landwehr Regiment. These elements were already in the line on the Lorraine front before the formation of the division. The 60th Landwehr Regiment, where Lt. Col. Fiedler was serving, beginning on August 11th, was assigned the security of the railroads of lower

Document 118   Authorization Certificate, Type 4, to Lt. Colonel Erich Feidler

Alsace. The division occupied the sector between Abaucourt and the Besange woods from May 1915 until February 1917. Except for a few raids, the division remained on the defensive during this long period.

Besitz-Zeugnis.

Dem

Oberstleutnant z.D. Erich Fiedler,

Vorstand des Versorgungsamts XXI. Armeekorps,

wurde für Verdienste im Felde am 21. Juli 1919

das

Eiserne Kreuz 1. Klasse

verliehen.

Saarbrücken, den 23. August 1919.

Versorgungs-Amt XXI. Armeekorps.

J. A.

Document 119   *Iron Cross 1st Class Authorization Certificate, Type 4, to Lt.Colonel Erich Fiedler*

This document shown at left, also of a very large format, measures 21.2 cm. wide x 33.0 cm. high. It is entirely handwritten in black ink including the signature.

It is interesting to note that directly under the word "merit" *(Verdienste)* written lightly in pencil, is the notation "bravery before the enemy" *(Tapferkeit vor d. Feind).*

In the lower right corner is the authenticating signature also in black ink. To the left of the signature is the dark purple ink official stamp of the Assistance Office of the XXIst Army Corps in Saarbrücken.

It was signed on 23 August 1919 awarding Lt. Colonel Erich Fiedler the Iron Cross 1st Class.

Für Verdienste im Felde

Exhibit 4   *Arrow indicates the enlargement of "bravery in action" penciled notation*

It is interesting to speculate as to the reason why Lt. Colonel Erich Fiedler did not receive a promotion during the war.

✠ ✠ ✠

The document shown below is an Authorization Certificate, Type 4, *(Besitzschein)* named to Corporal *(Unteroffizer)* **F. REDENBACH** serving in the 2nd Battalion, 22nd Infantry Regiment *(Fürst Wilhelm von Hohenzollern)*, 23rd Infantry Brigade, 11th Reserve Infantry Division.

Document 120   *Authorization Certificate, Type 4, to Unteroffizier Ferdinand Redenbach*

The plain document, entirely handwritten in black ink, measures 21.5 cm. wide x 16.5 cm. high. It was signed in black ink by the battalion commander on 1 May 1916. The text of the document shows that Unteroffizier Redenbach displayed "outstanding achievement on the battlefield" *(für seine besondern Leistungen im Felde)* and was awarded the Iron Cross 2nd Class on 1 November 1914. Interestingly there is no battalion or regimental stamp. It appears that this certificate was issued to and carried by Redenbach as a form of identification.

At the beginning of the war the 11th and 12th Reserve Infantry Divisions formed the 6th Reserve Corps. It belonged to the 5th Army of the Prussian Crown Prince. The division fought at Arrancy from 22-25 August 1914 and crossed the Meuse river on 21 September 1914. It was again engaged in the region of Cierges and by the end of September had established its position at the eastern edge of the Argonne (Varennes-Malancourt woods). It was during these actions that Unteroffizier Redenbach displayed bravery in action and was recommended for the Iron Cross 2nd Class. This was a very early award of the Iron Cross. The division occupied this area until the Verdun offensive in February 1916.

From January to December 1915 the division held the sector of Malancourt wood south of Montfaucon in the Argonne.

In February 1916, when the battle of Verdun began, the division was still in its sector on the left bank of the Meuse. In March it saw action near Bethencourt, which it captured on 9 April 1916. Relieved about 15 May after suffering 68% infantry casualties. It was withdrawn from the front and set to a rest area.

Unteroffizier Redenbach was transferred from the infantry to the flying service. He successfully completed flight training and become a pilot (flugzeugführer). He was then promoted to the rank of Acting Officer (Offizierstellvertrater). However, without his service record there is no way of knowing when this was accomplished.

The document shown below is a Preliminary Identification Certificate, Type 2, (Vorläufiger Ausweis) to **F. REDENBACH** showing that he is now serving in the "Group Wytschaete" on the western front.

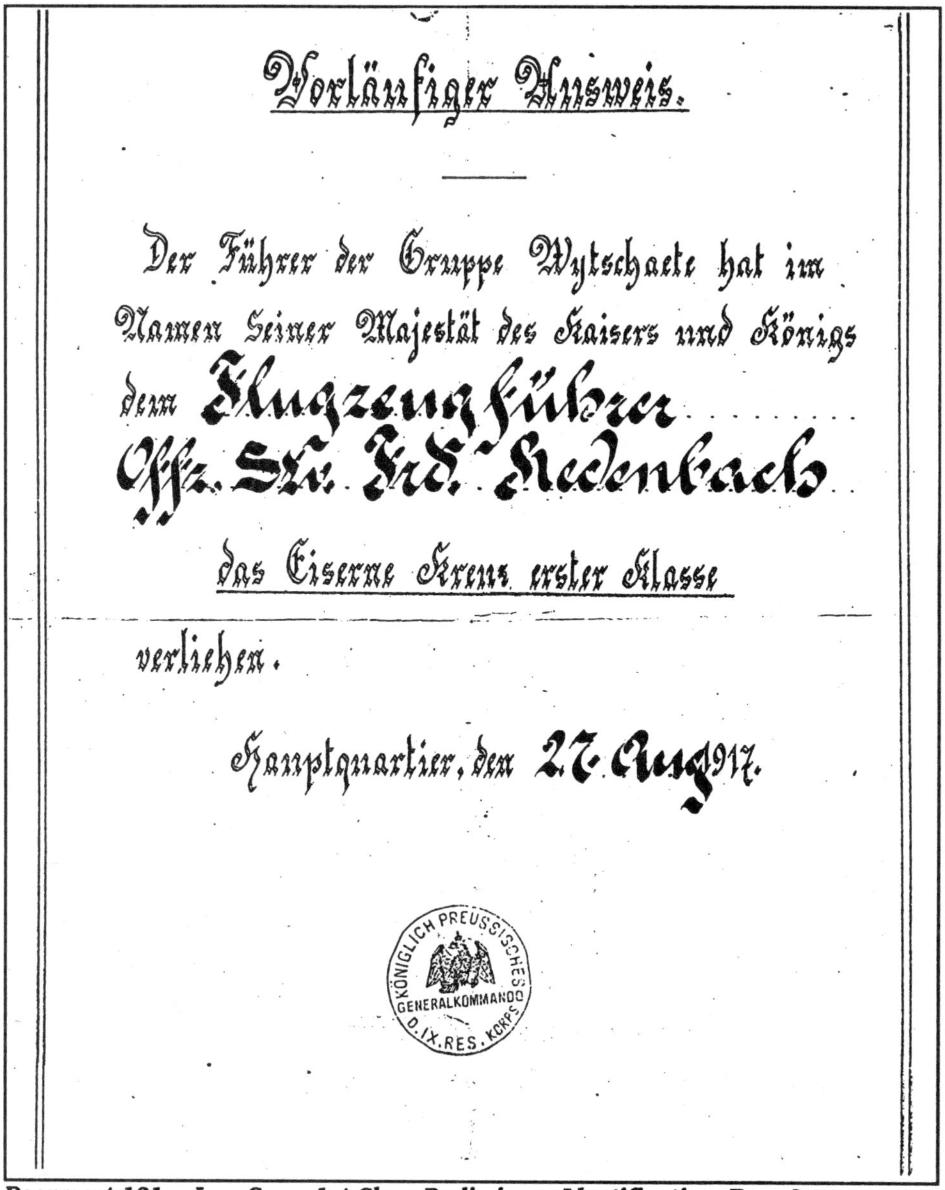

The document appears to have been hand-drawn and subsequently reproduced and printed in black ink.

The Preliminary Identification Certificate measures 21.0 cm. wide x 28.0 cm. high, however, the document appears to have been trimmed at the upper and lower edges.

It was authorized and awarded on 27 August 1917. In the lower center is the purple ink official stamp of the IXth Reserve Corps Command.

The signature, if there was one, is so badly faded it cannot be distinguished on this document.

**Document 121   Iron Cross 1st Class Preliminary Identification, Type 2,
to Offizierstellvertrater Redenbach**

✠ ✠ ✠

The document shown below is a Preliminary Identification Certificate, Type 2, *(Vorläufiger Ausweis)* named to Reserve Private First Class *(Oberjäger d.Res.)* **KURT DIESSNER**, serving at the time he received the Iron Cross 2nd Class in the 4th Company, 9th Lauenburg Light Infantry *(Jäger)* Battalion, 12th Landwehr Infantry Division.

Document 122   Preliminary Identification Certificate, Type 2, to Oberjäger d. Reserve Kurt Diessner

The document, in rather bad condition, measures 22.0 cm. wide x 18.3 cm. high. It was signed sometime in July 1916 in black ink by a Lt. General of the 12th Landwehr Infantry Division. To the left of the signature is the purple ink official stamp of the 12th Landwehr Infantry Division. In the left margin are the two typical punched holes indicating that this document was a part of the military record of Diessner.

Oberjäger Diessner appears to have served on the western front when awarded the Iron Cross 2nd Class. The 12th Landwehr Infantry Division was engaged in a major battle late in December 1915 at Hartmannswillwekopf where it sustained severe losses. After being withdrawn from the front, the division was sent to Belgium where it rested and was refitted and received replacements.

The 12th Landwehr Infantry Division held the Guebwiller-Cernay section from early 1916 to mid-September 1916. In October 1916 the battalions of Light Infantry *(Jägers)* including the 9th Lauenburg Light Infantry Battalion along with riflemen of the Guard Units were assigned to a new division in Macedonia on the eastern front.

Oberjäger Diessner was transfered from the infantry to flying school. Without his service record there is no way of determining when this took place. Diessner successfully completed flying school and became a pilot *(Flugzeugführer)* . On 13 December 1917, as a pilot and assigned to a flying unit, it appears he performed some notable action which warranted his being decorated with the Iron Cross 1st Class. There is no way of ascertaining whether the action was accomplished in the air or on the ground.

The document, shown below in actual size, is a Preliminary Identification Certificate, Type 2, *(Vorläufiger Ausweis)* named to **DIESSNER** now promoted to Reserve Senior Duty Sergeant *(Vizefeldwebel d.Res.)* serving as a pilot in the Aviation Unit 36 *(Flieger-Abteilung 36)*.

The plain typed document measures 16.0 cm. wide x 10.5 cm. high. It was signed in purple indelible pencil by the section chief on 16 December 1917 only a few days following his meritorious

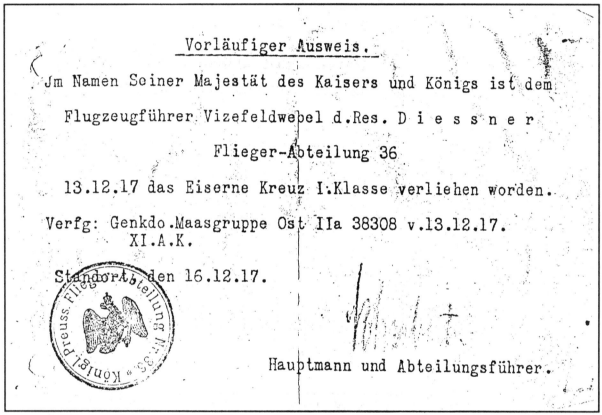

Document 123   Iron Cross 1st Class Preliminary Identification Certificate, Type 2, to Vizefeldwebel Diessner

action. The award was authorized through General Headquarters of Maas Group East *(Genkdo. Maasgruppe Ost)*. To the left of the signature block is the purple ink official stamp of the 36th Aviation Unit. In the left margin are the two punched holes indicating that this certificate was a part of the military record of Diessner.

✠ ✠ ✠

The document shown below is a Preliminary Authorization Certificate, Type 1, *(Vorläufiges Besitzzeugnis)* named to Corporal *(Unteroffizer)* **ARNO SCHICKEL** serving as a pilot *(flugzeugführer)* assigned to the 15th Field Aviation Unit *(Feldflieger Abteilung 15)*.

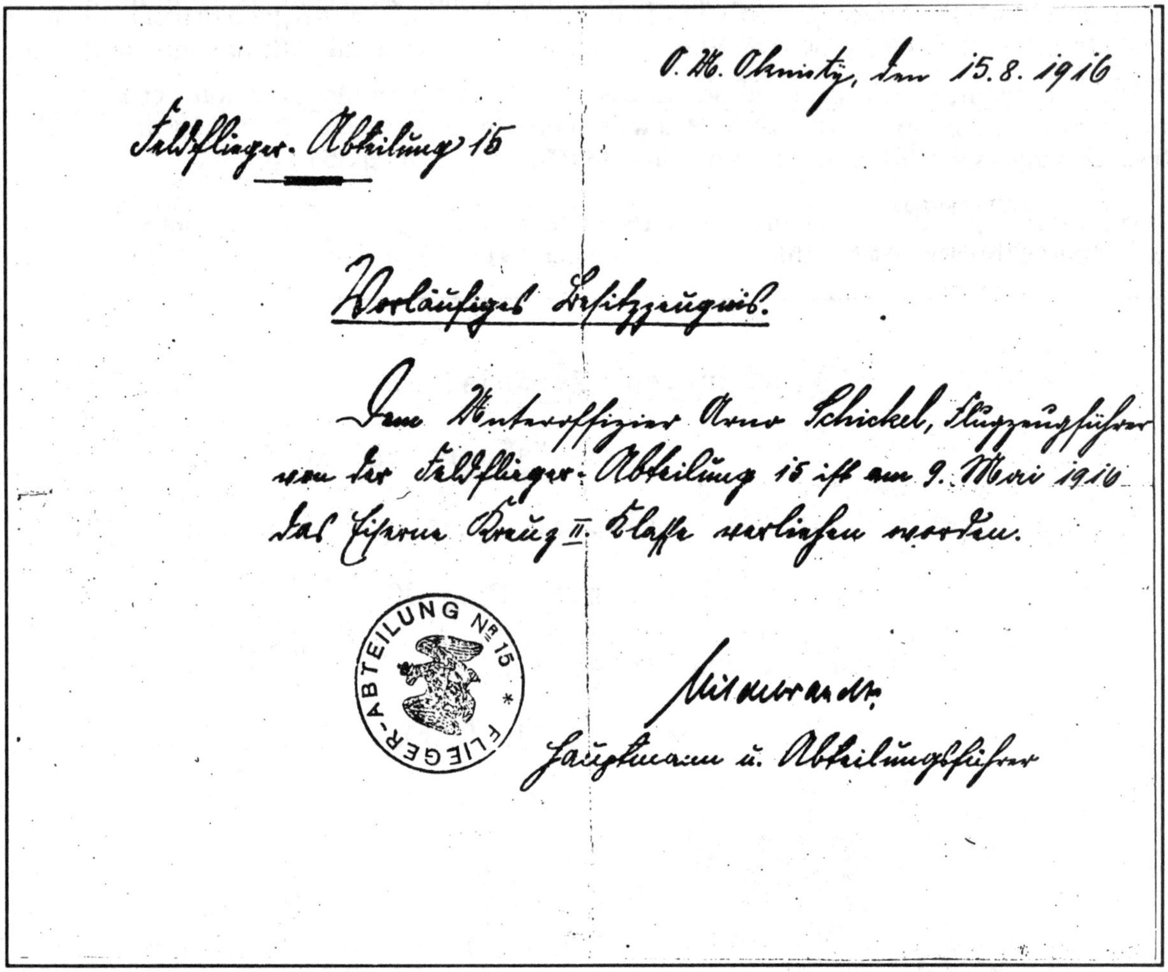

Document 124   Preliminary Authorization Certificate, Type 1, to Corporal Pilot Arno Schickel

The document is all handwritten in black ink and measures 20.7 cm. wide x 16.8 cm. high. It was signed in black ink, by the unit section leader on 15 August 1916 at the headquarters of the field aviation unit located,at the time, in Oknistÿ on the eastern front. To the left of the signature is the purple ink official stamp of the 15th Field Aviation Unit. The document shows that Unteroffizier Schickel was awarded the Iron Cross 2nd Class on 9 May 1916.

The document for the Iron Cross 2nd Class appears to have been carried by Schickel as a means of identification since there are no holes in the left margin to indicate it being a part of his military record.

A few days after receiving the Iron Cross 2nd Class authorization, Corporal Pilot Schickel was authorized the Iron Cross 1st Class on 22 August 1916.

The document shown below for the Iron Cross 1st Class to Corporal Pilot **ARNO SCHICKEL** is a Preliminary Authorization Certificate, Type 1, *(Vorläufiges Besitzzeugnis)* and was issued from the High Command of Army Section "Scholtz" on 22 August 1916.

The neat document measures 21.0 cm. wide x 17.6 cm. high. It was signed in black ink by a major representing the Chief of the General Staff. To the left is the black ink official stamp of the "Schlotz" Army Section.

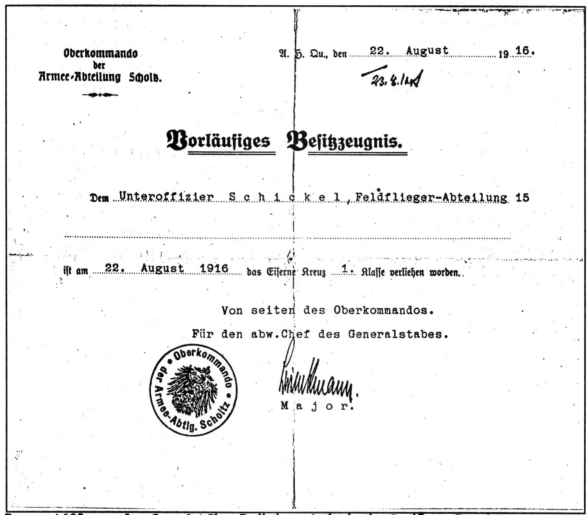

Document 125   *Iron Cross 1st Class Preliminary Authorization Certificate, Type 1, to Corporal Pilot Arno Schickel*

It is of interest to note that corporal pilot Schickel was awarded the Iron Cross 1st Class only **three and one-half** months after being decorated with the Iron Cross 2nd Class. Also of interest is that he was given the documents only seven days apart.

Without the service record of Schickel, and since he was a pilot, there is no way of knowing whether he was decorated with the Iron Cross 2nd and 1st Class for bravery in action in the air or on the ground. This allows one to speculate on the circumstances.

✠ ✠ ✠

Im Namen Seiner Majestät
des Kaisers und Königs

ist dem

Unteroffizier Gödecke

am 19. März 1916

das

Eiserne Kreuz

2. Klasse

verliehen worden.

Oberstleutnant und Kommandeur
des Kaiser Franz Garde Grenadier Regts. No 2

M 2499   Etappen-Druckerei 2 Armee 25.X.1916

Document 126   Official Certificate, Type 9, to Corporal Gödecke

Document 127   *Iron Cross 1st Class Official Certificate to Vizefeldwebel Heinrich Gödeke*

The documents shown on the preceding pages are both Official Documents, Type 9, named to **HEINRICH GÖDECKE**.

When awarded the Iron Cross 2nd Class on 19 March 1916, he was holding the rank of Corporal *(Unteroffizier)* and serving in the 2nd Guard Grenadier Regiment *(Kaiser Franz)* Regiment, 4th Guard Infantry Brigade, 2nd Guard Infantry Division.

The extremely large and attractive document, shown on page 154, measures 21.0 cm. wide x 32.3 cm. high. It was signed in black ink by the commander of the regiment and dated 19 March 1916. To the left of the signature block is the purple ink official stamp of the 2nd Guard Grenadier Regiment, a most impressive document. Note on the bottom right edge that the certificate was printed on 25 February 1916 by the supply unit printer of the 2nd Army.

Moving to the latter part of 1915, the division returned to the western front from the eastern front and arrived on September 20th. The division rested for one month in Belgium. On 25 October 1915 the division was assigned to the Orchies area and was engaged on 5 November in a heavy battle at Lorette Heights which lasted six days. The division suffered moderate casualties but was able to sustain itself. It finally went into the front line in the area between Noyon and Roye. It appears that during the time the regiment was in this sector Corporal Gödeke received the Iron Cross 2nd Class.

The 2nd Guard Division remained in the Noyon-Roye sector until August 1916. On 15 August 1916 the division was sent to the Somme region and engaged in several actions both to the north and south of Péronne. From 1 October until the end of December 1916, the division took part in several other actions south of Péronne.

At the end of January 1917 the division was sent to rest near Guise. After resting and receiving replacements, it was assigned to hold a sector of the Siegfried line near Roisel and St. Quentin for five or six days at the beginning of March 1917. From 16 March until 12 April 1917 the division rested and was refitted.

On 12 April 1917 the division was assigned to Sissonne where it went into the line between Hurtebise and Craonne supporting and relieving units of the 5th Guard Infantry Division. It remained in the area for three weeks and was engaged in several actions. On 11 May 1917 the division was dispatched to the Argonne where it was reorganized. It received replacements from the 613th, 614th and 615th Infantry Regiments, which were dissolved.

Withdrawn from the line at the beginning of July 1917 the division entrained for the eastern front where it took part in the attack on the Sereth on July 19th. It appears that Gödecke was awarded the Iron Cross 1st Class prior to the time the regiment left for the eastern front.

The extremely large and decorative Iron Cross 1st Class Official Certificate, Type 9, shown on page 155, measures 24.0 cm. wide x 37.7 cm. high. It shows that when Heinrich Gödeke was awarded the Iron Cross 1st Class, he had been promoted to the rank of Senior Duty Sergeant *(Vizefeldwebel)* and was serving in the 6th Company in the same 2nd Guard Infantry Regiment *(Kaiser Franz)*, 3rd Guard Infantry Brigade, 2nd Guard Infantry Division. The document is signed in black ink by the regimental commander and dated 6 June 1917. To the left of the signature is the purple ink official regimental stamp.

The division returned to the western front and remained there until the end of the war. The 2nd Guard Infantry Division was rated as a first class assault division by the US Intelligence Group. It participated in many heavy fighting actions, especially during 1918, and always acquitted itself very well. It was mentioned in several German official communiqués on several occasions.

✠ ✠ ✠

Notes:

The document shown below is a Preliminary Identification Certificate, Type 2, *(Vorläufiger Ausweis)* named to Reserve Medical Corpsman Corporal *(Sanitäts Unteroffizier der Reserve)* **HUGO OTTO LUDWIG ADRIAN** serving in the 9th Company, 3rd Battalion, 15th Reserve Infantry Regiment, 26th Reserve Infantry Brigade, 2nd Guard Reserve Infantry Division.

Document 128   Preliminary Identification Certificate, Type 2, to Sanitäts Unteroffizer Hugo Adrian

The document measures 20.9 cm. wide x 16.4 cm. high. It shows that Corpsman Adrian was 22 years old when awarded the Iron Cross 2nd Class on 5 September 1916. The document has been signed in purple indelible pencil by the commander of the 3rd Battalion. To the left of the signature is the blue ink official stamp of the 3rd Battalion, 15th Reserve Infantry Regiment.

At the top of the following page is the identification card that Corpsman Adrian carried showing he was a non-combatant medical corpsman and authorized to wear the Red Cross armband. The card, shown actual size, measures 13.7 cm. wide x 9.2 cm. high. It was required that front line medical personnel carry such identification. The card was issued by the Prussian Ministry of War.

Also shown is the Preliminary Identification Certificate, Type 2, awarding the Iron Cross 1st Class to Reserve Medical Corpsman Adrian on 14 September 1918. The document measures 20.2 cm. wide x 15.5 cm. high, and is signed with a purple indelible pencil by the battalion commander. To the left of the signature is the purple ink official stamp of the 3rd Battalion of the 15th Reserve Infantry Regiment. The document was printed by the 2nd Guard Reserve Division Field Printers. The document has been folded and appears to have been carried in a wallet by Corpsman Adrian.

Moving to the year 1916 when Corpsman Adrian was decorated with the Iron Cross 2nd Class, the 2nd Guard Reserve Division was relieved on 7 April from the Cuichy-Canal sector of La Bassée. After a rest in Belgium, the division was assigned in the Gommecourt sector of the Somme at the end of May.

Ausweis.

Name: *Hugo Adrian*

Dienstgrad: *Sanitäts-Unteroffizier d. Res.*

Truppenteil: *9. Kompagnie Res. Inf. Regiment No. 15*

ist gemäß Artikel 20 des Genfer Abkommens vom 6. Juli 1906 zum Tragen des Neutralitätszeichens, einer auf dem linken Arme befestigten von der Militärbehörde gestempelten Binde mit dem Roten Kreuze auf weißem Grunde, berechtigt.

Truppenteil: *III. Batl. Res. Inf. Reg. No. 15*

Kommandeur: (Unterschrift)

Zur Gegenprobe: (Unterschrift des Inhabers) *Hugo Adrian*

Document 129   Non-combatant Medical Corpsman Identification Card to Cpl. Adrian

The Franco-British offensive found the division in this sector on July 1st. It was heavily engaged from July to November 1916 and suffered 51% casulties and during one or more of these actions Corpsman Adrian received the Iron Cross 2nd Class.

Now moving to September 19-18, the division was sent to reinforce the front near the Arras-Cambrai road. It engaged in several actions and was relieved around the middle of September. It was during this time that Corpsman Adrian was again recognized for his bravery in administering medical aid under fire and was awarded the Iron Cross 1st Class.

✠ ✠ ✠

Vorläufiger Ausweis.

Dem *San.-Ustffz. d. R. Hugo, Otto, Ludwig Adrian*

von der *9. Kompagnie Reserve-Infanterie-Regiments Nr. 15*

geboren am *16. September 1894*

wurde vom Kommandeur der 2. Garde-Reserve-Division im Namen Seiner Majestät des Kaisers und Königs das

Eiserne Kreuz 1. Klasse

verliehen.

Im Felde, den *14. September 1918*

Hauptmann u. Batl.-Kommdeur.

Felddruckerei 2. Garde-Res.-Division.

Document 130   1st Class Iron Cross Preliminary Identification Certificate, Type 2, to Cpl. Adrian

The document shown below is a Preliminary Identification Certificate, Type 2, *(Vorläufiger Ausweis)* named to Corporal *(Unteroffizier)* **GERHARD GEORG DAMMEYER,** serving at the time he received the Iron Cross 2nd Class in the 3rd Battery, 34th Field Artillery Regiment, 33rd Artillery Brigade, 33rd Infantry Division, XVIth Army Corps.

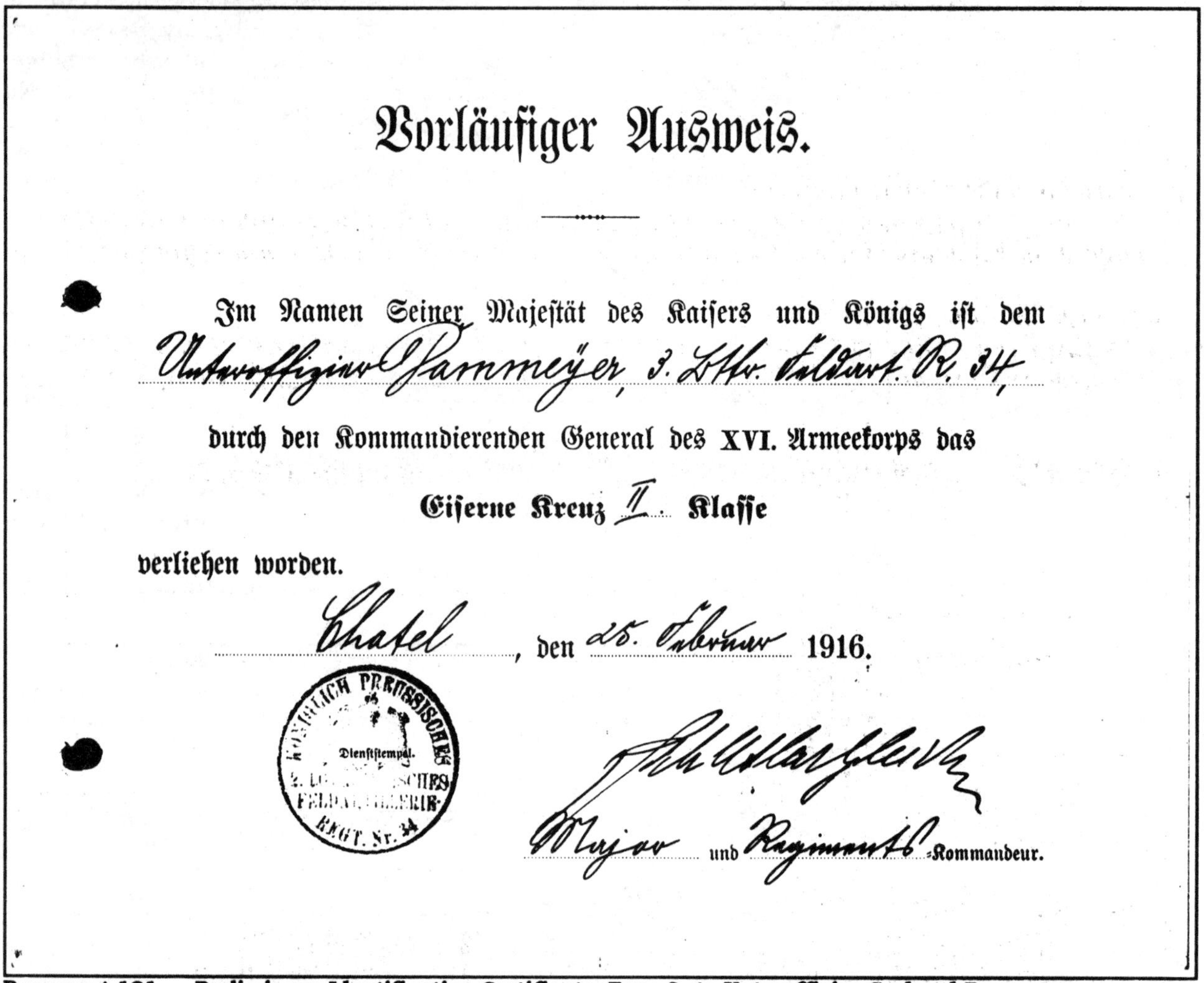

Document 131   *Preliminary Identification Certificate, Type 2, to Unteroffizier Gerhard Dammeyer*

The document measures 21.1 cm. wide x 16.6 cm. high. It was signed on 25 February 1916 in Chatel (France) by the regimental commander in black ink. To the left of the signature is the blue ink official stamp of the 34th Field Artillery Regiment.

At the outbreak of the war, the 33rd Infantry Division entered France by way of Audun le Roman, went north of Verdun, crossed the Meuse river at Givry on 1 September 1914 and advanced as far as Rambluzim and Heippes. After the battle of the Marne the division took positions in the Argonne. Its advance had been costly and the division suffered heavy casualties.

The 33rd Infantry Division remained in the Argonne sector from September 1914 until the middle of August 1915. It was while Unteroffizier Dammeyer was in the Argonne that he was awarded the Iron Cross 2nd Class. The 34th Field Artillery Regiment remained with the 33rd Infantry Division until the end of 1916 when it was transferred to the VIIIth Army Corps. The division to which it was assigned is not known. In 1918 while serving in the VIIIth Army Corps, Unteroffizier Dammeyer was awarded the Iron Cross 1st Class on 6 May 1918. The rather small document *(Document 132)* is an Official Certificate. It was signed in black ink by Lt. General Roderich von Schoeler,* commanding general of

---

* Lt. General Roderich von Schoeler was awarded the Prussian Pour le Mérite on 30 June 1918. The citation reads in part:

"... for outstanding leadership and distinguished military planning ... on the western front..."

he History of the Prussian Pour le Mérite Order, 1888-1918, " Volume III, W.E. Hamelman, p. 585, entry 604.

the VIIIth Army Corps. The document measures 19.8 cm. wide x 12.0 cm. high. To the left of the signature is the purple ink official stamp of the High Command of the VIIIth Army Corps.

Im Namen Seiner Majeſtät
des Kaiſers und Königs

iſt dem ___Unteroffizier Gerhard, Georg D a m m e y e r,___

___Feldartillerie-Regiment 34,_____3.Batterie___

das Eiſerne Kreuz I. Klaſſe

an ___6. M a i 1918_____ verliehen morden.

Der Kommandierende General des VIII. Armeekorps.

Generalleutnant

Document 132   Iron Cross 1st Class Official Certificate, Type 9, to Unteroffizier Dammeyer

On 21 September 1918, Gehard Dammeyer, promoted to Senior Duty Sergeant (Vizewachtmeister), received the Wound Badge Identification Certificate shown below. It has been made on a duplicator (Ditto) machine the text being in light blue.

The document measures 21.8 cm. wide x 17.0 cm. high and was signed in purple indelible pencil by the regimental commander. To the left of the signature is the black ink official stamp of the 34th Field Artillery Regiment.

Note that all three documents have in their left margins two punched holes indicating they were a part of the military file of Vizewachtmeister Gerhard Dammeyer.

✠ ✠ ✠

Ausweis.

Der Inhaber dieses Besitzzeugnisses

Vizewachtmeister Dammeyer, Feldart. R. 34, 3.Btr.

hat am 24.9.18 das Abzeichen für Verwundete

in ſchwarz

verliehen erhalten.

Im Felde, den 21. September 1918

Major und Regiments-Kommandeur.

Document 133   Wound Badge Identification Document to Vizewachtmeister Dammeyer

The document shown below is a Preliminary Authorization Certificate, Type 1, *(Verläufiges Besitzzeugnis)* named to Reserve Private First Class *(Gefreiten d. Reserve)* **GEORG MÖLLER** serving in the 223rd Artillery Spotter Aviation Unit *(Artillerie-Flieger-Abteilung 223)*, attached to the 2nd Infantry Division.

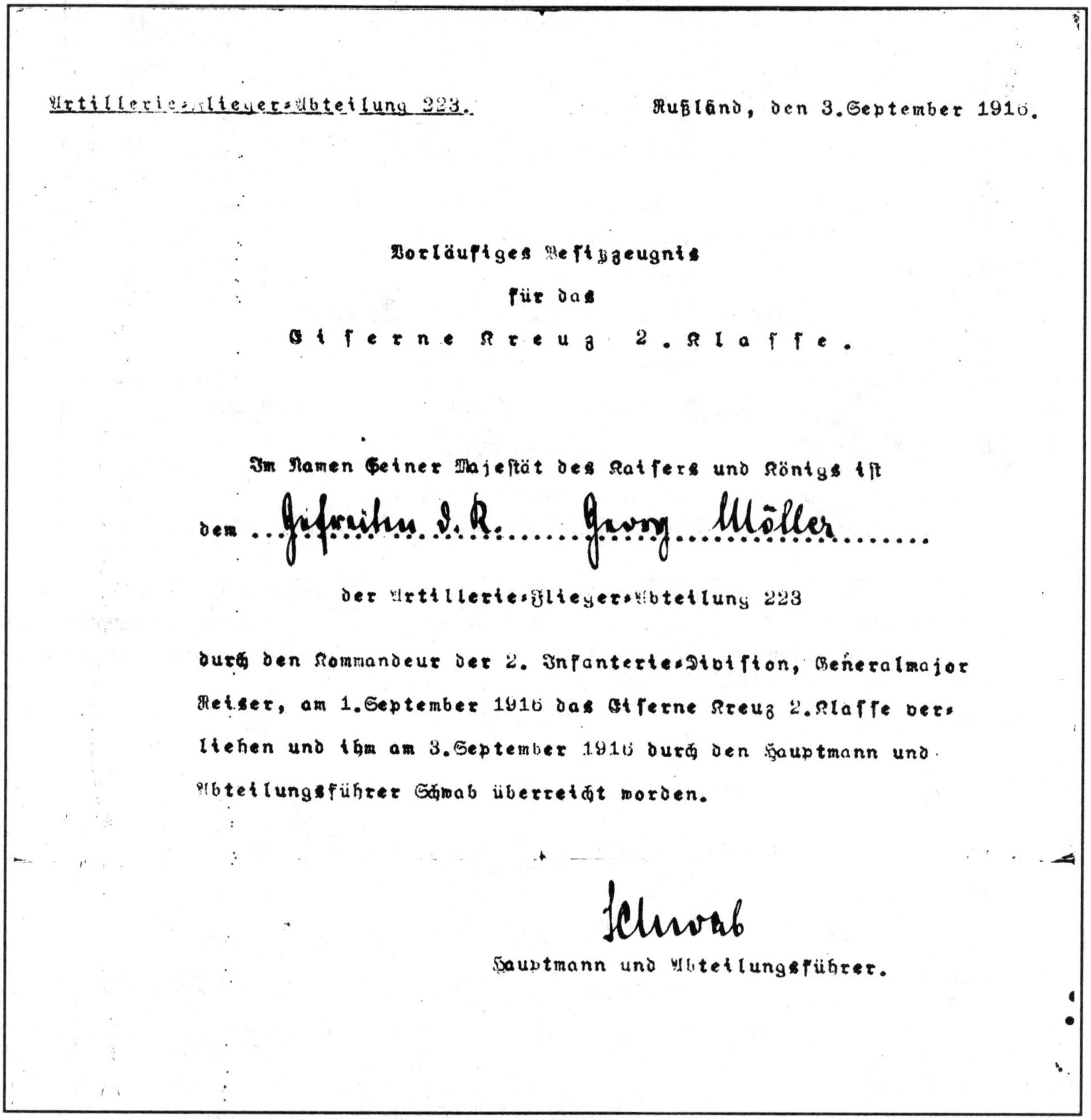

Artillerie-Flieger-Abteilung 223. Rußland, den 3.September 1916.

Vorläufiges Besitzzeugnis

für das

Eiserne Kreuz 2. Klasse.

Im Namen Seiner Majestät des Kaisers und Königs ist

dem Gefreiten d. R. Georg Möller

der Artillerie-Flieger-Abteilung 223

durch den Kommandeur der 2. Infanterie-Division, Generalmajor Reiser, am 1.September 1916 das Eiserne Kreuz 2.Klasse verliehen und ihm am 3.September 1916 durch den Hauptmann und Abteilungsführer Schwab überreicht worden.

Schwab

Hauptmann und Abteilungsführer.

Document 134 Preliminary Authorization Certificate, Type 1, to Gefreiten d. Res. Georg Möller

The document is a typed single-page carbon copy of the Preliminary Authorization Certificate for the Iron Cross 2nd Class given Gefreiten Möller. The Gothic lettering of the typewriter is quite beautiful and unusual. It measures 21.0 cm. wide x 32.8 cm. high. *(The example shows only the text area.)* The document was signed in black ink by Captain Schwab, the section leader, who also appears to have filled in the recipient's name. It was authorized by the 2nd Infantry Division at its Russian headquarters on 1 September 1916 and given on 3 September 1916. In the upper left corner the unit name is typed in red.

Between 1916 and 1918 when Möller attended Aircraft Mechanic School, he had been promoted to the rank of Corporal *(Unteroffizier)*.

Flugzeugmeisterei Adlershof.
Werkmeisterschule.

Zeugnis

über die bestandene Prüfung als Werkmeister für die Fliegertruppen.

Der .... Vizefeldwebel Georg M ö l l e r

geboren am .....25.2.91.... in ....H a m b u r g

hat am....15..Werkmeister-Ausbildungs-Kursus der Werftschulen der Flugzeugmeisterei Adlershof

vom.......1. Febr.18..... bis zum ....15. Mai 1918.......... teilgenommen.

Seine praktischen Fähigkeiten wurden mit

.......-- gut --

die theoretischen Kenntnisse mit

.......-- fast gut --

bewertet.

.......Auf Grund der am ...14.u.15.Mai 1918........... vor der unterzeichneten Kommission
abgelegten, mit

.......-- genügend --

beurteilten mündlichen Prüfung, erhält er das

Gesamtzeugnis

.......-- g e n ü g e n d --

Adlershof, den ......30. Mai............ 191 8

Die Prüfungskommission: _Stacker_

[signatures in pencil]

Berlin, den ....3. Juni.................. 1918.

Major u. Kommandeur der Flugzeugmeisterei.

Document 135   *School Certificate to Vizefeldwebel Möller*

Shown at the left is an Official Certificate, showing that Vizefeldwebel Georg Möller completed an Aircraft Mechanics course at the Technical School located at Adlershof. The document measures 21.0 cm. wide x 33.0 cm. high. He attended the school from 1 February until 15 May 1918. He was 27 years old at the time.

The document shows that his practical application was "good" *(gut)* and the theoretical knowledge was "very good" *(fast gut)*. He also successfully passed an oral examination. He passed all examinations satisfactorily *(genügend)* and was given this certificate on 3 June 1918.

The document has been signed in pencil by five instructors and the commander of the school. To the left of the signature and under the date is the purple ink official stamp of the school.

Vizefeldwebel Möller was eventually returned to his 223rd Artillery Aviation Unit where he served until the war ended.

Vizefeldwebel Möller also received the Hamburg War Merit Cross on 30 April 1918. It appears that he received this award while attending the Aircraft Mechanic School at Adlershof. From the Hamburg document, his rank appears to be that of Corporal *(Unteroffizier)* when he entered the school and when the course was completed, Möller was promoted to Vizefeldwebel.

The document shown below is the Authorization Certificate, Type 4, *(Bestizzeugnis)* for the Iron Cross 1st Class awarded to Georg Möller. It measures 21.0 cm. wide x 16.4 cm. high. The document is signed in black ink by a unit representative of the Field Artillery Regiment "von Scharnhorst."

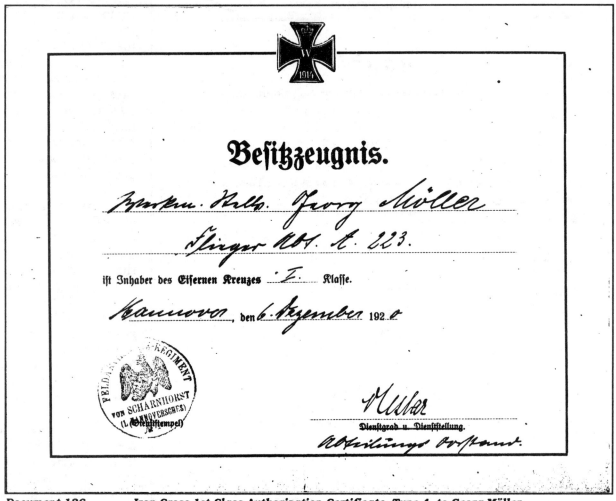

Document 136   *Iron Cross 1st Class Authorization Certificate, Type 4, to Georg Möller*

The document shows that it was signed in Hanover on 6 December 1920. To the left of the signature is the purple ink official stamp of the Field Artillery Regiment "von Scharnhorst."

On 20 March 1935 Georg Möller, residing in Harburg-Wilhelmsburg, received the Honor Cross for Front Combatants *(Ehrenkreuz für Frontkämpfer).*

✠ ✠ ✠

1914 First Class Iron Cross Documents

One of the unfortunate aspects of collecting documents is that more often than not the collector will be able to come by only one or two documents to the same individual. So in showing the reader only the 1st Class Iron Cross document in this section simply means that the author was unable to obtain other documents such as the individual's Iron Cross 2nd Class document.

The document shown below is a Preliminary Identification Certificate, Type 2, *(Vorläufiger Ausweis)* named to Territorial Reserve Lieutenant *(Leutnant d. Landwehr)* **STRATMANN**. There is no indication of his unit.

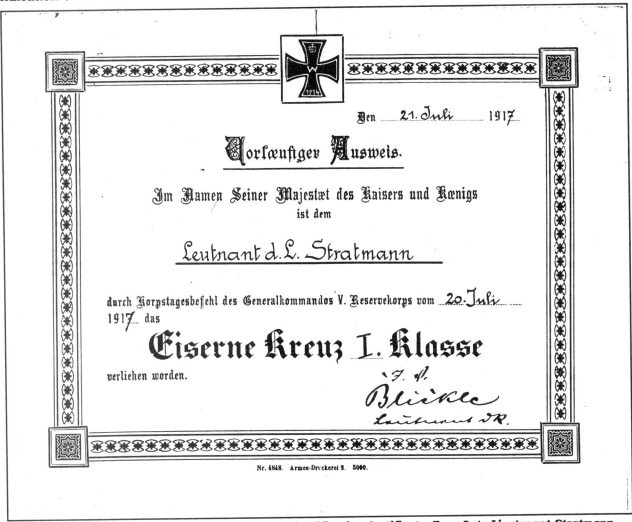

Document 137   Iron Cross 1st Class Preliminary Identification Certificate, Type 2, to Lieutenant Stratmann

The decorative document authorizing the Iron Cross 1st Class to Lt. Stratmann measures 21.6 cm. wide x 17.0 cm. high. It was issued on 21 July 1917, and authorized from the 20 July 1917 "Corps Orders of the Day" *(Korpstagesbefehl)* of the High Command of the Vth Reserve Corps. It has been signed in black ink by a Reserve Lieutenant. It is interesting that there is no official unit stamp. However, it is not absolutely necessary to have a unit stamp.

✠ ✠ ✠

The documents shown to the right and on the following page were authorized from the same headquarters of the 6th Army.

The document shown at right is an Official Certificate, Type 9, authorizing the Iron Cross 1st Class to Reserve Lieutenant *(Leutnant der Reserve)* **GÖTZ**. No unit is indicated.

The large document measures 21.2 cm. wide x 33.0 cm. high. It is dated 26 May 1917.

In the lower right corner is the purple ink official stamp of the High Command of the 6th Army.

There is no signature nor is there any indication that one is necessary on this particular form used by the 6th Army Headquarters.

It is of interest that both of the documents shown were dated on the 26th of the month.

Document 138 **Iron Cross 1st Class Official Certificate, Type 9, to Lt. Götz**

✠ ✠ ✠

The document shown at left is an Official Certificate, Type 9, authorizing the Iron Cross 1st Class to Territorial Reserve Lieutenant *(Leutnant der Landwehr I)* **OVERHAMM**. No unit is indicated.

The large document measures 21.2 cm. wide x 33.0 cm. high. It is dated 26 June 1917.

In the lower right corner is the black ink official stamp of the High Command of the 6th Army.

There is no signature nor is there any indication that one is necessary on this particular form used by the 6th Army Headquarters.

Document 139   Iron Cross 1st Class Official Certificate, Type 9, to Lt. Overhamm

J. Eicher Collection

✠ ✠ ✠

The document shown below is an Indentification Certificate, Type 4, *(Ausweis)* named to Senior Duty Sergeant *(Vizefeldwebel)* **MÜLLER I**, who was serving in the 4th Guard Field Engineers Company (*4. Garde Feldpionier Komp.)*, 100th Engineer Battalion, 5th Guard Infantry Division.

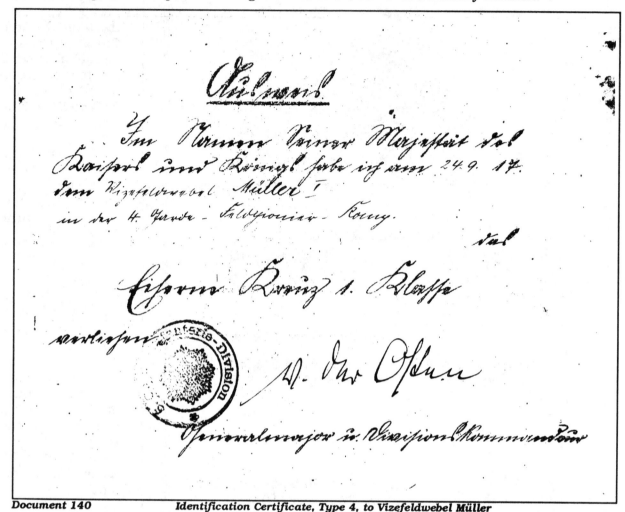

Document 140   *Identification Certificate, Type 4, to Vizefeldwebel Müller*

The poorly printed document measures 21.0 cm. wide x 16.5 cm. high. It is dated 24 September 1917 and, most interestingly, has been signed in black ink by Major General von der Osten, the division commander. To the left of the signature is the green ink official stamp of the 5th Guard Infantry Division.

The 5th Guard Infantry Division was organized February 1917. It appeared for the first time on the front line about 20 March 1917 between Craonne and Hurtebise where it suffered heavy losses during an engagement between 16 and 18 April 1917. Relieved on 4 May 1917, the division went to a calm sector in the region of Preqmontreq. On 5 June 1917, it was sent to rest in the region north and northwest of Laon. On 20 June 1917 it was located in the region of Sissonne, where it remained until 7 July 1917. On 7 July 1917, the division arrived in the Californie Plateau sector where it executed a violent attack against enemy positions on 19 July 1917. It was relieved on 27 July, reinforced and rested in the region of Mauregny en Haye and Barenton sur Cerre. Around 20 August 1917 the division relieved the 43rd Reserve Infantry Division on the Chemin des Dames sector between Pantheon and La Royere where the division suffered heavy casualties during the French offensive of 23 October 1917. It was during this period that Vizefeldwebel Müller was awarded the Iron Cross 1st Class having previously been decorated with the Iron Cross 2nd Class. In the region of Vervins at the beginning of November, the division went into the front line near Hargicourt at the end of November 1917. According to US military intelligence sources the 5th Guard Infantry Division was considered to be one of the best units of the German Army.

✠ ✠ ✠

The document shown below is a Preliminary Identification Certificate, Type 2, *(Vorlaeufiger Ausweis)* to First Lieutenant *(Oberleutnant)* **REINHARD EBUR**, serving in the 52nd Fighter Squadron *(Jagdstaffel 52)*.

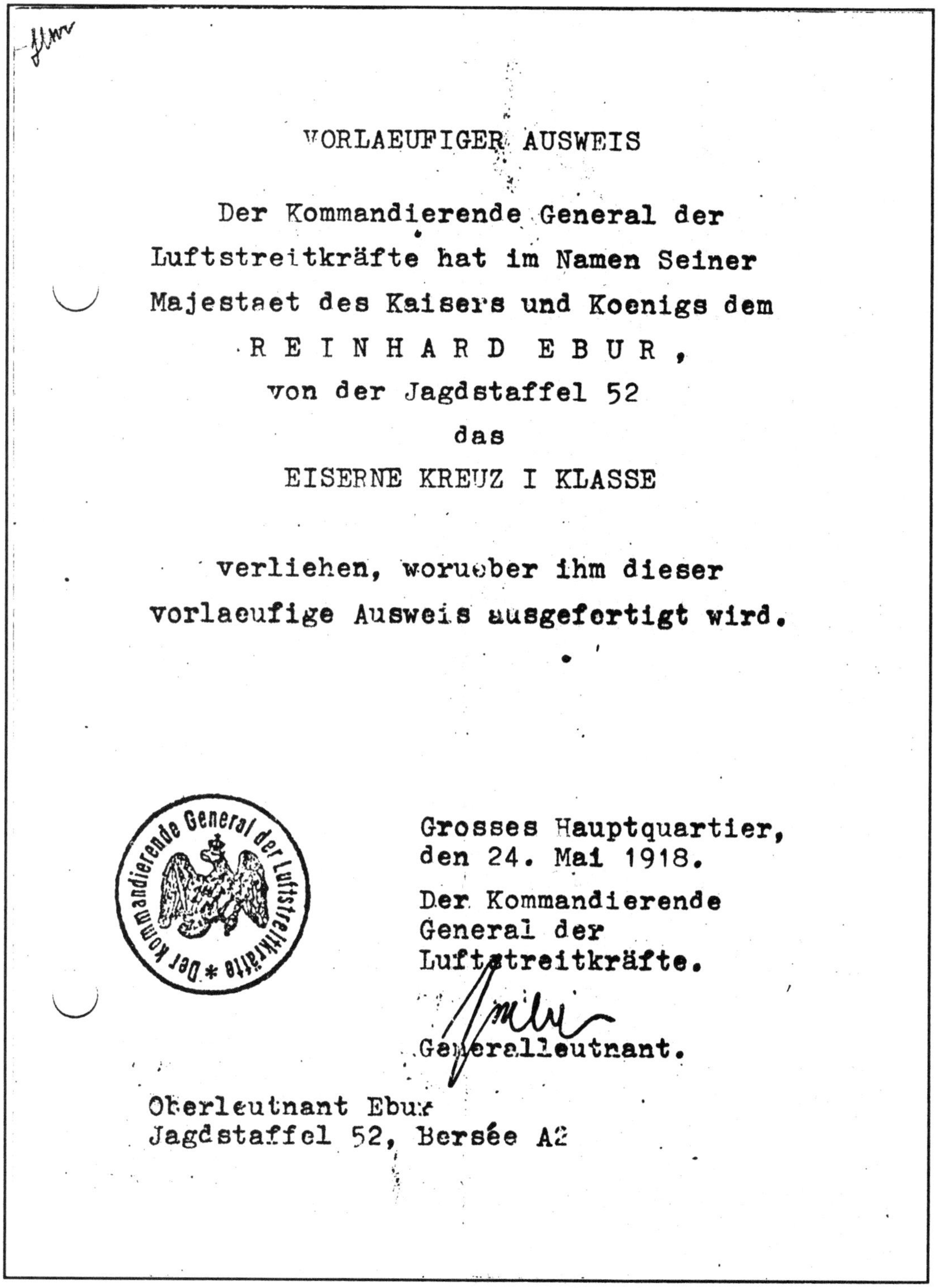

VORLAEUFIGER AUSWEIS

Der Kommandierende General der Luftstreitkräfte hat im Namen Seiner Majestaet des Kaisers und Koenigs dem

R E I N H A R D E B U R ,

von der Jagdstaffel 52

das

EISERNE KREUZ I KLASSE

verliehen, worueber ihm dieser vorlaeufige Ausweis ausgefertigt wird.

Der Kommandierende General der Luftstreitkräfte *

Grosses Hauptquartier,
den 24. Mai 1918.

Der Kommandierende
General der
Luftstreitkräfte.

Generalleutnant.

Oberleutnant Ebur
Jagdstaffel 52, Bersée A2

Document 141 Preliminary Identification Certificate, Type 2, to Oberleutnant Reinhard Ebur

The document, shown in actual size, measures 14.2 cm. wide x 19.2 cm. high.

The cetificate appears to have been typed. It was signed at the Supreme Headquarters of the Commanding General of the Air Service.

The document is dated 24 May 1918 and signed in black ink by a Lt. General. To the left of the signature is the purple ink official stamp of the Headquarters of the Commanding General of the Air Service.

In the left margin are seen the two punched holes which indicate that this document was a part of the military service record of Lt. Ebur.

The 52nd Fighter Squadron was stationed on the western front. There is no indication whether 1st Lt. Ebur was a flying or an administrative officer.

✠ ✠ ✠

The document shown below is an Authorization Certificate, Type 4, *(Besitz-Zeugnis)* named to Sergeant *(Sergeanten)* **ALFRED LEHMANN**, who, when decorated with the Iron Cross 1st Class was serving in the 10th Grenadier Regiment, 21st Infantry Brigade, 11th Infantry Division.

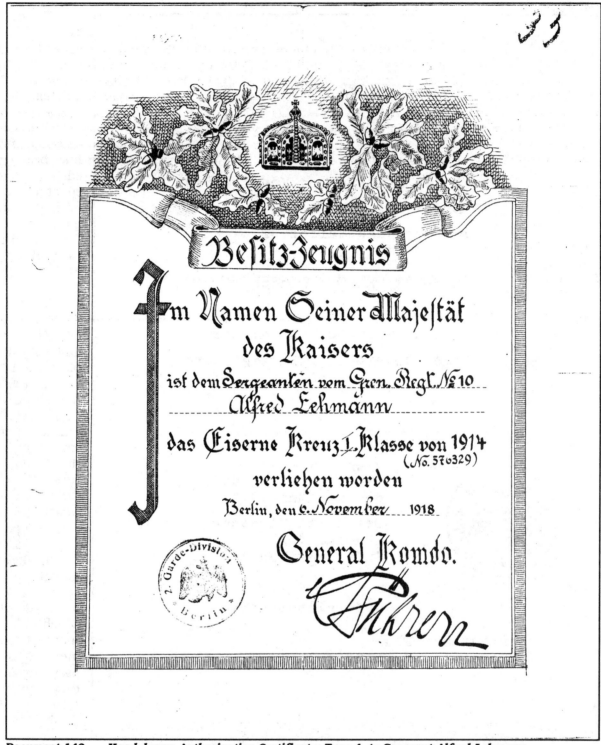

Document 142   Hand-drawn Authorization Certificate, Type 4, to Sergeant Alfred Lehmann

What makes this document very unique is that it has been entirely **_hand-drawn_** in dark red ink. The name, date, number and signature are in black ink. This beautiful document measures 21.4 cm. wide x 25.8 cm. high. It is dated 6 November 1918 and was signed in Berlin by a representative of the High Command. To the left of the signature is the purple ink official stamp of the 2nd Guard Infantry Division in Berlin. Records available show that the 10th Grenadier Regiment was attached to the 11th Infantry Division from the beginning until the end of the war and the 2nd Guard Infantry Division did not show the 10th Grenadier Regiment in the Table of Organization. Another question is what the meaning is of the *"No. 576329"* that appears to have been added. In the left margin is the usual two punched holes indicating that this document was a part of the military service record of Sergeant Lehmann.

On 1 March 1918, the division relieved the 51st Reserve Infantry Division in the Butte de Mesnil and held that sector until it was relieved on 15 April 1918. Returning to the front again on April 20th, the division was replaced by the 202nd Infantry Division on 23 May 1918. The division rested in the Cuiscard area for about 10 days. On June 9th, the division reinforced the Montdidier-Noyon battlefront south of Thiescourt west of Noyon. The 11th Infantry Division, as an assault division, attacked on the first day of the offensive on a 1500 yard front. Compiegne was to be its objective; however, it succeded in occupying Machemont. During this major attack, the division suffered heavy losses. The division was relieved and rested for a short time and then returned to the frontline action near Rubescourt on 19 July 1918. In this action, the division again suffered many casualties. The division was still on the front when the war ended.

✠ ✠ ✠

The document booklet shown below is a Preliminary Identification Certificate, Type 2, *(Vorlaeufiger Ausweis)* that was carried by Second Lieutenant *(Leutnant)* **M. DANIELS** who was serving in the 3rd Single Seater Fighter Unit *(Kampfeinsitzerstaffel 3)*.

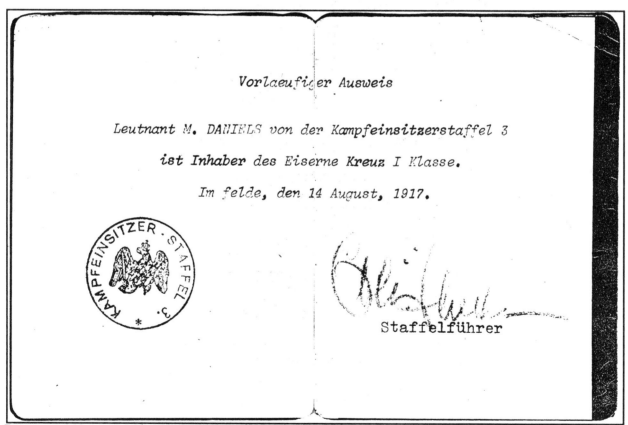

Vorlaeufiger Ausweis

Leutnant M. DANIELS von der Kampfeinsitzerstaffel 3

ist Inhaber des Eiserne Kreuz I Klasse.

Im felde, den 14 August, 1917.

Staffelführer

Document 143   *1st Class Iron Cross Preliminary Identification Booklet carried by Lt. Daniels*

The document booklet authorizing the 1st Class Iron Cross measures 16.6 cm. wide x 10.8 cm high. It is composed of an inside sheet, typed and signed in purple indelible pencil by the unit commander and dated in the field on 14 August 1917. To the left of the signature is the purple ink official stamp of the 3rd Single Seater Fighter Unit. This has had a cover made from a file cover onto which the certificate was pasted. This type of identification was carried by the recipient.

✠ ✠ ✠

Besitz-Zeugnis.

Im Namen Sr. Majestät des Kaisers und Königs wurde
am _15. August_ 1918, dem
Leutnant Richter
Führer der 7. Komp. F. R. 390
für hervorragende Tapferkeit vor dem Feinde das unterm
6. August 1914 gestiftete

Eiserne Kreuz _I_ Klasse

verliehen, über dessen rechtmäßigen Besitz ihm dieses Zeugnis ausgefertigt worden ist.

Für die Richtigkeit:

Leutn. u. Regts. Adj.

Document 144   **1st Class Iron Cross Authorization Certificate, Type 4, to Lt. Richter**

The document shown on the facing page is an Authorization Certificate, Type 4, *(Besitz-Zeugnis)* to Second Lieutenant *(Leutnant)* **RICHTER** who received the Iron Cross 1st Class while serving as the company commander of the 7th Company, 390th Infantry Regiment, 211th Infantry Brigade, 211th Infantry Division.

The document appears to have had the edges cut down, however, an identical document is seen on page 59 *(Document 43)* which measures 20.4 cm. wide x 33.3 cm high. The recipient's name, date, and assignment as well as the regimental adjutant's title are written in black ink. The document is dated 15 August 1918 and signed in purple indelible pencil by the regimental adjutant. To the left of the signature is the purple ink official stamp of the 390th Infantry Regiment.

The 211th Infantry Division was organized on 15 September 1916. The 390th Infantry Regiment joined the division, after being transferred from the 16th Reserve Division, during January 1917. The division held the Soissons sector until around March 20th. On this date it was assigned to the line at Vauxaillon where it opposed the French attack of 16 April 1917.

Moving ahead to 1918 when Lt. Richter was decorated with the 1st Class Iron Cross, having already received the 2nd Class, the division was relieved on 8 March 1918 in the Chamouille area and went to rest near Laon until the 19th. It marched toward its assigned sector east of La Fere by Crepy en Laonnois, arriving there on 20 March 1918. It followed up the attack against the French lines at La Fere, crossing the Oise river near Travecy, until the 22nd, when the division was again engaged west of Travecy. The division advanced through Farguiers, Quessy, Liez, Chauny, Quirezy, and Varesnes until the line was stabilized near the Aisne Canel at Manicamp and Champs. It held this sector until 27 May 1918. After the French retreat following the German advance to the Marne river, the division advanced as far as Moulin sous Touvent-Nampcel. It held that sector until the beginning of July when it withstood a French attack on 3 July 1918. After this attack, the division was relieved by the 15th Infantry Division.

The division rested and was returned to the line on 20 July 1918 at Mercin-Vauxbuin to oppose the Allied counterthrust and remained in the line until 3 August 1918. It was during these actions that Lt. Richter was cited for outstanding leadership and bravery in action and rewarded with the 1st Class Iron Cross.

After the division's withdrawal from the front it was sent to Charleville and disbanded*. The men of the 390th Infantry Regiment were sent as replacements to the 42nd Infantry Division.

✠ ✠ ✠

---

* When the effective strength of a division has reached a minimum, it is disbanded.

The Document shown below is a Preliminary Identification Certificate, Type 2, *(Vorlaeufiger Ausweis)* to Second Lieutenant *(Leutnant)* **FRIEDRICH LINDNER**, who, when awarded the 1st Class Iron Cross, was serving in the 2nd Battalion, 351st Infantry Regiment, 245th Infantry Brigade, 123rd Infantry Division.

Den *25. April* 191*8*

Vorlæufiger Ausweis.

Im Namen Seiner Majestæt des Kaisers und Kœnigs

ist dem

Leutnant Friedrich Lindner, J.R. 351,

durch Korpstagesbefehl des Generalkommandos V. Reservekorps vom

21. April 191*8* das

Eiserne Kreuz 1. Klasse

verliehen worden.

Major z. Dtstn.

Document 145   ***Iron Cross 1st Class Preliminary Identification Certificate, Type 2, to Lt. Friedrich Lindner***

The plain printed document measures 21.0 cm. wide x 16.5 cm. high. It was signed in purple indelible pencil by a major who was the battalion commander on 25 April 1918. The award was authorized by the Corps Orders of the Day *(Korpstagesbefehl)* of the Headquarters Command of the Vth Reserve Infantry Corps *(Generalkommandos V. Reservekorps)* on 21 April 1918. Adjacent to the signature is the purple ink official stamp of the Saxon 2nd Battalion of the 351st Infantry Regiment.

During 1916 the 351st Infantry Regiment became part of the 88th Infantry Division. The division was holding a position on the Drisviaty Lake on the eastern front. It occupied this position from September 1915 until September 1917. In May 1917, the 123rd Infantry Division exchanged the 425th Infantry Regiment for the 351st Infantry Regiment. The 351st was now a part of the 123rd Infantry Division.

Around November the division was transferred from the eastern front to the western front and on 22 November 1917 took its position on the Verdun front south of Bezonvaux. It stayed the entire winter and held the Bezonvaux sector until 3 June 1918 when it was relieved by the 7th Reserve Infantry Division. While in this sector, Lt. Lindner displayed outstanding leadership and bravery in action and received the 1st Class Iron Cross. He had previously received the Iron Cross 2nd Class.

✠ ✠ ✠

The document shown below is a Preliminary Identification Certificate, Type 2, *(Vorläufiger Ausweis)* named to Reserve Sergeant *(Vizefeldwebel d. Reserve)* **WILHELM DEHNBOSTEL,** who, when awarded the 1st Class Iron Cross, was serving in the 3rd Company, 32nd Machine Gun Sharpshooter Unit *(3. Komp. Maschinengewehr Scharfschützen Abteilung 32),* attached to the 4th Guard Infantry Division.

Document 146   *Iron Cross 1st Class Preliminary Identification Certificate, Type 2,*   D. Pirozzo Collection
to Vizefeldwebel Wilhelm Dehnbostel

The plain printed document measures 20.8 cm. wide x 16.5 cm. high. It was signed in black ink by the unit commander who was a captain. The document is dated 16 August 1918 and was issued in the field *(Im Felde).* In the left lower corner in the area marked with the inscription "Service Stamp" *(Dienststempel)* is seen the purple ink official stamp of the 32nd Machine Gun Sharpshooter Unit.

The 32nd MG Unit was attached to the 4th Guard Infantry Division sometime in 1917. In 1918 when Sgt. Dehnbostel was decorated with the Iron Cross 1st Class, the division was engaged 27 July 1918 southeast of Fere en Tardenois. It fell back toward Fismes on 1-2 August, from where the division was assigned to the Courlandon-Breuil sector where the division held from 14 August to the beginning of September 1918. It was during this action that Sgt. Dehnbostel was cited for bravery and awarded the Iron Cross 1st Class. He had already received the Iron Cross 2nd Class.

✠ ✠ ✠

The document shown below is a Preliminary Identification Certificate, Type 2, *(Vorläufiger Ausweis)* to Cavalry Captain *(Rittmeister)* **PAUL KLINGER**, who, when awarded the Iron Cross 1st Class, was serving as the commandant of the staff attached to the High Command of the XVth Bavarian Reserve Corps.

Vorläufiger Ausweis.

Im Namen Seiner Majestät des Kaisers wurde vom Kommandierenden General XV. bayer. Reserve-Korps

dem *Rittmeister Paul Klinger, Kommandant der K. G. Qu. beim Gen. Kdo. XV. bay. Rf Korps* das

Eiserne Kreuz I. Klasse

verliehen.

K. H. Qu., den *1. Mai* 191*7*.

(Dienstsiegel.)

Document 147 *Iron Cross 1st Class Preliminary Identification Certificate, Type 2,*
to Rittmeister Paul Klinger

The attractive document measures 20.4 cm. wide x 16.5 cm. high. It was signed on 1 May 1917. To the right of the date is the purple ink official stamp of the High Command of the XVth Bavarian Reserve Corps. There is no signature on the document. To the left of the stamp is the initial of the recorder.

Rittmeister Klinger had previously been awarded the Iron Cross 2nd Class.

Shown below is the Authorization Certificate for the Black Wound Badge given to Rittmeister Klinger who was still serving at the headquarters of the XVth Bavarian Reserve Corps.

General - Kommando
XV. bayer. Reserve-Korps.

Besitzeugnis

über das dem _Rittmeister Klinger des Generalkommandos_

XV.bayer. Reserve - Korps

am _23. Mai_ 1918 verliehene

Abzeichen für Verwundete in _schwarz._

K.H.Qu., _23. Mai 1918._

Major
und Chef des Generalstabs.

Document 148   **Wound Badge Certificate to Rittmeister Klinger**

The document measures 20.7 cm. wide x 16.5 cm. high. It was signed in pencil by Major von Reichert, Chief of the General Staff on 23 May 1918. In the lower center is the purple ink official stamp of the headquarters of the XVth Bavarian Reserve Corps. The stamp is the same as seen on the Iron Cross 1st Class document to Rittmeister Klinger on the facing page.

The document shown below is a Preliminary Authorization Certificate, Type 1, *(Vorläufiges Besitzzeugnis)* named to Reserve Second Lieutenant *(Leutnant der Reserve)* **BRUNO BRINKMANN**, serving at the time he was decorated with the Iron Cross 1st Class in the 3rd Company, 232nd Reserve Infantry Regiment, 213th Infantry Brigade, 107th Infantry Division.

Document 149   *Preliminary Authorization Certificate, Type 1, to Reserve Lt. Bruno Brinkmann*

The attractivly drawn and printed document measures 25.0 cm. wide x 20.9 cm high. It was signed in purple indelible pencil by the commander of the 107th Infantry Division on 21 December 1917. The document was issued in the field *(Im Felde).* To the left is the purple ink official stamp of the 107th Infantry Division. Along the upper border are two punched holes indicating that the document was a part of the military service record of Lt. Brinkmann.

In January 1916 the 107th Infantry Division was in reserve in the vicinity of Dvinsk on the Russian front until 15 March 1916. On March 18th the division took over the sector north of Postavy. From May until 20 June it secured the sector near Smorgoni. At the end of June the division was assigned to meet the Russian offensive in Volhynia. Between 21 June until the middle of July the division was engaged in several actions in the area between the Styr and the Stokhod. In August and September it was still in Volhynia near the Koval-Rovno railroad. The division stayed in this region and occupied the sector west of Kachovka until the beginning of November 1917.

Relieved from the Russian front, the division was reassigned to the western front on 9 November 1917. It detrained near Cambrai on the 18th of November. From November 21st the division was engaged in several actions southwest of Cambrai and was relieved from the front around the end of

December 1917. It was in one of these actions that Lt. Brinkmann was cited for leadership and awarded the Iron Cross 1st Class. He had already been decorated with the Iron Cross 2nd Class.

The unusual document shown below is a Black Wound Badge Authorization Certificate *(Besitzzeugnis)* to Lt. Bruno Brinkmann showing that he had been wounded in action on 11 May 1918. He was still serving at the time in the 3rd Company of the 232nd Reserve Infantry Regiment.

Document 150   *Wound Badge Certificate to Leutnant Bruno Brinkmann*

The document measures 19.0 cm. wide x 26.2 cm. high. It is dated 11 May 1918 and issued in the field (Im Felde). In the right lower corner is the purple indelible pencil signature of the regimental commander. In the lower left corner is the purple ink official stamp of the 232rd Reserve Infantry Regiment. Along the upper edge are two punched holes indicating that this certificate was a part of the military record of Lt. Brinkmann.

During 1918 when Lt. Brinkmann was wounded in action his unit was on the front at Gonnelieu. On 21 March 1918, a German offensive began and the 232rd Reserve Infantry Division advanced by way of Mesnil and Avelny Woods. It was relieved and sent to rest on 16 April 1918. Returning to the front on May 16th, the division took up positions at Morlancourt and held this sector until the 24 May 1918. It was during the German offensive that Lt. Brinkmann was wounded.

✠ ✠ ✠

The document shown below is a Transcript *(Abschrift)* of the Authorization to wear the Pilot Badge *(Abzeichen für Flugzeugführer)* indicating Corporal *(Unteroffizier)* **KARL GREGOR** is a qualified pilot. He was assigned at the time to the 210th Artillery Spotter Aviation Unit *(Artillerie Fliegerabteilung 210)*.

Abschrift

Der Kommandierende
General Der Luftstreitkräfte

Gr.H.Qu, den 7. April.1917

Ich verleihe

dem   Unteroffizier GREGOR

Artillerie   Fliegerabteilung   210

das Abzeichen für   FLUGZEUGFÜHRER

Document 151   *Transcript of Authorization to wear Pilot Badge by Unteroffizier Gregor*

The document measures 20.3 cm. wide by 14.5 cm. high. It was dated on 7 April 1917 at High Headquarters of the German Air Service. It was signed in ink by Lt. General Ernst Wilhelm von Hoeppner,* the commanding general of the German Air Service. In the lower left corner is the red ink official authenticating stamp of the Headquarters of the Commanding General. It could be that at this time Pilot Corporal Gregor was assigned to the 210th Artillery Spotting Aviation Unit as a pilot.

It appears that shortly after being assigned to the Artillery Spotter Aviation Unit, Pilot Corporal Gregor was cited for outstanding and brave actions which resulted in his being recommended and awarded the Iron Cross 1st Class. He had previously been decorated with the Iron Cross 2nd Class.

* Lt. General Ernst von Hoeppner was appointed as Commanding General of the German Air Service on 15 November 1916. He was awarded the Prussian Pour le Mérite Order in recognition of his development, planning and operations of the German Air Service between 15 November 1916 and 8 April 1917.

"The History of the Prussian Pour le Mérite Order, 1888-1918," Volume III, by W.E.Hamelman, page 484, entry 217.

Lt. General Ernst Wilhelm von Hoeppner

The document shown below is a Preliminary Identification Certificate, Type 2, *(Vorläufiger Ausweis)* named to Pilot Corporal *(Flugzeugführer Unteroffizier)* **KARL GREGOR**. He was serving at the time of his being decorated with the Iron Cross 1st Class in the 210th Artillery Spotter Aviation Unit that was attached to the XVIIth Army Group.

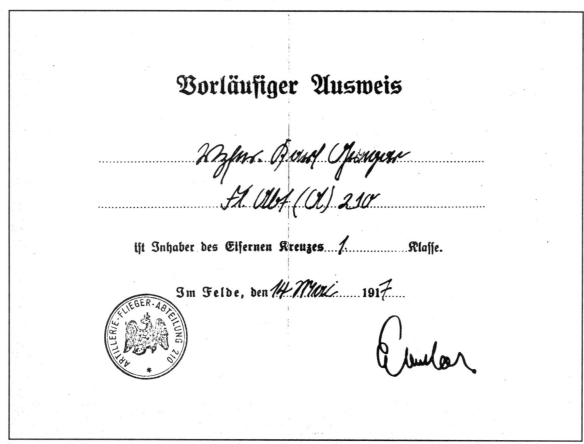

Document 152   ***Iron Cross 1st Class Preliminary Identification Certificate, Type 2, to Pilot Corporal Gregor***

The plain document is printed on a yellowish-brown enameled paper and measures 20.0 cm. wide x 15.0 cm. high. It is signed in ink by, presumably, the unit commander and dated 14 May 1917. Across to the left is the purple ink official stamp of the 210th Artillery Spotting Aviation Unit.

✠ ✠ ✠

The document shown below is a Preliminary Authorization Certificate, Type 1, *(Vorläufiges Besitzzeugnis)* named to Captain *(Hauptmann)* **ERICH ANDERSON** awarding him the Iron Cross 1st Class. Captain Anderson was serving in the 401st Infantry Regiment, 402nd Infantry Brigade, 201st Infantry Division.

201. Inf.=Division   **D.St.Q., den** 27. 1. **19**17.

Vorläufiges Besitzzeugnis
♔ ♔ ♔

Auf Befehl Seiner Majeſtät des Kaiſers und Königs habe ich dem *Hauptmann Erich Anderson vom Infanterie-Regiment 401* das **Eiſerne Kreuz** *erſter* Klaſſe verliehen.

Generalleutnant und Diviſions=Kommandeur.

Otto Kircher, herzogl. Hofbuchdr., Blankenburg am Harz.

Document 153   *Preliminary Authorization Certificate, Type 1, to Hauptman Erich Anderson*

The attractive document measures 20.8 cm. wide x 16.5 cm. high. It was signed by a representative of the commanding officer at Staff Headquarters of the 201st Infantry Division on 27 January 1917. On the lower left side is the purple ink official stamp of the 201st Infantry Division. The document shows in the left margin two punched holes indicating the document had been placed in the military file of Captain Anderson. He had previously been awarded the Iron Cross 2nd Class.

The 201st Infantry Division was formed, mostly of recruits from various army depots, at the beginning of July 1916. This was the time of the start of the Russian Broussilov offensive on the eastern front. The 401st Infantry Regiment* along with 402nd, 403rd, and the 404th Infantry Regiments were assigned to the division. When the division was complete it was sent to the eastern front to counter the Russian advance north of Baranovitchi.

Here the division held its assigned sector from July 1916 until December 1917. During this period, the division was engaged in two major actions, one in November 1916 and the other in November 1917. It was during the November 1916 action that Captain Anderson was cited for distinguished leadership and bravery in action.

By 15 December 1917 the 201st Infantry Division was transferred to the western front and assigned to the right bank of the Moselle northeast of Pont a Mousson. By February 1918 Captain Anderson was transferred from the 401st to the 403rd Infantry Regiment where he commanded the 1st Infantry Battalion.

---

* Previously called the Allenstein Regiment.

During 1918, the 201st Infantry Divison was engaged in several major engagements on the western front and suffered heavy losses.

On 2 June 1918, Captain Anderson, commanding the Ist Battalion, 403rd Infantry Regiment, received his fifth wound in action and was awarded the Golden Wound Badge *(see below)*.

After suffering extremely heavy losses, the 201st Infantry Division was dissolved on 22 October 1918 and the remaining troops were assigned to other regiments until the end of the war.

Shown below is the Authorization Certificate for the Golden Wound Badge *(mattgelbe Abzeichen für Verwundete)* given to Captain Anderson.

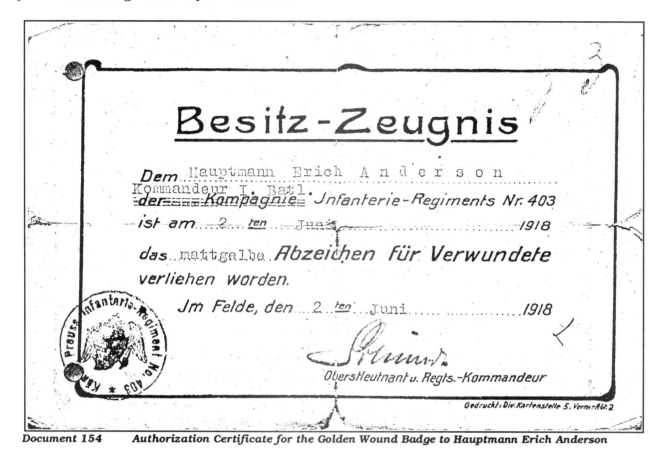

Document 154   *Authorization Certificate for the Golden Wound Badge to Hauptmann Erich Anderson*

The document, shown actual size, measures 16.8 cm. wide x 11.0 cm. high. It was signed in purple indelible pencil by the regimental commander and is dated 2 June 1918. It was given while the regiment was in the field *(Im Felde)*. In the left bottom corner is the purple ink official stamp of the 403rd Infantry Regiment. At the left edge are the two punched holes indicating that this document had been placed in the military records of Captain Anderson.

Other awards to Captain Erich Anderson during the war included the Hamburg War Merit Cross from the City of Hamburg on 25 February 1918. On 29 April 1918 he also received the Prussian Royal Hohenzollern House Order Knights Cross with Swords *(das Kreuz der Ritter des Königlichen Hausordens von Hohenzollern mit Schwerten)*.

After the war, on 28 August 1933 Erich Anderson, now holding the rank of Major, was awarded the East Prussian Cross *(Ostpreußen-Kreuz)* in recognition of his military leadership in Danzig and East Prussia. On 24 May 1935 he received the Honor Cross for Combatants *(Ehrenkreuz für Frontkämpfer)* while he was living in Berlin-Steglitz.

The Hungarian War Commemorative Medal *(die Ungarische Kriegserrinnerungs Medaille)* was given to Major Anderson on 7 January 1937.

Another interesting document to Anderson during the war is shown below. It is a Transmittal Letter advising Captain Anderson, serving at the time as commander of the Ist Battalion of the 403rd Infantry Regiment, that he has been awarded the Friedrich August Cross 1st and 2nd Classes *(Friedrich August Kreuz I. und II. Klasse)*. It originated from the Military Chancellory of the Grand Duke of Oldenburg on 25 June 1918.

Militär-Kanzlei
S. K. H.
des Großherzogs von Oldenburg.

Oldenburg, den 25. Juni 1918.

Seine Königliche Hoheit der Grossherzog haben Euer Hochwohlgeboren als Mitglied des Deutschen Schulschiffvereins und Jnhaber des E.K.I und II "das Friedrich August Kreuz I. und II. Klasse" verliehen, deren Abzeichen hiermit übersandt werden.

J.V.

Major und Flügeladjutant.

An

Herrn Hauptmann Erich A n d e r s e n ,

Kommandeur I /403

B e r l i n W.

Kaiser Allee 108.

Document 155   **Transmittal Letter to Captain Erich Anderson**

The document states that Captain Anderson as a member of the German School Ship Association* *(Mitglied des Deutschen Schulschiffvereins)*, and holder of the Iron Cross 1st and 2nd Classes *(Inhaber des E.K.I und II)*, is elgible for the Friedrich August Cross 1st and 2nd Classes.

The document measures 20.5 cm. wide x 16.5 cm. high. It has been typed and is signed in black ink by an aide-de-camp.

☩ ☩ ☩

---

* How a membership in a School Ship Association has any bearing on being decorated with the Frederick August Cross 1st and 2nd Classes, a military decoration, remains a mystery.

Presentation of the Iron Cross 1st Class by Emperor Wilhelm II

The photo at left shows Ludwig Jeckert, indicated by the arrow, with his unit before he attended Flying School becoming a pilot and subsequently assigned to the 56th Fighter Squadron. He went on to score four aerial victories before the war ended.

✠ ✠ ✠

The document shown below is a Preliminary Identification Certificate, Type 2, *(Vorlaeufiger Ausweis)* given to Pilot Corporal *(Flugzeugführer Unteroffizier)* **LUDWIG JECKERT,** who was serving at the time of his being decorated with the Iron Cross 1st Class in the 56th Fighter Squadron *(Jagdstaffel 56).*

```
              VORLAEUFIGER AUSWEIS

     Der Kommandierende General der Luftstreitkräfte
     hat im Namen Seiner Majestaet des Kaisers und Koenigs
                        dem
             UNTEROFFIZIER LUDWIG JECKERT ,
              von der Jagdstaffel 56
                        das
             EISERNE KREUZ I KLASSE
           verliehen, worueber ihm dieser
     vorlaeufige Ausweis ausgefertigt wird.

                    Grosses Hauptquartier,
                    den 22. August 1918.

                    Der Kommandierende
                    General der
                    Luftstreitkräfte.
```

Document 156   *Iron Cross 1st Class Preliminary Identification Certificate, Type 2, to Unteroffizier Ludwig Jeckert*

The simple typed document on rather heavy textured paper measures 20.7 cm. wide x 13.3 cm. high. It was typed at the Headquarters of the Commanding General of the German Air Service, dated 22 August 1918 and authorized with a black ink stamped facsimile signature of Lt. General Ernst Wilhelm von Hoeppner. To the left of the signature block is the blue ink official stamp of the Headquarters of the Commanding General of the German Air Service.

The studio photo at right shows Ludwig Jeckert wearing only the Black Wound Badge. This could indicate the photo was taken before his receiving the Iron Cross 1st Class or becoming a pilot.

The **Cross & Cockade Journal, Volume I, Number 4, Winter 1960,** contains an excellent article by Heinz Nowarra regarding the "War Diary of the Royal Prussian Jagdstaffel 56." It shows that the 56th Fighter Squadron was formed at the Squadron School at Paderborn on 20 October 1917. By January 1918 the newly formed squadron transferred to the front and established its first base in France. On 3 February 1918, the first flights of the squadron commenced and by February 9th the first aerial combats took place.

Studio Photo of Ludwig Jeckert

On 12 July 1918 Unteroffizier Ludwig Jeckert was assigned to the 56th Fighter Squadron. It appears that he was a qualified pilot at the time of his arrival into the squadron. On 31 July 1918, Pilot Corporal Jeckert successfully shot down a British Camel over Ypres at 18:45. This was his first aerial victory.

On 5 September 1918, Jeckert scored his next victory by shooting down a second Camel over Lenvelere at 18:25. This brought the squadron's total victories to 49.

Jeckert scored again by bringing down an A.R. over Morswede at 8:00 in the morning of 28 September 1918. This brought his score to three. An R.E. 8 was brought down over Zonnebeeke at 8:30 am by Pilot Corporal Jeckert, making his total aerial victories four. This was the last victory for Jeckert and by 12 November 1918, the squadron aircraft were returned to Germany. On 14 November 1918, the 56th Fighter Squadron was demobilized in Königsberg, East Prussia, having achieved a total of 63 aerial victories.

The document shown below is a Transcript (*Abschrift*) of the authorization to wear the Pilot Badge (*Abzeichen für Flugzeugführer*) and indicates Corporal Ludwig Jeckert was a qualified pilot.

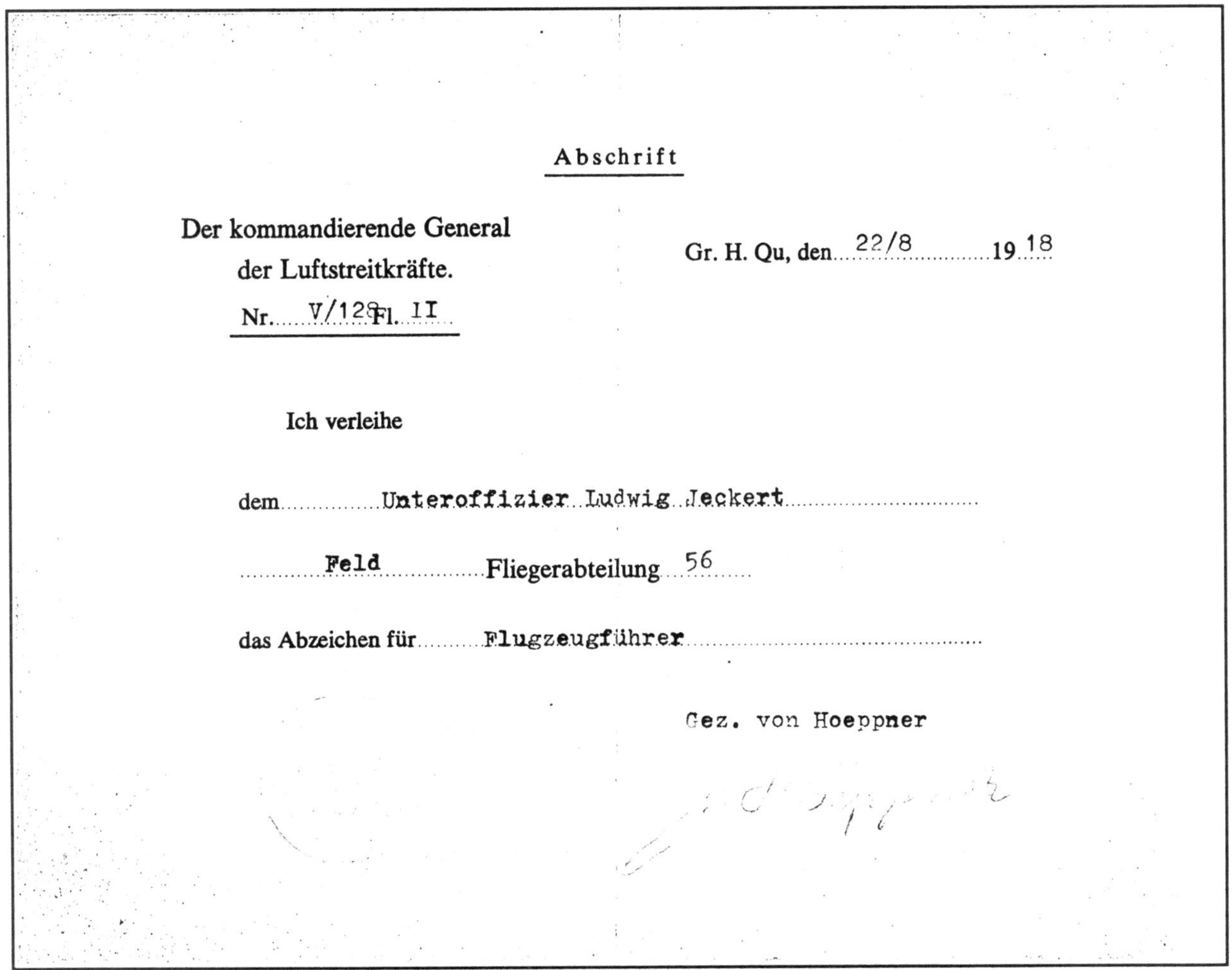

Abschrift

Der kommandierende General
der Luftstreitkräfte.

Nr. V/12 Fl. II

Gr. H. Qu, den 22/8 19 18

Ich verleihe

dem Unteroffizier Ludwig Jeckert

Feld Fliegerabteilung 56

das Abzeichen für Flugzeugführer

Gez. von Hoeppner

Document 157 **Transcript of Authorization to wear Pilot Badge by Unteroffizier Ludwig Jeckert**

The document measures 22.0 cm. wide x 17.0 cm. high. It has been printed on heavy card stock. The document is dated 22 August 1918 and authorized with the facsimile signature stamp of Lt. General Ernst Wilhelm von Hoeppner, which is barely visible. To the left of the signature is the blue ink official stamp of the Headquarters of the Commanding General of the German Air Service, also barely visible.

✠ ✠ ✠

The following documents are those of Reserve Lieutenant **PAUL WILHELM BÄUMER**, a German flying ace of WWI.

Lt. Paul Bäumer

In the **"Cross & Cockade Journal," Volume 5, Number 4, Winter 1964,** is the fine and informative article *"Paul Bäumer - Iron Eagle"* by A. Imrie which follows the civil and military career of Paul Bäumer until his death in an aircraft accident 15 July 1927 in Copenhagen, Denmark. Some information from this article has been extracted and condensed here.

Paul Wilhelm Bäumer was born at Duisburg on 11 May 1896. At an early age, Bäumer realized he wanted to become a flyer. His mother, however, was not too keen on his becoming a flyer when he could become successful in some "safe" profession, so she apprenticed young Paul to a local dentist. Bäumer found a friend in the dentist who also, strangely enough, had a secret desire to take to the air. He helped Bäumer make the necessary contacts to get a start in flying.

He was able to get enough training flights completed that he was ready to apply to to be examined by the Aero-Club of Germany and receive an Aviators Certificate when, unfortunately, World War I began thus preventing his being licensed as a pilot.

Bäumer wanted to become a military pilot and applied at the Navy Aviation Unit (Marine Fliegerabteilung) in Holtnau without success. He then applied to various military flying units in Döberitz, Darmstadt, and Trier, again without success. He was told, "too many volunteers, too few aircraft and too busy."

Fearing the war would be over before he could become a military flyer, he enlisted on 20 August 1914 as a volunteer in the 70th Infantry Regiment. Bäumer thought that later he would be able to transfer into a flying unit. However, in October 1914, his unit, the 70th Infantry Regiment, 32nd Infantry Brigade, 31st Infantry Division, which was a part of the 21st Army Corps, had taken part in several fierce engagements on the western front. At the end of October 1914 the division took over the front of Fouquescourt-Chaulnes and stayed in this sector until the end of January 1915.

Around 25 January 1915, the division left the Somme for the eastern front and detrained at Tilsit, East Prussia. At the beginning of February the division became a part of the Hindenburg Army. On 14 February 1915 the division left the area of Augustowo and began an advance to the east. Bäumer was wounded in the left arm during the hand-to-hand combat on 28 February 1915.

He was returned to Germany for recovery. While in the Brunswick Military Hospital, he applied for a transfer to the flying service but without success. His wound healed and he was sent to a reserve battalion. During a muster, technical personnel were asked to fall-out to be assigned as mechanics for the flying units. Even though he was a dental "mechanic" he stepped forward and was accepted. He was transferred to the 1st Aviation Replacement Unit *(Flieger Ersatz Abteilung 1)* in Döberitz on 17 August 1915, one day before he was to return to the front as a reserve infantryman.

Since he came from the infantry, he was assigned sentry duties upon his arrival in the unit. This did not set well with Bäumer so he applied to his commanding officer giving all details of his previous flying experiences and stating that if he could not be given flying duties he would rather return to his old regiment. His application was approved and on 30th September 1916, after only a few flights, he successfully took the pilot examination. The unit transferred to Altenburg where he trained in various aircraft. Prior to being reassigned to a fighter squadron, Bäumer had a two month hospital stay as the result of his aircraft having a carburetor fire at 3300 ft. Unable to extinguish the flames, he crashed while making a forced landing. Most of the fabric had been burned off the bottom wing.

On 24 October 1916, Private Paul Bäumer was assigned as a pilot to 1st Army Aircraft Center *(Armee Flugpark 1)* where his duties consisted of being a flying instructor, ferrying aircraft, and other special assignments.

Bäumer was promoted to Private First Class *(Gefreiter)* on 19 February 1917 and reassigned to the 7th Aviation Unit *(Flieger Abteilung 7)* ,located in the area of Lille, on 26 March 1917. He received another promotion to Corporal *(Unteroffizier)* on 29 March 1917. It was on 15 May 1917 that Unteroffizier Bäumer received the Iron Cross 2nd Class as well as his authorization to wear the pilot badge since he had completed 20 operational flights.

Abschrift.

Der kommandierende General
der Luftstreitkräfte.

Nr. V/12743 Fl II

Gr. H. Qu, den......15. Mai........1917..

Ich verleihe

dem ....Unteroffizier Bäumer............................

.........................Feld-.........Fliegerabteilung...7...:.

das Abzeichen für ....Flugzeugführer..........................

Gez. von Hoeppner,
Der Kommandierende General
der Luftstreitkräfte.

Generalleutnant.

Document 158   *Transcript of Authorization to wear the Pilot Badge by Unteroffizier Paul Bäumer*

Prussian Pilot Badge as worn by Corporal Paul Bäumer

The document shown above is a Transcript *(Abschrift)* of Authorization to wear the Pilot Badge given to Unteroffizier Paul Wilhelm Bäumer. It measures 21.5 cm. wide x 17.7 cm. high. It was signed in ink by a representative of Lt. General Ernst Wilhelm von Hoeppner, Commanding General of the German Air Service. The document is dated 15 May 1917 and has the registration number V/12743. To the left of the signature block is the purple ink official stamp of the Commanding General of the German Air Service.

In his spare time Bäumer worked on a captured Nieuport 17 *(B' 1514)*, and, after restoring the aircraft to flying condition, he had it repainted and flew it on several flight over the front lines. It was probably the light handling and maneuverability of this single seater Nieuport that helped him decide that he would prefer to transfer to the scouts or single seater fighters.

On 11 June 1917 he was reassigned to 4th Army Aircraft Center *(Armee Flugpark 4)* and was immediately attached to the Fighter Squadron School *(Jastaschule)* in Valenciennes for single seater fighter training.

On completion of the Jastaschule training, Unteroffizier Paul Bäumer was transferred back to Jagdstaffel "Boelke." Two days later he was reassigned to Jagdstaffel 5 at Bois-trancourt. Following some time with Jasta 5, Bäumer gained valuable experience and scored a few victories. On 15 August 1917 he was again transferred back to Jasta "Boelke."

Within the first few weeks of his returning to the Boelke squadron, he had shot down three allied aircraft. Unteroffizier Bäumer was awarded the Iron Cross 1st Class on 4 September 1917.

The document shown to the right is an Authorization Certificate, Type 4, (Besitzzeugnis) to Unteroffizier Paul Bäumer. It measures 17.4 cm. wide x 25.5 cm. high. It is dated 4 September 1918 and has the purple ink official stamp of the Headquarters of the Commanding General of the German Air Service. Note that the document does not have a signature, however, this was not unusual for the certificates not to be signed.

Befitzeugnis

Im Namen
Seiner Majeftät des Kaifers

habe ich

dem

UNTEROFFIZIER BÄUMER'

Jagdstaffel BOELCKE

das eiferne Kreuz I. Klaffe von 1914 verliehen.

den ___4 September___ 191 7

Nr. 2172 der Ordensfifte der Armee Flugpark 4

Spezialfabrit für Militärformulare Gebr. Saupe, Zweiggeschäft Metz. Inh. Karl Dießmann.

Document 159 *Iron Cross 1st Class Authorization Certificate, Type 4, to Unteroffizier Paul Bäumer*

Bäumer was promoted to Sergeant (Vizefeld-webel) on 31 October 1917. In the month of November 1917, Vizefeldwebel Bäumer had nine aerial victories and six of these were shot down during a four day period. His total victories were now 15 allied aircraft.

Due to the number of victories obtained by Bäumer, his successes were somewhat resented by some of the officers in his squadron, especially since he was the only non-commissioned pilot in the

Since every successful fighter pilot chose his own personal emblem to be painted on his aircraft, so Bäumer chose as his emblem the Edelweiss.

*Exhibit 5 Paul Bäumer in his Edelweiss marked Albatros D V while in the 5th Fighter Squadron**

*Exhibit 6   Obverse and Reverse of the
Prussian Golden Military Merit Cross*

Still holding non-commissioned officers rank, Paul Bäumer was awarded the highest bravery award Prussia could give to an enlisted man: the Golden Military Merit Cross, number 68, which he received on 12 February 1918.

On 10 April 1918, Vizefeldwebel Paul Bäumer was commissioned a Reserve Second Lieutenant (Leutnant der Reserve). His aerial victories now stood at 22.

On 29 May 1918, Lt. Bäumer crashed landed and suffered a complicated lower jaw fracture. He was sent to the 602nd Field Hospital and was later moved to the larger medical facility at the Military Hospital at Landau. He finally recovered while at the 1st Reserve Hospital in Düsseldorf, where another patient, Lothar von Richthofen, was also recovering.

* "German Air Aces of World War One" by Alex Imrie, Vintage Warbirds No. 8, Arms & Armor Press, Great Britian, 1987

Paul Bäumer standing beside his Albatros D V

On 16 August 1918 Lt. Bäumer received the Black Wound Badge.

In early October 1918, Lt. Bäumer was eventually able to get reassigned back to the "Boelke" Fighter Squadron. He started scoring and on 6 September 1918 another British plane was shot down. By the end of the month his victories had reached 38, and in one day he had shot three enemy aircraft out of the sky *(see following chart)*. Bäumer was able to shoot down three adversaries in one day on three separate occasions.

Lt. Bäumer had his last aerial victory on 9 October 1918, and he left the front on reassignment to special duties at Adlershof. On 2 November 1918, in recognition of his 30th aerial victory, Lt. Bäumer was decorated with the Prussian Pour le Mérite Order (Ordre Pour le Mérite).

He went on to achieve a total of 43[1] confirmed aerial victories (sources seem to disagree with the total number) and five unconfirmed. Lt. Bäumer was mustered out of the military service on 30 November 1918.

Paul Bäumer was a very special man and pilot. He was able to receive the highest bravery awards his country had to offer as both an enlisted man and officer. He became one of Germany's leading flying aces of World War I and at the end of the war he ranked seventh[2].

Exhibit 7 Prussian Pour le Mérite Order

---

1 "The History of the Prussian Pour le Mérite Order, 1888-1918" Volume III, by W. E. Hamelman, page 630, entry 793, shows the total aerial victories to be 44.

2 "Air Aces of the 1914-1918 War," edited by B. Robertson, Aero Publishers, Inc. Fallbrook CA, 1959.

Lt. Paul Wilhelm Bäumer
List of Confirmed Aerial Victories*

No.	Date		Aircraft Type	Place
1.	12 July	1917	Balloon	Nurlu
2.	13 July	1917	Balloon	Marteville
3.	15 July	1917	Balloon	Trefcon
4.	9 September	1917	R.E. 8	Mannessvaere
5.	20 September	1917	Martinsyde	Ramscapelle
6.	21 September	1917	Sopwith	Boesinghen
7.	5 November	1917	Sopwith	St. Julien
8.	6 November	1917	Spad	E. of Zonnebeke
9.	6 November	1917	Sopwith	Vierlavenhoek
10.	7 November	1917	R.E. 8	SW. of Moorslede
11.	8 November	1917	Sopwith	N. of Zonnebecke
12.	8 November	1917	Sopwith	N. of Zillebeke
13.	18 November	1917	R.E. 8	Zillebeke Lake
14.	19 November	1917	R.E. 8	NW. of Dixmude
15.	28 November	1917	R.E. 8	N. of Gheluvelt
16.	7 December	1917	Spad	Zonnebeke
17.	16 December	1917	R.E. 8	N. of Boesinghen
18.	18 December	1917	Sopwith	W. of Becelaire
19.	9 March	1918	Sopwith	N. of Zonnebeke
20.	23 March	1918	Sopwith	S. of St. Léger
21.	23 March	1918	R.E. 8	N. of Tilloy
22.	23 March	1918	R.E. 8	N. of Beugnatre
23.	5 September	1918	Bristol Fighter	S. of Douai
24.	6 September	1918	D.H. 9	W. of Cantaing
25.	14 September	1918	R.E. 8	Area of Cantaing
26.	16 September	1918	Bristol Fighter	NE. of Henin-Liétard
27.	20 September	1918	Sopwith	E. of Rumancourt
28.	21 September	1918	D.H. 9	E. of Bourlon Woods
29.	21 September	1918	D.H. 9	E. of Lagnicourt
30.	21 September	1918	D.H. 9	E. Morchies
31.	24 September	1918	Sopwith	Sailly
32.	24 September	1918	D.H. 9	SW. of Clary
33.	27 September	1918	Single Seater (?)	S. of Cisy
34.	27 September	1918	D.H. 9	W. of Cambrai
35.	27 September	1918	S.E. 5	W. of Cambrai
36.	29 September	1918	Bristol Fighter	Marcoing
37.	29 September	1918	S.E. 5	Bourlon Woods
38.	29 September	1918	Sopwith	S. of Sailly
39.	3 October	1918	Bristol Fighter	Rumilly
40.	4 October	1918	Bristol Fighter	Cambrai
41.	4 October	1918	S.E. 5	Montbehain
42.	8 October	1918	Sopwith	Bautigny
43.	9 October	1918	Bristol Fighter	Preseau

---

* "Paul Bäumer - Iron Eagle" by A. Imrie, Cross & Cockade, Volume 5, Number 4, Winter 1964.

Notes:

POST 1918 SECOND CLASS IRON CROSS DOCUMENTS

After World War I, during the "no decorations" *(Ordenslos)* period of the Weimar Republic, all royal Orders, decorations and medals were abolished; however, the new government still authorized and awarded the Iron Cross to those who had been recognized and recommended for the bravery award, and also the Wound Badge for those having been wounded in action during the war. The following section shows those documents which had been authorized and awarded after 1918. Many late awards and documents were awarded almost up to the beginning of World War II.

✠ ✠ ✠

The following document is very interesting as it tells a story of the sailor recipient. With the document showing the U-Boats he served aboard, his career can almost be traced. A short history of the submarines on which Machinist Mate Georg Ludwig served will be presented so we can share his adventures.

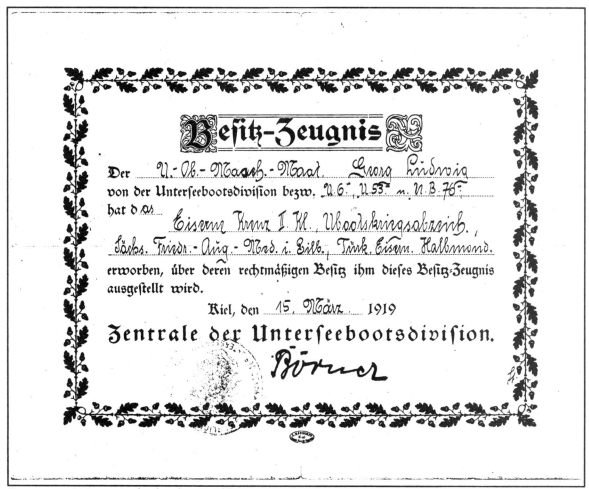

Document 160   *Authorization Certificate, Type 4, to U-Boot Obermaschinistmaat Georg Ludwig*

The document shown above is an Authorization Certificate, Type 4, *(Besitz-Zeugnis)* named to Submarine Machinist Mate 1st Class *(Unterseeboot Obermaschinistmaat)* **GEORG LUDWIG**. He served during WWI on the submarines U-6, U-53, and the UB-76.

The document also shows that he was awarded, besides the Iron Cross 2nd Class, the Saxon Silver Friedrich August Merit Medal, the Turkish War Medal, often erroneously called the *"Gallipoli Star,"* and the Submarine Service Badge.

The attractive document measures 20.8 cm. wide x 16.5 cm. high. It was signed on 15 March 1919 at the Submarine Division Operations Center *(Zentrale der Unterseebootsdivision)* by an officer named Börner. Adjacent to the signature is the purple ink official stamp of the Submarine Division Operations Center.

U-6

Machinist Mate Ludwig started his wartime career on the U-6, under the command of Kapitanleutnant Reinhold Lepsius. The U-6 was commissioned on 18 May 1910. It carried a crew of 29. The U-6 was 188' long, 18'3" wide, and 11'3" high and displaced 506 tons.

Interior of a WWI U-Boat showing the cramped interior   Imperial War Museum

During February 1915, the U-6, working with the U-20, the submarine credited with sinking the *Lusitania*, and the U-27 were patroling the English channel. On 28 February 1915, the U-6, traveling submerged off Beachy Head, sighted a 500 ton coaster, *Thordis*, under the command of Captain John Bell. Lt. Lepsius took the U-6 across the bow of the *Thordis* from starboard to port in order to launch a torpedo. The *Thordis* took evasive action and the torpedo missed. Captain Bell steered his coaster toward the U-6 in order to ram her. Lt. Lepsius reacted by turning the U-6 away and attemped to submerge. The submarine, being old, responded slowly and was hit by the Thordis which smashed into the conning tower, broke off one periscope and bent the second periscope, rendering it unusable. The conning tower was smashed and an oil tank was ruptured. Finally, the U-6 was able to dive out of danger. Seeing the oil slick and knowing that they rammed the submarine, the Thordis crew was sure that it had sunk its enemy. If true, it would have been the first time a merchantman had accomplished that. Captain Bell and his crew were subsequently fêted in London, and Captain Bell was even given £500 as a prize by the city of London.

However, Kapitanleutnant Reinhard Lepsius and the crew were able to repair some of the damage and steering blindly successfully returned to Wilhelmshaven where the U-6 was repaired. Fortunately for Machinist Mate Ludwig, he was transferred before the U-6 hit a mine in the English Channel on 18 December 1915 and did indeed sink.

Ludwig was then assigned aboard the U-53, captained by Kapitanleutnant Hans Rose. The U-53 was commissioned on 8 December 1915. It displaced 712 tons and carried a crew of 35. The U-53 was 214' long, 21' wide, and 11'9" high.

The following are a few of the highlights of the U-53 while Machinist Mate Ludwig was serving aboard her. In August 1916 while on patrol, Kapitanleutnant Rose was instrumental in warning Admiral Sheer, steaming in the North Sea with the High Seas Fleet, that the U-53 had sighted "a great pall of smoke" and realized it was the British Grand Fleet. Only 40 miles separated the two fleets which could have made naval history. Sheer turned the German fleet back and saved it for another day.

Aware that a number of British warships were patroling the US Eastern coast line trying to sink the German submarine *Deutschland*, Kapitanleutnant Rose and the U-53 were ordered to patrol off the east coast of America to attack British ships. The U-53 made the crossing and arrived off Newport, Virginia, on 7 October 1916. The British withdrew their ships and left the field wide open for the U-53. The U-53 sank three British, one Norwegian, and one Dutch ship. Completing the patrol with success, the U-53 returned to Germany. The USS Jacob Jones, an American destroyer, was sunk by the U-53 in 1917.

At some point Petty Officer Ludwig was transferred to the UB-76, a coastal submarine. It carried a crew of 34 and was commissioned on 5 May 1917. It appears that PO Ludwig finished the war on the UB-76. It was surrendered to the British on 12 February 1919 and was scrapped during 1922 at Rochester, England. It is interesting that Machinist Mate Ludwig was awarded the Iron Cross 2nd Class one month later. Could it be that he was one of the crew that delivered the submarine to the British? We don't know but it's something to ponder.

Note: After the armistice the U-53 under a new captain named von Schrader, was to have surrendered the submarine to the British on 1 December 1918. Instead, the crew chose to take the U-53 to Sweden where it was interned. Eventually the British received the submarine, and the U-53 was scrapped at Swansee, England in 1922.

The document shown below is an Authorization Certificate, Type 4, *(Besitz-Zeugnis)* named to **GUSTAV PARCHAU.** He probably served in the Imperial Navy. It appears that his rank has been altered on the document so none can be determined.

Document 161   ***Authorization Certificate, Type 4, to Gustav Parchau***

The document measures 15.8 cm. wide x 21.0 cm. high. It shows Parchau was authorized the Iron Cross 2nd Class on 20 February 1920. The document was signed on 24 March 1920 at the Naval base in Kiel. In the lower left corner in the purple ink stamp of Naval Command in Kiel. Note that the "Imperial" *(Kaiserlich)* word on the naval stamp has been removed, leaving a blank space. Also note the two punched holes in the left margin where it appears that the certificate had been a part of the record of Parchau.

✠ ✠ ✠

The document shown on the following page is also a Naval certificate. It is an Authorization Certificate, Type 4, *(Besitz-Zeugnis)* named to Senior Naval Ordnance Inspector *(Marine Waffenwerk-meister)* **SCHMEIER**, serving at the Garison Machine Manufacturing Center, Feldhausen Arms Factory, Wilhelmshaven. *(Garison Maschinen Bauamt, Waffenwerk Feldhausen, Wilhelmshaven).*

The document has a dark red border and measures 20.0 cm. wide x 32.1 cm. high. It was signed in ink by a representative of the Office of the Naval Superintendent *(Marine Indendantur)* on 29 December 1919. Note that the prior office was the "Command of the Naval Station on the North Sea" *(Kommando der Marinestation der Nordsee)* and has been lined out. To the left of the signature is the black ink official stamp of the Office of the Naval Superintendent. The document shows that Inspector Schmeier was awarded the Iron Cross 2nd Class on 10 December 1919. What is interesting is that written on the certificate is a notation that the Iron Cross is on the black-white ribbon *(schwarz-weiss band)*. It is unusual to specify the combatant ribbon on a document.

✠ ✠ ✠

Besitz-Zeugnis

Dem _Marine-Waffenwerksinspektor_

Schmeier

von _dem Garnison-Waffen-Amt Wilhelmshaven_

(Waffenwerk Feldhausen)

ist am _10. Dezember_ 1919 das

Eiserne Kreuz _II_ **Klasse**

am schwarz-weißen Band

verliehen worden. _lfg. der Chef der Admiralität_

_M 7890 v. 16. II. 1919._

Wilhelmshaven, den _29. Dezember_ 1919.

~~Kommando der Marinestation~~
~~der Nordsee~~

Marine-_____

[signature]

The document shown below is very interesting and extremely rare. It is an Authorization Certificate, Type 4, (Besitz-Zeugnis) named to Corporal (Unteroffizier) **KARL WISSWÄSSER**. The document does not indicate the unit Unteroffizier Wisswässer was serving in, but it can be assumed that he was serving in one of the German Sea Battalions that was stationed in the German Protectorate of Tsingtau, China.

BESITZ-ZEUGNIS

Dem   Unteroffizier in Tsingtau

Karl Wisswässer

ist durch Verfügung vom 16. September 1920 — PU 7586 — das

Eiserne Kreuz II. Klasse

verliehen worden.

Berlin, den 25. Oktober 1920.

Reichswehrministerium
Chef der Marineleitung
J. V.

Document 163   *Authorization Certificate, Type 4, to Unteroffizier Karl Wisswässer*

The document measures 19.0 cm. wide x 14.5 cm. high, and was signed in black ink by a representative of the Chief of Naval Department (Chef der Marineleitung), State Defense Ministry (Reichswehrministerium). As sometimes seen on other documents, there is no official stamp.

Unteroffizier Wisswässer was one of the more than 4,000 German soldier and sailors who defended Tsingtau against the Japanese when they declared war on Germany on 23 August 1914. The intent of the Japanese was to take the German Protectorate and at the same time gain a foothold on mainland China to establish their claim to a Chinese port. On 2 September 1914, the Japanese landed an invasion force of 65,000 troops on the north coast of Shantung Province, slowly advancing toward Tsingtau. By the 28th of September, the Japanese had completely isolated Tsingtau by land and sea.

The Japanese began a nine day bombardment with their ships and land artillery. During the night of 6-7 November 1914, the German defenders fired their last shell at the enemy. On 7 November 1914 Naval Captain Clemens Friedrich Meyer-Waldeck, serving as Governor of Tsingtau, surrendered the German garrison to the allied forces.

Unteroffizier Wisswässer was one of the 2,300 German defenders taken by the Japanese. Captured German soldiers and reservists were assembled at the Bismarck Barracks and afterwards

Naval Captain Meyer-Waldeck

the troops marched past Naval Captain Meyer-Waldeck, in parade formation. It was a sad but proud moment for the defenders. Wasting little time with the German prisoners, the Japanese put them aboard several old and filthy ships for their journey to Japan and captivity. The German POW's spent the next five years in various Japanese prison camps. By mid-1919, the surviving Germans had been returned to Germany and Unteroffizier Karl Wisswässer was among them. In recognition of his bravery in action and for having survived the Japanese prisons, he was recognized by being awarded the Iron Cross 2nd Class.

✠ ✠ ✠

The document shown below is an Authorization Certificate, Type 4, *(Besitzzeugnis)* named to Replacement Reservist *(Ersatz Reservist)* **OTTO TSCHAMMER**. There is no indication of his wartime unit.

> ### Besitzeugnis.
>
> Durch Verfügung des Befehlshabers des Wehrkreiskommandos III vom
>
> - I a Kv. 1617 -
>
> ist dem Ersatz-Res. Otto Tschammer,
>
> geboren am 29. 12. 1889 in Berlin.
>
> das Eiserne Kreuz II. Klasse
>
> verliehen worden.
>
> Berlin-Schöneberg, den 7. 8. 19 20.
> General-Papestraße.
>
> Form. Nr. XXXX ²

Document 164   *Authorization Certificate, Type 4, to Ersatz Reservist Otto Tschammer*

The document had been framed and is badly faded. It is pasted to cardboard. It measures 21.3 cm. wide x 16.5 cm. high. The award of the Iron Cross 2nd Class to Otto Tschammer was authorized by Military Area Command III and issued by the Personnel Assistance Office. It is signed in ink by a personnel officer and dated 7 August 1920. Tschammer was 31 years old when awarded the Iron Cross 2nd Class.

✠ ✠ ✠

The document shown below is an Authorization Certificate, Type 4, *(Bestizzeugnis)* named to Private First Class *(Gefreiten)* **HERMANN CLAGES**. There is no indication of his wartime unit.

Document 165   *Authorization Certificate, Type 4, to Gefreiten Hermann Clages*

The document measures 16.0 cm. wide x 20.7 cm. high. It was authorized by the Defense Ministry and signed with an indelible purple pencil on 6 March 1924 by the commander in chief of the 1st Army Group Command. In the lower left corner of the document is the purple ink stamp of the 1st Army Group Command. The document awards the Iron Cross 2nd Class to Gefreiten Clages for merit in the field *"für Verdienst im Felde."* On the left margin are the two punched holes which indicated that the document was a part of Hermann Clages personnel record but does not rule out it being a part of his military record of this time period.

Shown at the top of the following page is the reverse of the upper half of the Iron Cross document to Gefreiten Clages. It shows the purple stamp of State Association of German Railroad Veterans of 1914-1918 *"Reichsbund Deutscher Eisenbahner Kriegsteilnehmer 1914-1918 a.V."* It is numbered 266. Also on his 1934 document for WWI combatant veterans *(Ehrenkreuz für Frontkämpfer)*, it states that Clages' title is a Reserve Locomotive Engineer *(Reserve Lokomotivführer)*.

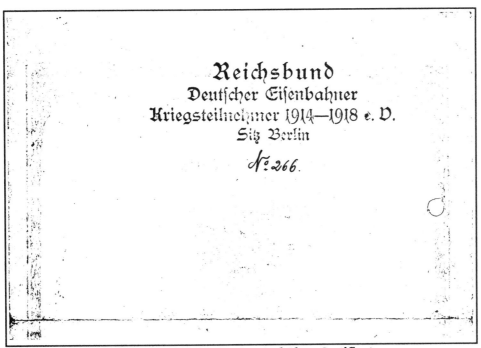

Document 166   *Reverse of the Iron Cross 2nd Class Certificate to Gefreiten Hermann Clages*

Im Namen des Führers und Reichskanzlers

Dem *Reserve-Lokomotivführer Hermann Clages in Neumünster*

ist auf Grund der Verordnung vom 13. Juli 1934 zur Erinnerung an den Weltkrieg 1914/1918 das von dem Reichspräsidenten Generalfeld=marschall von Hindenburg gestiftete

Ehrenkreuz für Frontkämpfer

verliehen worden.

Neumünster, den 15. Dezember 1934.

Der Oberbürgermeister

Nr. C/27 /34.

Document 167   *1934 Merit Cross for Combatant Certificate to Hermann Clages*

This indicates Hermann Clages served in the Railway troops during World War I and continued this career in civilian life. Also note that the 1934 Merit Cross certificate has at the left margin the two punched holes indicating that this document was also a part of the personnel records of Hermann Clages.

✠ ✠ ✠

The document shown below is an Authorization Certificate, Type 4, *(Besitz-Zeugnis)* named to Corporal *(Unteroffizier)* **EMIL HODSKE**. There is no indication of his wartime unit.

Document 168   *Authorization Certificate, Type 4, to Unteroffizier Emil Hodske*

The attractive document measures 16.5 cm. wide x 21.4 cm. high. It was authorized by Military District V and signed in black ink by a representative of the Personnel Affairs Office of the former *(früheren)* XVIII Army Corps. To the left of the signature is the purple ink official stamp of the former XVIII Army Corps. Unteroffizier Hodske was authorized the Iron Cross 2nd Class on 31 March 1920.

✠ ✠ ✠

The document shown below is an Authorization Certificate, Type 4, *(Besitz-Zeugnis)* named to Private *(Musketier)* **VALENTIN WEISSENSTEIN**. There is no indication of his wartime unit.

Document 169 *Authorization Certificate, Type 4, to Musketier Valentin Weissenstein*

The attractive document, identical to the document on the preceding page, measures 16.5 cm. wide x 21.4 cm. high. It was authorized by Military District V and signed in black ink by a representative of the Personnel Affairs Office of the former *(früheren)* XVIII Army Corps. To the left of the signature is the purple ink official stamp of the former XVIII Army Corps. Musketier Weissenstein was authorized the Iron Cross 2nd Class on 14 November 1920.

✠ ✠ ✠

Notes:

Post 1918 Iron Cross 2nd Class Documents
for Noncombatants

Recipients of the Iron Cross on the "noncombatant" *(Nichtkämpfer)* ribbon were usually decorated for outstanding successful endeavors which did not actually involve battlefield action. It was awarded to medical personnel and nurses behind the lines and in recognition of distinguished achievements in the war effort on the homefront. As shown by the following documents, government officials were recognized for their efforts and awarded the Iron Cross 2nd Class on the "noncombatant" or the white ribbon with black edge stripes.

✠ ✠ ✠

The document shown below is an Authorization Certificate, Type 4, *(Besitzzeugnis)* named to Government Auditor *(Rechnungsrat)* **WILLIBALD SEIFFERT** serving in the State Ministry of Justice when awarded the Iron Cross 2nd Class on the noncombatant *(white with black edge stripes)* ribbon.

Document 170   ***Authorization Certificate, Type 4, to Senior Auditor Willibald Seiffert***

The document measures 26.3 cm. wide x 20.7 cm. high. It was authorized through the State Ministry of Justice *(Reichsjustizministerium)* on 20 April 1920. The document authorized Auditor Seiffert the Iron Cross 2nd Class on the white ribbon with black edges *(weißen Bande mit schwarzer Einfassung)* on 23 March 1920.

This type of document was awarded during the war through the General Orders Commission and has the facsimile signature of Kanitz who was the Orders Commissioner. The reverse of the document shows in the upper left-hand corner the registration number **2959** (shown as Exhibit 8 on the right) and the date the award was given to Auditor Seiffert. Notice also that the Bureau of the General Orders Commission *(Büro der Generalordenskommission)* was marked out since during this period of the Weimar Republic all imperial Orders were now obsolete. The document is signed in ink by the State Minister of Justice *(der Reichsminister der Justiz)* or his authorized representative.

2959

Exhibit 8

Document 171   *Reverse of the Authorization Certificate to Auditor Willibald Seiffert*

Also notice that Berlin has been marked out and no indication is given as to where the State Justice Ministry is located. However, it seems in all likelihood the Ministry was located in Berlin.

✠ ✠ ✠

The document shown at the top of the following page is an Authorization Certificate, Type 4, *(Besitzzeugnis)* named to Senior Government Administrative Official *(Oberregierungsrat)* Dr. **GUSTAV HEINRICH EUGEN GROLMAN** serving in the government service in Düsseldorf. He held the degree of Doctor of Laws.

The document measures 26.5 cm. wide x 21.0 cm. high. It was authorized through the president of the Düsseldorf governing administration *(Der Regierungs Präsident)*. It is dated 15 December 1919 and has the facsimile signature of Kanitz who was the Orders Commissioner.

The reverse of the document shows in the upper left hand corner the registration number **174** (shown as Exhibit 9 on the following page). The date when he received the certificate is 7 February 1920. Notice that the Bureau of General Orders Commission *(Büro der Generalordenskommission)* has been marked through and replaced with the purple ink stamp of the Governing President *(Der Regierungs Präsident)*. The certificate has been signed in black ink by a representative of the president. To the left of the signature is the purple ink official stamp of the government of Düsseldorf.

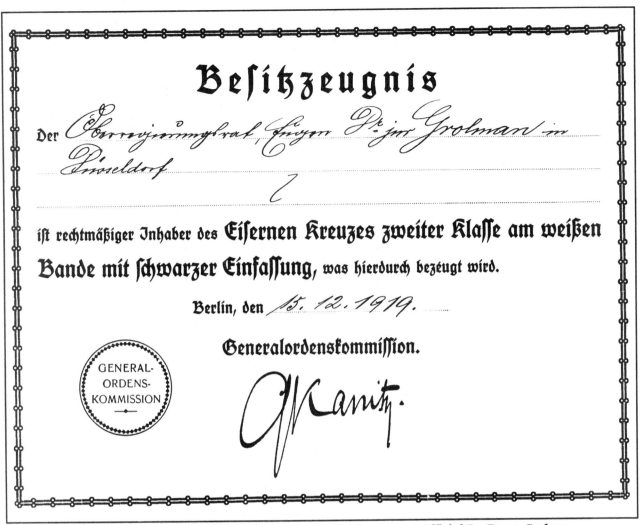

Beſitzeugnis

Der *Oberregierungsrat Eugen Dr. jur. Grolman in Düsseldorf*

ist rechtmäßiger Inhaber des **Eiſernen Kreuzes zweiter Klaſſe am weißen Bande mit ſchwarzer Einfaſſung**, was hierdurch bezeugt wird.

Berlin, den *15. 12. 1919.*

Generalordenskommiſſion.

GENERAL-
ORDENS-
KOMMISSION

Document 172   Authorization Certificate, Type 4, to Senior Government Official Dr. Eugen Grolman

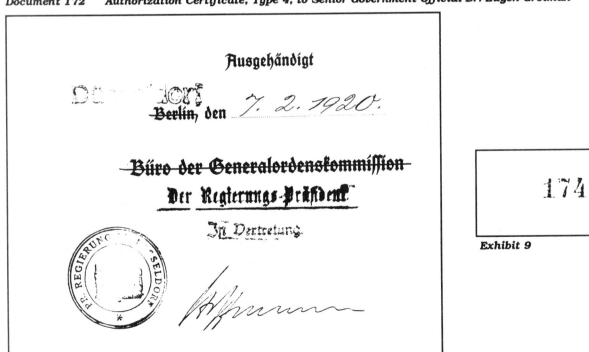

Ausgehändigt

~~Berlin,~~ den *7. 2. 1920.*

~~Büro der Generalordenskommiſſion~~

~~Der Regierungs-Präſident~~

In Vertretung

174

Exhibit 9

Document 173   Reverse of Authorization Certificate to Dr. Eugen Grolman

The document shown below is a Militia Military Long Service Award 2nd Class Certificate (die II. Klasse der Landwehr Dienstauszeichnung) to Second Lieutenant (Second Lieutenant) Eugen Grolman serving in the Reserve of the 5th Westphalian Lancer Regiment (Westfälischen Ulanen Regiment No. 5).

It appears that Dr. Grolman was active in the reserves prior to WWI. Note that the name has been spelt with double "n."

The large, hand-drawn and subsequently printed document measures 21.0 cm. wide x 33.0 cm. high.

It is dated 13 March 1894 and signed in Münster by the commanding General of the VIIth Army Corps. To the left of the signature is the purple ink official stamp of the Commanding General of the VIIth Army Corps.

On the following page is shown the Authorization Certificate to the Merit Cross for War Help awarded to Dr. Eugen Grolman on 19 May 1917.

The document measures 26.5 cm. wide x 21.0 cm. high. It has the facsimile signature of Kanitz and was awarded through the Prussian General Orders Commission.

Document 174   *Reserve Long Service Certificate to 2nd Lt. Eugen Grolman*

* The first Merit Cross for War Help was awarded by Emperor Wilhelm II to General Field Marshal von Hindenburg.

Beſitzeugnis

Auf Allerhöchſten Befehl Seiner Majeſtät des Königs bezeugt die Generalkommiſſion in Angelegenheiten der Königlich Preußiſchen Orden hierdurch, daß Seine Majeſtät

dem Oberregierungsrat Dr. Eugen Grolman bei

der Regierung in Düſſeldorf

das Verdienſtkreuz für Kriegshilfe zu verleihen geruht haben.

Berlin, den *19. Mai 1917*

Generalkommiſſion in Angelegenheiten der Königlich Preußiſchen Orden

Document 175   *Merit Cross for War Help Authorization Certificate to Dr. Eugen Grolman*

On the reverse is a rather interesting notation (seen below). It indicates that the document was given to Dr. Grolman on 21 May 1918. This is either a mistake in the entry of the date or else it took a year for Dr. Grolman to receive the certificate for the award.

The reverse was signed by a representative of the governing president of Düsseldorf. To the left is the purple ink official stamp of the government of Düsseldorf.

Ausgehändigt

Düſſeldorf, den *28. Mai 1918.*
Der Regierungs-Präſident.

Document 176   *Reverse of the Merit Cross for War Help Authorization Certificate to Dr. Eugen Grolman*

Der Regierungs-Präsident.

\C.B.I. 644.

Düsseldorf, den 8. März 1919.
Postfach:

> Beifolgend übersende ich Euerer Hochwohlgeboren das Besitzzeugnis über das Ihnen verliehene österreichische Kriegskreuz für Zivilverdienste II.Klasse.

An

Herrn Oberregierungsrat

Dr. G r o l m a n

hier.

Document 177 Transmittel Letter to Dr. Eugen Grolman

Shown at the left is the Transmittal Letter to Dr. Eugen Grolman advising him of his being awarded the Austrian Civil Merit War Cross 2nd Class.

Note that it was signed by the same official who signed the Prussian War Help Cross (see document 176).

To the right is shown the document for the Austrian Civil Merit War Cross 2nd Class named to Dr. Eugen Grolman.

It measures 19.8 cm. wide x 31.8 cm. high. It is signed in ink by a representative of the Imperial and Royal Foreign Ministry (k. und k. Ministerium des Außern).

To the left of the signature is the black ink official stamp of the ministry.

Document 178 Austrian Civil Merit War Cross 2nd Class to Dr. Eugen Grolman

✠ ✠ ✠

Post 1918 Iron Cross 1st Class Documents

After World War I, Germany was allowed to continue several small armed forces and small naval stations.These naval installations were maintained basically in order to expedite the surrender to the allies any capital ships remaining in the Imperial German Navy. The naval bases functioned also to support coastal patrol vessel activity.

✠ ✠ ✠

The document shown below is an Authorization Certificate, Type 4, *(Besitzzeugnis)* named to Naval Senior Paymaster *(Marine Oberzahlmeister)* **SCHULTE** serving at the time of his being awarded the Iron Cross 2nd Class at the Naval Station on the Baltic Sea in Kiel, Germany.

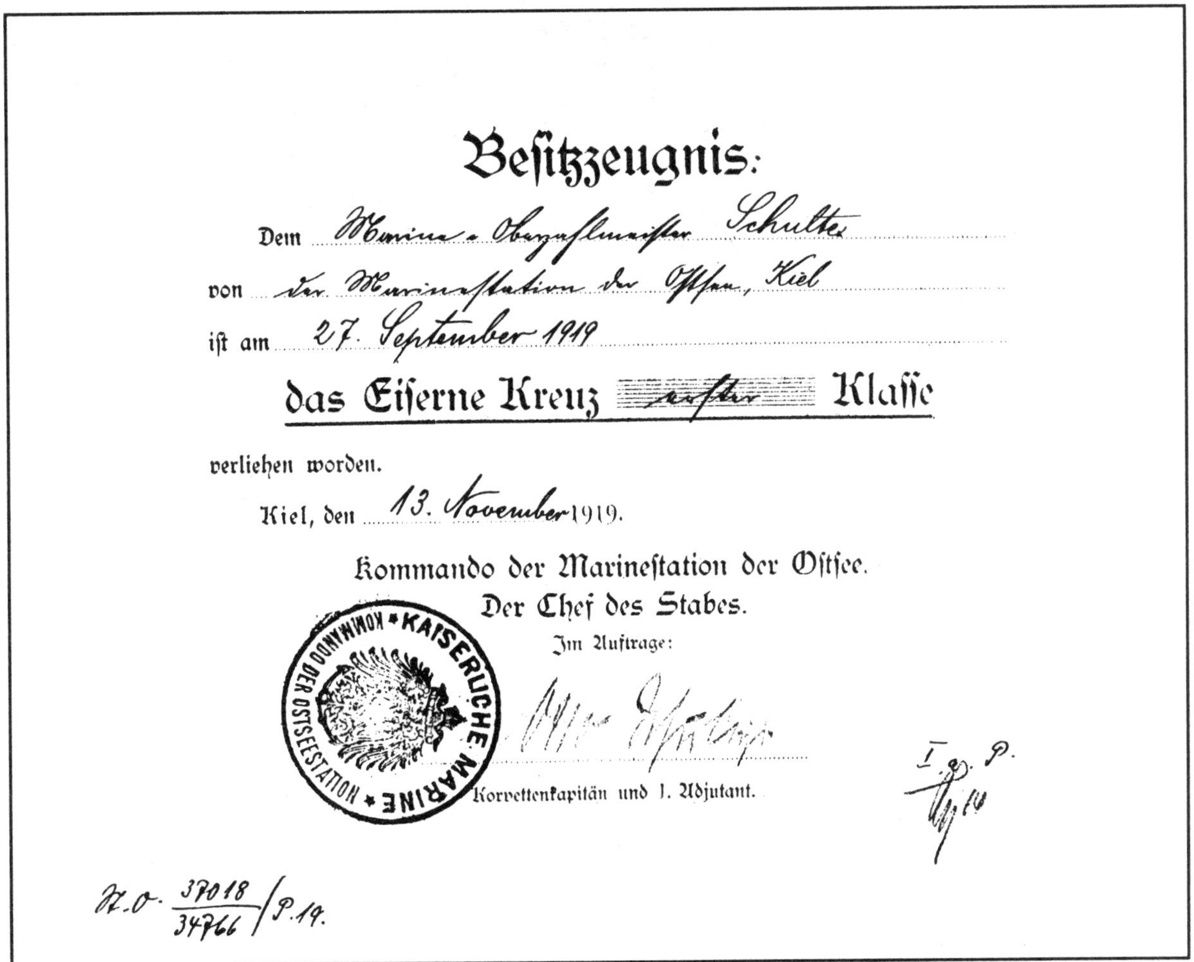

Besitzzeugnis.

Dem Marine-Oberzahlmeister Schulte

von der Marinestation der Ostsee, Kiel

ist am 27. September 1919

das Eiserne Kreuz ~~erster~~ Klasse

verliehen worden.

Kiel, den 13. November 1919.

Kommando der Marinestation der Ostsee.

Der Chef des Stabes.

Im Auftrage:

Korvettenkapitän und I. Adjutant.

KOMMANDO DER OSTSEESTATION * KAISERLICHE MARINE *

Document 179 ***Authorization Certificate, Type 4, to Naval Senior Paymaster Schulte***

The document is printed on brown paper and measures 20.9 cm. wide x 16.5 cm. high. It was signed in pencil by the adjutant of the staff of the Naval Station on13 November 1919 and authorized Paymaster Schulte the 1st Class Iron Cross on 27 September 1919. To the left of the signature is the red ink official stamp of the East Sea Command of the Navy. What is of interest is that the word "Imperial" *(Kaiserliche)* was still being used a year after the abdication of the Emperor. Seen in the left margin are the two punched holes indicating the document was a part of the personnel record of Schulte.

✠ ✠ ✠

✠ Name Directory ✠

✠ ✠ ✠

✠✠✠

✠ SELECTED BIBLIOGRAPHY ✠

Bowen, Ezra, *KNIGHTS OF THE AIR*, Time-Life Books, 1980.

von Dellmensingen, K. K., *DAS BAYERNBUCH VOM WELTKRIEG 1914-1918*, Chr. Belser A.G., 1930.

Graudenz, Karlheinz, *DIE DEUTSCHEN KOLONIEN*, Südwest Verlag, 1982.

Hamelman, William E., *THE HISTORY OF THE PRUSSIAN POUR LE MÉRITE ORDER, VOLUME III, 1888-1918*, Matthaeus Publishers, 1986.

Imrie, Alex, *GERMAN AIR ACES*, Vintage Warbirds No. 8, Arms & Armour Press, 1987.

Imrie, Alex, *PAUL BÄUMER - IRON EAGLE*, Cross & Cockade Journal, Volume 5, Number 4, Winter 1964.

Nowarra, J. H., *VON RICHTHOFEN AND THE FLYING CIRCUS*, Aero Publisher, Inc., 1964.

Preston, Antony, *SUBMARINES*, Bison Books Ltd. 1982.

Preston, Antony, *U-BOATS*, Excalibur Books, 1978.

Puglisi, William, *WAR DAIRY OF ROYAL PRUSSIAN JAGDSTAFFEL 56*, Cross & Cockade Journal, Volume 1, Number 4, Winter 1960.

Rimell, Raymond L., *THE GERMAN ARMY AIR SERVICE IN WORLD WAR ONE*, Vintage Warbirds No. 2, Arms & Armour Press, 1985.

Taylor, John C., *GERMAN WARSHIPS OF WORLD WAR I*, Doubleday & Company, Inc., 1970.

von Zobeltiz, Hanns, *VOLKSBÜCHER DER GESCHICHTE DAS EISERNE KREUZ*, Velhagen & Klasing, ?

Multiple Authors, *EUROPE AT WAR*, Doubleday, Page & Company, 1914

Multiple Authors, *HISTORIES OF TWO HUNDRED AND FIFTY-ONE DIVISIONS OF THE GERMAN ARMY WHICH PARTICIPATED IN THE WAR (1914-1918)*, Government Printing Office, 1920.

Multiple Authors, *DER KRIEG 1914/16 IN WORT UND BILD, VOLUME 2*, Deutsches Verlagshaus Bong & Co., 1916.

✠ ✠ ✠

INDEX

Notes:

Notes: